The Vietnam Experience

Tools of War

by Edgar C. Doleman, Jr.
and the editors of Boston Publishing Company

Boston Publishing Company/Boston, MA

Boston Publishing Company

President and Publisher: Robert J. George
Vice President: Richard S. Perkins, Jr.
Editor-in-Chief: Robert Manning
Managing Editor: Paul Dreyfus

Senior Writers:
Clark Dougan, Edward Doyle, David Ful-
ghum, Samuel Lipsman, Terrence Maitland,
Stephen Weiss
Senior Picture Editor: Julene Fischer

Researchers:
Jonathan Elwitt, Sandra W. Jacobs, Christy
Virginia Keeny, Denis Kennedy, Michael
Ludwig, Anthony Maybury-Lewis, Carole
Rulnick, Nicole van Ackere, Robert Yar-
brough

Picture Editors:
Wendy Johnson, Lanng Tamura
Assistant Picture Editor: Kathleen A. Reidy
Picture Researchers:
Nancy Katz Colman, Robert Ebbs, Tracey
Rogers, Nana Elisabeth Stern, Shirley L.
Green (Washington, D.C.), Kate Lewin
(Paris)
Archivist: Kathryn J. Steeves
Picture Department Assistant:
Suzanne M. Spencer

Historical Consultants:
Vincent Demma, Lee Ewing
Technical Consultant: Steven Zaloga
Picture Consultant: Ngo Vinh Long

Staff Editor: Gordon Hardy
Production Editors:
Kerstin Gorham, Patricia Leal Welch

Editorial Production:
Sarah E. Burns, Karen E. English, Pamela
George, Elizabeth Campbell Peters,
Theresa M. Slomkowski, Amy P. Wilson

Design: Designworks, Sally Bindari
Design Assistants: Sherry Fatla, David Ver-
gara

Marketing Director: Jeanne C. Gibson
Business Staff: Amy Pelletier

Special Contributors to this Volume:
John Batchelor (illustrations), Donald Dale
Jackson (editorial), Anne Masters (design),
Sara Schneidman (picture editor), Linda
Yates (picture assistant)

About the editors and authors

Editor-in-Chief *Robert Manning*, a long-time
journalist, has previously been editor-in-chief
of the *Atlantic Monthly* magazine and its press.
He served as assistant secretary of state for
public affairs under Presidents John F. Kennedy and Lyndon B. Johnson. He has also
been a fellow at the Institute of Politics at the
John F. Kennedy School of Government at
Harvard University.

Author: *Edgar C. Doleman, Jr.* was a company
commander and intelligence officer with the
1st Cavalry Division (Airmobile) in Vietnam
and later served as an infantry unit adviser
with the 5th ARVN Division. He has a B.S. in
physics from Virginia Military Institute and
has done graduate work in history at the University of Richmond.

Historical Consultants: *Vincent H. Demma*, a
historian with the U.S. Army Center of Military
History, is currently working on the center's
history of the Vietnam conflict. *Lee Ewing*, editor of *Army Times*, served two years in Vietnam as a combat intelligence officer with the
U.S. Military Assistance Command, Vietnam
(MACV) and the 101st Airborne Division.

Technical Consultant: *Steven Zaloga*, a defense writer and illustrator, is the author of numerous books on military technology.

Picture Consultant: *Ngo Vinh Long* is a social
historian specializing in China and Vietnam.
Born in Vietnam, he returned there most recently in 1980.

Cover Photo:

High-tech warfare. A Russian-made SA-2 surface-to-air radar-guided missile sits in a rice field
near Hanoi. Although the Communists at first
fought the war with defensive guerrilla tactics and
rudimentary weapons, as the U.S. brought its modern arsenal to Southeast Asia the North Vietnamese and Vietcong relied increasingly on advanced
weaponry supplied by their allies.

Library of Congress Catalog Card Number: 84-
72888

ISBN: 0-939526-13-1

10 9 8 7 6
5 4 3 2 1

Contents

Preface

It is a given in war that opposing forces will bring to bear all the ingenuity and technological know-how at their command. That did not quite happen in Vietnam—the United States withheld its ultimate nuclear weapons. In most respects, though, the Vietnam War brought out all the tools of war that soldiers, scientists, and tinkerers of the 1960s and 1970s could devise. The Americans brought to bear tremendous firepower against an enemy that, early in the fighting, used some of the same primitive weapons and tactics their forebears had used long before to end 1,000 years of Chinese occupation.

But as the war—and American technology—escalated, so did the weaponry of the North Vietnamese, who acquired from their Chinese and particularly their Soviet backers air, antiaircraft, and ground weapons, many of them equal in modernity and sophistication to those employed by the Americans and South Vietnamese. It was in the end a highly technological war, but one in which will rather than technology played the decisive role.

This volume of THE VIETNAM EXPERIENCE attempts to portray for the layman some of the astonishing variety and ingenuity of the weapons and counter-weapons and what it was like to use them, or face them, in Vietnam. Some were modern versions of weapons decades, even centuries, old. Some were departures for which Vietnam was merely the testing laboratory. Some were expensive, even ludicrous duds.

It would take a volume far thicker and far more technical than this one to detail them all.

—The Editors

The Technological Edge

In the beginning it looked like a modern version of David and Goliath: the most economically productive, technologically advanced, and militarily powerful nation on earth taking on an army of peasant soldiers equipped with little more than an assortment of small arms and homemade booby traps. Indeed, when U.S. combat troops first joined the Vietnam War in the spring of 1965, the technological gap between the two opposing sides was so great that the eventual outcome seemed to many to be preordained. Through the combined application of its vastly superior firepower, mobility, communications, and logistics, the part of the mighty American war machine committed to Vietnam would seek out and destroy the enemy or at least wear him down to the point where he would be forced to sue for peace. Or so it was confidently assumed by U.S. military leaders in Saigon and Washington.

Erroneous as that assumption proved to be, it was based not so much upon hubris as history.

Ever since the victory of the Union over the Confederacy in the Civil War, American military planning had been shaped in large part by the nation's extraordinary productive capacity. In World War II, the U.S. "arsenal of democracy" had turned the tide, overwhelming the enemy with quantities of war materiel—aircraft and tanks, ships and artillery, rifles and uniforms—that could not be matched. When President Franklin Roosevelt called for the manufacture of 50,000 airplanes at the outset of World War II, the Germans dismissed it as a propaganda ploy. Yet by 1944 American factories were turning out nearly 100,000 planes *per year*, in addition to providing the bulk of supplies required by America's allies.

Quality over quantity

If the Second World War confirmed the advantages of unsurpassed productivity, it taught another lesson as well: that superior quality in weaponry could neutralize or overcome superior quantity. The most awesome technological development of the war, the atomic bomb, seemed to prove this with two quick strikes over Hiroshima and Nagasaki, hastening the surrender of Japan. But throughout World War II, scientists on both sides had spawned military breakthroughs with dramatic consequences for their own fight and for fights to come. Developments in radar and jet aircraft were to be the opening acts of a drama that later played itself out over Vietnam.

As the world war approached in the 1930s it was obvious that command of the sky had become critical. But air superiority could be neutralized if the defenders on the ground could track invading aircraft before they reached their targets; interceptor planes could then be sent up to engage the invaders. While American scientists invented radar, first testing it in 1932, German and British scientists were also homing in on it in the mid–1930s. By the time hostilities began in 1939 both nations had radar networks, but it was British radar that proved decisive, if only because radar was a defensive tool and in the early years of the war Britain was the defender.

English scientists proved in a secret experiment in 1935 that a plane passing through a radio field reflected radio waves back to their point of origin and thus permitted the craft's location and course to be calculated. From there, the British constructed a chain of radar stations along the coast that monitored aircraft bound for England. Each station had a 350-foot-high transmission tower with a maximum range of 120 miles. Among the several criteria for site location was a concern that the stations would not "interfere unduly with grouse shooting."

Preceding page. *America's ingenuity goes to war. Portable fuel bladders, which allow helicopters to be fueled anywhere, dot the 1st Air Cavalry's heliport at An Khe, South Vietnam, in January 1966.*

When the Germans spotted the towers in the spring of 1939 they sent a zeppelin loaded with electronic equipment on a reconnaissance cruise to find out if the British had radar, but for reasons unknown their monitoring devices failed to detect the radar signals. A few weeks later British radar picked up a squadron of more than fifty planes that approached to within seven miles of the coast and then turned back, apparently a prewar rehearsal for the bombing raids that would soon begin.

The German Luftwaffe was still unaware of the radar system the British called "Chain House" when the Battle of Britain began in the summer of 1940. A ground control network connected radar operators with British Royal Air Force pilots long before Nazi planes reached England. Also assisting British air defenses was "Ultra," or the "Turing engine," named for its developer, cryptanalyst Alan Turing. Kept secret until the end of the war, Ultra was an ingenious device used to break the Germans' highly complex system of codes. With the information provided by radar and the decoding of German messages, the pilots could concentrate their outnumbered forces—the Germans had a five-to-one edge at the beginning—where it would pay off. "I was astonished," a German airman admitted later, "to find that each time we crossed the Channel there was always an enemy fighter force in position." Along with the Ultra decoder, radar was the equalizer that resulted in the destruction of 1,736 German planes as against RAF losses of 915. Technology in this instance had saved a nation from disaster.

Three years later it was British pilots who were trying to dodge German radar over the Fatherland, and this time ingenuity served aggression. British experts discovered that strips of aluminum foil precisely thirty centimeters long interfered with German radar. Bundles of foil tossed from British planes filled German radar screens with a blizzard of signals that made the receivers useless, a technique at the time given the code name "Window" and later called "chaff." With German fighters thus forced to scramble blindly, a fleet of 722 British bombers slammed Hamburg in July 1943 with one of the most devastating aerial barrages ever unleashed. Nine square miles of the city were consumed in the first-ever firestorm that resulted in 50,000 people dead and 1 million homeless.

At about the same time, Germans and Americans were involved in a high-technology duel over the skies of Italy. In 1943, the Germans began deploying a number of types of radio-guided glide bombs and missiles, launched from aircraft, against Allied shipping in the Mediterranean. These were the first true precision guided munitions and the precursors to the "smart bombs" first used by the U.S. in Vietnam. In August 1943, the British sloop HMS *Egret* was sunk by an Hs-293 missile, and subsequently this type of missile knocked out one Greek and four British destroyers. The German Fritz X glide bomb also damaged or destroyed a number of warships. In response to this aerial threat, the Naval Research Lab developed the first radio jamming system and used it to interfere with the channels over which the German weapons were guided. This was deployed aboard American destroyers in October 1943, and was very successful in cutting down the effectiveness of the German missiles.

Almost a year to the day after the bombardment of Hamburg, RAF pilot Alan Wall was approaching Munich in his Mosquito photo reconnaissance plane when he spotted a craft unlike anything he had ever seen closing on his tail at blazing speed. Wall tried to outmaneuver his attacker, but the German pilot overtook him repeatedly and blasted away with 30MM cannons, scoring several hits before Wall found sanctuary in a cloud bank and escaped to Italy. The streamlined, swift plane Wall encountered that morning in July 1944 was the Messerschmitt 262, the world's first operational jet fighter. With a top speed of 540 miles per hour, it was 70 mph faster than any of the Allies' propeller-driven craft. The Me-262 was quite simply the best airplane in existence and a weapon that could well have affected the outcome of the war.

Jet propulsion, like radar, was a notion that scientists in several countries pursued in the decade before the war. But German researchers, aided by early government backing, were first to prove that a plane could be propelled by the thrust from a turbojet engine, first to test fly a jet plane (in 1939), and first to embark on production (1944). Though Britain, the U.S., and Japan all developed jets before the war ended, the Germans were the leaders.

Allied commanders quickly saw the danger that the Me-262 represented. Squadrons of German jets attacked Allied installations and armored columns on the western front from just above treetop level. The speed of another German jet, the Ar-234, enabled it to fly photo reconnaissance missions with little fear of interference, and the resultant intelligence contributed to the success of the German counteroffensive in the Ardennes in late 1944. American and British fighters had to scramble to keep the jets in sight; hitting them was almost impossible.

The Germans cleverly dispersed and camouflaged manufacturing sites and jet bases to make them more difficult to spot, but by April 1945 Allied bomber crews were regularly lambasting the jet bases and soon afterward Me-262 squadrons had to scatter to far-off fields. It was none too soon. As Allied troops advanced into Germany they repeatedly came upon rows of newly built jet fighters awaiting delivery to now-defunct Luftwaffe squadrons. The main reason the Messerschmitts had not been used widely was that U.S. bombers had wiped out their fuel. The jet was also very difficult to pilot.

In the final weeks of the war, both U.S. and Soviet forces seized several Me-262s along with their factories and technical files. Designers in both countries saw that the jet's powerful engines made its extraordinary speed possible. Combining this with still-experimental swept-

Top. *A British worker examines a pile of radar-foiling aluminum strips early in World War II.* Below. *The "chaff" is tossed from a British Lancaster bomber during a raid on Essen, Germany, in March 1945.*

back wings and some of their own ideas, Russian engineers came up with the MiG-15, which made its public debut in 1948. In the U.S. the North American Aviation Company incorporated the swept wing design into its F-86 Sabrejet, which at 675 miles per hour became the speediest operational American fighter, although it was slower than the MiG. A few years later these two stepchildren of the Me-262 tangled in the sky over North

Korea in a closely matched contest that their successors would repeat over Vietnam.

"More bang ..."

The lessons of military innovations during World War II were not lost on the American defense establishment, and, as a result, during the postwar period U.S. military planners began to emphasize the need for increasingly sophisticated military technology. In addition to the improvement and expansion of its atomic arsenal, including the creation of the thermonuclear H-bomb, the U.S. introduced a wide range of new weapons and munitions designed to pro-

could fit into a small space—like a GI's rucksack. Another advancement in electronics was the digital computer, first introduced in the early 1950s. The second development identified by Dickson was the appearance of "remotely manned systems"—machines operated from a distance, via electronics. Examples abound, but one of the most dramatic was the Cable Controlled Underwater Research Vehicle, or CURV, an unmanned submarine equipped with a television camera and a remote-controlled "arm." CURV was used on April 7, 1966, to retrieve an H-bomb lost by the U.S. in the Mediterranean near Spain. Third, Dickson lists the emergence of bionics, in which scientists began to study and imitate systems occurring in nature,

The German Messerschmitt 262 Schwalbe (Swallow) equipped for a night mission with radar antennas on its nose.

vide, as President Dwight D. Eisenhower's Secretary of Defense Charles Wilson once put it, "more bang for the buck": long-range, high-altitude bombers and supersonic jet fighters, nuclear-powered submarines and, by the early 1960s, the first nuclear-powered aircraft carrier.

The advent of what has often been called "the third industrial revolution" in the late 1950s and early 1960s further bolstered the American commitment to technological warfare. Military visionaries had begun to imagine ways to automate warfare, replacing men on the battlefield with machines. According to Paul Dickson in his book *The Electronic Battlefield*, three specific developments were to enable these visions to become real. The first was the general revolution in electronics, which produced among many other innovations the integrated circuit. "Large scale integration" allowed electrical engineers to reduce thousands of circuits to a very small size, leading to the development of highly complex electronic equipment that

especially the nervous systems of various creatures. Bionic engineers began in the early sixties to build machines based on animal systems and organs—frogs' eyes, human noses, a beetle's flight system—in the hope that they could be used to detect and transmit specific kinds of information. These three innovations and other dramatic advances, such as those in optics and laser, opened new vistas of possibilities, many of which were exploited when the Kennedy administration began to modernize the nation's conventional war-making capabilities.

Spurred by a growing concern that excessive reliance on nuclear deterrence had crippled the United States' capacity to wage limited war and by the realization that many American weapons had become obsolete, the campaign to upgrade the armed forces across the board gathered momentum after the Berlin crisis of 1961 and Cuban missile crisis of 1962. The result was the creation of perhaps the most formidable, and certainly the most technologically advanced, arsenal of weaponry in the history of warfare.

By early 1965, on the eve of the American combat involvement in Vietnam, the U.S. Air Force had at its disposal 630 B-52 long-range heavy bombers, each capable of flying up to 10,000 miles without refueling while carrying 54,000 pounds of ordnance, as well as some 280 B-47 and B-58 medium bombers. The fighter force, which had expanded more than 50 percent during the Kennedy-Johnson years, consisted of 1,600 aircraft, designated "F" for fighter, organized into twenty-three tactical wings, including sixteen squadrons of brand-new "Mach 2"* F-4 Phantoms, twelve squadrons of F-105 Thunderchiefs, and twenty squadrons of F-100 Supersabres. For tactical transport there was the C-130 Hercules and the smaller C-123 Provider. For reconnaissance there were RF-101 Voodoo jets and specially equipped RF-4Cs. And for search and rescue missions there were A-1 Skyraiders, which also came to be used as attack aircraft.

In addition, American forces in Vietnam could call on the support of the 125 ships and 64,000 men of the U.S. Navy's Seventh Fleet, whose Task Force 77 at the time included the attack carriers *Hancock*, *Coral Sea*, and *Ranger*. It was from these three ships that the U.S. launched its first bombing missions against North Vietnam, the Flaming Dart reprisal raids in February 1965, as well as many of the Rolling Thunder missions that followed. Equipped with steam catapults and enormous angled flight decks, each of the carriers could accommodate a mixed group of strike, interceptor, and reconnaissance aircraft: F-4 Phantoms, A-4 Skyhawks, A-1 Skyraiders, and, soon, A-6 Intruders. The oldest and smallest of the three, the *Hancock*, operated with between sixty and seventy aircraft, while the *Coral Sea* carried a maximum of eighty aircraft and the *Ranger* ninety. In addition to the "blue-water" navy, the U.S. had older ships in mothball fleets that could be used for other purposes, such as slowing the movement of enemy supplies along the South Vietnamese coast and patrolling inland waterways, primarily in the Mekong Delta.

Although not as impressive as the air and sea power the Americans brought to Vietnam, the weaponry with which they equipped their ground forces seemed more than up to the task at hand. Although the first U.S. combat troops to arrive in-country carried M14 rifles, these were soon replaced by much lighter, fully automatic M16s. Most U.S. infantry units were also equipped with M60 machine guns, M79 grenade launchers, and "claymore" mines. Further firepower was provided by 4.2 inch mortars, 106MM recoilless rifles, M48 tanks, and a variety of heavy artillery pieces. To move the troops there were standard two and a half-ton trucks, M113 armored personnel carriers, and, most

important of all, helicopters. Helicopters had been used for medical evacuation in World War II, albeit briefly, and Korea, but these early choppers were severely handicapped by their short range and mechanical unreliability. With the development of the turbine-powered, single-rotor UH-1 Iroquois "Huey" in the early 1960s, however, the helicopter's potential was dramatically increased.

Communist preparations

By contrast, the enemy that the U.S. faced in the spring of 1965 possessed little that could match the awesome firepower and unprecedented mobility of the American forces in Vietnam. The Vietcong insurgents in South Vietnam had no aircraft whatsoever, while the North Vietnamese Air Force at the time consisted of a single interceptor regiment of fifty-three Soviet-made subsonic MiG-15s and MiG-17s soon to be augmented by the supersonic MiG-21. The North Vietnamese navy included only eighteen ex-Chinese and ex-Russian motor torpedo boats and a motley collection of some sixty patrol craft and mine sweepers. Communist ground forces were somewhat better equipped, though even here their arsenal was decidedly inferior to that of the Americans. While many North Vietnamese infantrymen were now equipped with Soviet- and Chinese-made AK47s, a weapon deemed by many experts to be the most successful assault rifle ever designed, most Vietcong units still relied on a wide variety of stolen or captured small arms: antiquated French bolt-action rifles and submachine guns, Garand M1 rifles and M1 carbines, and a few Soviet RPG2 rocket-propelled grenades. To contend with American air power, VC antiaircraft batteries had nothing more sophisticated than 12.7MM and 14.5MM heavy machine guns, while "artillery" support was provided by 82MM and 120MM mortars. The North Vietnamese did have some heavy artillery and a small number of aging Soviet T34 tanks, but none of these weapons were as yet deployed in the South.

Nor could the Communists count on the kind of logistical support available to their American adversaries. With its highly industrialized economy and its giant fleet of aircraft and ships, the U.S. could provide and transport seemingly limitless quantities of equipment to and around South Vietnam with relative ease. Communist forces, on the other hand, had to depend on the largesse of their Soviet and Chinese allies for the bulk of their supplies and then move them southward by sampan and junk along the Vietnamese coastline or by foot and bicycle along the rugged Ho Chi Minh Trail. In either case, they were forced to run a gauntlet of American interdiction efforts.

For all the problems and limitations they faced in early 1965, however, the Vietnamese Communists were clearly preparing for a long fight, as they responded to the influx of American troops and materiel with a build-up of their own. By early 1965 many Vietcong Main Force units were

---

* "Mach" designates an aircraft's ability to fly at the speed of sound, 334 miles per hour. Mach 2 means an aircraft can fly twice the speed of sound.

The Philippine Insurrection

Vietnam was not the first American counterinsurgency war in Asia. In 1898, American forces had fought in the Philippines, then a Spanish colony, alongside the *insurrectos* led by Don Emilio Aguinaldo who had been in rebellion against Spain since 1896. But the treaty ending the Spanish-American War gave the Philippines to America, not the insurgents, and the Philippine Insurrection against the U.S. began February 4, 1899. With old rifles and few support weapons, U.S. troops did not fare well even though lopsided conventional battles drove Aguinaldo into the countryside. The American force's search and destroy tactics killed many presumed insurgents but cost hundreds of American lives, fed Filipino hatred of the U.S., and secured no end to the war. The *insurrectos* were defeated in 1901, but the struggle against Moro tribesmen of the southern islands blundered on until President McKinley appointed William Howard Taft as governor with total civil and military authority. Taft's astute efforts gradually won over the Filipinos and the war died out by 1916.

Above. *A patrol wades a creek in pursuit of Filipino insurgents.* Right. *A group of Americans poses with one of the few new weapons at their disposal for fighting the rebels, a Gatling gun.*

Above. *After clearing out its inhabitants, American soldiers have set fire to houses in this Manila suburb.*

Left. *American troops engage in a firefight with insurgents.*

being reequipped with AK47s and other advanced weaponry, while the number of NVA regulars infiltrating into the South was steadily increasing. An intricate network of antiaircraft artillery (AAA) and ground radar already guarded North Vietnam from the inevitable U.S. bombing campaign. More portentous still, in June 1965 the first battery of highly sophisticated Soviet SA-2 missiles was set up in Hanoi to protect the capital against air attacks.

None of this daunted American military planners in Washington and Saigon, who did not even find out about the North's AAA defenses until the first Rolling Thunder missions in March 1965. They were convinced that the military advantages they enjoyed would ultimately enable them to subdue the enemy and to achieve their principal objective: a free and independent South Vietnam. They were equally confident that whatever obstacles they might run into could be overcome by the application of American technological know-how. As early as 1961, in fact, the U.S. decided to help the South Vietnamese establish a testing center to "develop, with modern technology, new techniques against Viet Cong forces." A similar charge was later given to the U.S. Army Concept Team in Vietnam (ACTIV), which evaluated and sought technical solutions to problems confronted by army units in the field.

Some of the problems, like the weather and terrain of South Vietnam, were permanent and unchanging. Nearly two-thirds of the country was covered by densely foliated jungles, forests, and mountains that were annually saturated with monsoon rains. Not only did this provide a built-in shield for enemy troop movements, but it also inhibited the use of many U.S. vehicles and weapons that had originally been designed for plains warfare in Europe. Tanks, trucks, and armored personnel carriers, for instance, were useless in many parts of Vietnam, while some jet fighters, such as the F-4 Phantom, were too fast and unmaneuverable to be used against fleeting targets.

Most U.S. attack and fighter aircraft, until the development of the A-6, were less effective in bad weather.

Communist guerrilla tactics compounded the problem. With their preference for operating at night and mingling with the civilian population by day, and for fighting and fleeing rather than engaging in set battles, Communist units made it exceedingly difficult for the Americans to find and fix, and ultimately destroy, their enemy. Moreover, when U.S. forces encountered a sizable enemy force, the Communists soon learned to "hug" the American troops so close that to use close air and artillery support, U.S. commanders risked hitting their own men.

Limited vs. total war

Beyond these concrete tactical issues, there were larger strategic questions to be addressed. In 1965 it was still uncertain, for instance, just how far the leaders of the Soviet Union and the People's Republic of China were prepared to go in their support for the Vietnamese Communist cause or, for that matter, how far the U.S. was prepared to let them go. President Johnson had made it clear that he was willing to throw the enormous weight of the American military behind the government of South Vietnam, yet he had also made it clear that he did not want to provoke a war with either of the major Communist powers. He was willing to order American forces to bomb North Vietnam, yet he placed strict limitations on the pilots' tactics and he would not authorize them to strike certain targets, including the capital city of Hanoi, for fear of rousing international protest. He wanted to interdict the movement of North Vietnamese men and supplies to the South, but he did not want to violate the neutrality of the bordering states of Laos and Cambodia.

For the Americans, in short, this was to be a limited war fought for limited ends. To achieve its objectives, the U.S.

At the U.S. Air Force base in Bien Hoa, an ordnance man loads bombs onto an A-1 Skyraider, its wings folded for storage. Designed during World War II and flown first in 1946, the A-1 seemed outmoded by the newer, faster jet aircraft. But its accuracy, durability, and ability to carry heavy bomb loads suited it better than some of its modern cousins for the task of supporting ground troops in Vietnam.

would have to operate within the context of constraints imposed by its own concept of the international political scene on the one hand and by American domestic politics on the other. America's nuclear weapons were to remain sheathed, and there was to be no national mobilization. Instead, the U.S. would rely on its superior technology to serve as a "multiplier" of its force and to reduce the sacrifice of American lives in a distant land. For as President Johnson realized, however much the American people might support the cause of South Vietnamese autonomy, they would not tolerate a long and costly war.

For the North Vietnamese and the Vietcong, however, this was a total war, fought in their own back yard with every means and resource at their disposal. With their rudimentary industrial base and near-total dependence on foreign military aid, they knew that in one sense they were no match for the affluent Americans. But they also knew that the relative "backwardness" of their economy and technology in some ways made them less vulnerable to American power. The relative lack of concentrated industry in North Vietnam, for instance, made the country less susceptible to strategic bombing, while their primitive means and myriad avenues of transport were easy to rebuild and thus limited the impact of U.S. aerial interdiction efforts. Similarly, while they did not have the Americans' capacity to move troops quickly over great distances, on the battlefield itself their lightly burdened soldiers were able to move more deftly than their heavily laden adversaries. They could also hide more easily—in the villages and cities as well as in the countryside.

It would not be easy to subdue the Vietnamese Communists. Yet in 1965 there was little reason to doubt that the Americans would find a way. Backed by the world's most advanced technology, a technology deeply interwoven into the fabric of American culture, they seemed supremely well prepared to overcome whatever obstacle the enemy might throw in their path. To help find the enemy they would use seismic sensors, chemical "people sniffers," and electronic communications intercepts. To "take the night away from Charlie," they were developing ground radar, infrared sensors, and television cameras that operated in low light. To increase the destructiveness of their firepower they were to use more accurate and lethal bombs, such as "smart" bombs and cluster bombs. To coordinate tactical air and artillery support for ground forces they would develop the most sophisticated communications ever used in warfare. And to quantify and analyze the progress being made they would use computers. As much as possible, in short, they would attempt to replace men with machines—a new way of war, but one in keeping with the American way of war.

Battling the elements. South Vietnamese marines slog toward an American CH-47 Chinook that will carry them into battle in Phuoc Tuy Province in the Mekong Delta on July 20, 1967.

17

Technology in the Great War

The trenches of World War I created battlefields bloodier than perhaps any others in history. As the "Great War" began, commanders of both forces hoped tactical measures including surprise, maneuver, or overwhelming mass could generate sufficient momentum in an initial assault to overcome the entrenched enemy. But nothing seemed to break the muddy embrace of trench warfare. The Germans tried to advance at Verdun in 1914, but ten months of battle later nothing had changed except that 698,000 men had been killed or wounded in an area the size of Manhattan. In all of 1915, the Allies never gained more than three miles of territory.

The technology of the time played a large part in commanders' hopes, but a host of new weapons was brought to the front to little avail. The tank, introduced by the British, made its first appearance but was so unreliable that it had little effect on any battle. At Cambrai in 1916, for example, tanks broke through the German line but mechanical failure and lack of reserves prevented them from sustaining the attack.

Of all the major forces the Americans came the least technologically prepared. When they joined the war in 1917, they had no tanks or artillery and had to use French machine guns and aircraft. Still, in the ultimate war of attrition, the Americans, with their fresh courage and sheer numbers, proved the final straw for an exhausted Germany.

A British Mark I "male" tank advances in the Somme on September 15, 1916. Inset. At Bellicourt in 1918, Mark IV tanks advance carrying metal fascines to drop across trenches. World War I tanks had an average speed of two mph and a range of fifteen to twenty miles.

Firepower

At first there will be increased slaughter on so terrible a scale as to render it impossible . . . to push the battle to a decisive issue. . . . At the end it is very doubtful whether any decisive victory can be gained.

So wrote Ivan S. Block, a Warsaw banker, before World War I, predicting the effect the heavy firepower of turn-of-the-century weapons would have on warfare. The war proved him correct. The repeating rifle, the machine gun, and rapid fire artillery, all newly introduced, proved killing machines of unprecedented dimensions. Observers of warfare had also sensed the growing ascendency of defensive tactics owing to increases in firepower, and the trenches of World War I seemed to support their views. As the British military historian J. F. C. Fuller wrote, "Their carefully planned war was . . . smashed to pieces by firepower so devastating that . . . there was no choice but to go under the surface . . . like foxes."

Right. British gunners use cart wheels as an antiaircraft mount for their Lewis machine gun. One wheel is buried while the other allows the gun to pivot.

German gunners fire the "Paris gun" toward the French capital. The one-of-a-kind monster could hurl a 264-pound shell eighty-two miles. Although it was militarily ineffective, its propaganda value was great.

Left. German crewmen operate a Maxim machine gun, one of World War I's most effective killing machines. Invented by the American Hiram Maxim, the gun was first sold to the Germans after the U.S. Army ordnance purchasers scorned Maxim's offer to sell it to them.

Below. The German flame thrower was risky to its operators but effective against British tanks.

Gas

Armies of wars past had attacked from behind smoke screens. To try to break the impasse in World War I, however, both sides employed a far deadlier screen: gas. The Germans introduced chlorine at Ypres in 1915, and the opposing forces subsequently wrought tremendous misery with a variety of the poisonous substances. But neither force was able to exploit the temporary advantages clouds of gas sometimes gave them. Ironically, one of the deadlier gases introduced in the war provided an unexpected medical boon when, in 1942, it was discovered that the active ingredient in mustard gas could reverse some types of lymphatic cancer. But so terrible was the suffering rendered by gas during World War I that the Geneva Protocol of 1925 declared it illegal as a weapon.

Top. German soldiers tend special smoke fires to screen activity from enemy eyes. Both sides used smoke to hide maneuvers and attacks, but depended on the wind to blow screens in the right direction.

American doughboys accustom themselves to British-made gas masks.

Below. German infantrymen attack out of a cloud of their own phosgene gas.

Communications

Armies took advantage of wireless radio and the telephone for the first time during World War I. Both sides relied on the telephone, and both sides tried to wipe out the other's telephone lines with intense artillery barrages. Because these barrages were often successful, wireless radio sets appeared at the front in increasing numbers. In addition, naval vessels carried radios, as did reconnaissance aircraft—planes, balloons, and zeppelins—for communication with the ground. Radios were also fitted to tanks, like the Mark IV, that were then used to coordinate other tanks and infantry.

Right. *A wireless station at the front.* Below. *An American officer shouts through his gas mask, relaying orders he has just received from the field telephone operated by the two seated soldiers.*

Shadow of the Future

Perhaps the most significant technological breakthrough in the war was the use of aircraft, albeit in experimental, often unsuccessful roles. Airplanes were used in every way commanders on the two sides could imagine, chiefly for aerial reconnaissance, but also for bombing civilian areas and defending troop positions. The war's memorable dogfights were carried out to protect—or shoot down—intelligence aircraft. Although no aircraft proved decisive in a battle, the destruction they could create foreshadowed aerial bombardment of the future. When British aircraft hit one of the Germans' key communications links in 1918, the Thionville railroad yards, they left their target a shambles.

Right. The "Kettering bug," a radio-guided torpedo airplane. The Allies tested this early pilotless bomb but were unable to employ it successfully on the battlefield.

Aerial bombing techniques. Left. In 1914, the copilot of a British BE-2 shows an early bomb release method. Right. A crew attaches bombs to wing racks on a British De Havilland late in the war.

Opposite. *The Thionville rail yards lie in ruins after the British air attack in 1918.*

Ground Weapons

Helicopters filled the morning sky over the jungle near the Cambodian border. Dragonflylike OH-13 Loaches darted close to the green foliage. Above and behind them came strings of troop-carrying UH-1D "slicks" flanked by their gunship escorts and behind them big CH-47 Chinook helicopters toting 105mm howitzers in slings. Above the helicopters were air force observation planes, part of the aerial armada rumbling into combat in Vietnam's central highlands, and above the observation planes flew F-4 and F-100 fighter-bombers loaded with rockets, bombs, napalm, and 20mm cannons. This was not an air but an infantry action, Vietnam style. Operation Paul Revere II, spearheaded by men from the 1st Air Cavalry Division, had begun in the early days of August 1966.

Intelligence reports had indicated that at least one and possibly two North Vietnamese regiments—the 66th and 33d—hardened veterans of the fierce fighting in the Ia Drang the previous

November, were moving back into the highlands from Cambodia. Captured documents and prisoners had given hints of the enemy move into Pleiku Province. Radio direction finders had picked up transmissions from new locations as the NVA headquarters moved to the east. Analysis of the radio signals helped identify the North Vietnamese units. Photographs taken from high-altitude reconnaissance planes revealed freshly used trails. Infrared cameras detected fresh camouflage, and heat sensors revealed signs of campfires beneath the jungle canopy.

The general outline if not the specific details had become clear: The NVA was headed back to the Ia Drang, the battleground its leaders had abandoned after their fateful clash with the 1st Air Cavalry. From there they could draw American forces stationed at isolated bases like Plei Me and Duc Co into carefully prepared ambushes. The North Vietnamese might also attack the vulnerable outposts and cut the roads, choking off a sizable section of the highlands.

The fight that now seemed imminent would be directed on the enemy side according to traditional doctrine. A commander in a headquarters bunker close to his troops and the fighting would strictly implement a plan meticulously drawn up, and, in some aspects, rehearsed. The routes to the intended battlefield would have been scouted, and ammunition, food, and medical supplies would have already been stored in caches along the way. Equally important, the routes of withdrawal would have been studiously planned, for battlefield retreat was a significant element in the enemy tactics. The North Vietnamese chose to attack only when they held the numerical advantage. With the Americans' capacity for rapid reinforcement through air mobility, the battlefield advantage might quickly shift and force a retreat. Thus the North Vietnamese carefully prepared for eventual withdrawal.

By contrast, the American commanders were acting according to a more flexible military doctrine made possible by air mobility and communications. The battalion and brigade officers flew 2,000 feet above the ground in Huey helicopters packed with radio consoles and cluttered with binoculars and maps. The commanders anxiously scanning the ground wore headsets that linked them to every element in the invading force—jets, choppers, company officers on the ground, artillery crews, division headquarters in the rear. Their airborne operations centers were known in army parlance as command and control ships; to the grunts they were C&Cs, or "Charley-Charleys." Their blend of speed, vantage, and communications technology added a new dimension to commanding men in combat.

The pilots in the little Loaches buzzing the treetops served as the operation's point men. They scouted ahead of the main force to find the enemy, draw his fire, and force him to expose his position. A suspicious movement on the forest floor, even a shadow, could send a chopper and its gunship escort slicing down for a closer look. Sometimes an enemy soldier, afraid that he had been spotted even if he had not, might move or even fire at the helicopters. The firefight the aerial scouts hoped for would begin. In the color code of the cavalry the Loaches were the white teams. The gunships, ready to open up with guns and rockets at the first sign of the enemy, were the red teams. The infantrymen traveling to battle in the trailing slicks were the blue teams.

The firefight began by the book: a quick movement between the trees, a blast from a gunship, return fire from below. Before the echoes of the first shots died, word of the fight's beginning flashed to the hovering brigade Charley-Charley. The message came in on a radio frequency monitored by the battalion commanders in the separate helicopters, by the USAF airborne forward air controllers—the FACs—coordinating the fighter-bombers, and by the division command post on the ground. A decision had to be made instantly: Should the fighter-bombers be diverted from their preassigned targets? Should the troop-carrying slicks scheduled to move in after the bombing raid be detoured to the site of the firing? The F-100s were already closing on their targets. The decision came quickly: Proceed as planned.

The FACs rolled the light observation planes—O-1 Birddogs—into near vertical dives over the first designated landing zone and fired white phosphorus rockets. Brilliant white smoke billowed up, marking the site for the bombers. The controllers used their UHF radios to tell the jet jockeys which way to come in and out and where the target was in relation to the white phosphorus cloud. The jets dove for the spot and dropped their bombs in pairs, the forest ceiling shuddered as a compression wave swept through them. And dirty gray smoke now mingled with the white puffs billowing up from the jungle floor.

Seconds after the bombs had been dropped, a fresh series of orange flashes enveloped in gray-brown erupted near the landing zone. The commanders in the Charley-Charleys had ordered eight-inch and 175MM guns at a firebase sixteen kilometers away to open fire. On another radio network all pilots were warned of the shells' trajectories so they could avoid them. Before the artillery smoke cleared, two helicopter gunships angled in and plastered the fringe of the landing zone with rockets. Fire now ringed the tangled clearing. The Charley-Charley coordinated the attack, orchestrating the complex beginnings of the battle from inside the helicopter flying 2,000 feet above the battle at 100 miles an hour. A stream of orders snapped out over the command frequency to the firebase, the gunships, and the slicks now bearing in on the landing zone with their cargo of 1st Cav soldiers tensing for the attack.

The slicks came in low, just above treetop level. The gunships on their flanks fired salvos of rockets, then began peppering the ground with 40MM grenade launchers in their chin turrets. Grenades popped along the tree line and amid the waving grass of the shell-pocked landing zone. Finally door gunners loosed a fusillade of machine-gun fire at the surrounding shadows. The lead slick eased down to within a few feet of the ground and six soldiers leaped out, some stumbling as they hit the ground but bouncing up to gallop toward the edge of the LZ. Another slick dropped down to unload, and then another, and in about ninety seconds a 100-man rifle company was on the ground. A group of three men who appeared to be glued together scudded across the clearing like some giant six-legged insect with two antennae: This was the company command group, the commander and two RTOs, radio telephone operators carrying the VHF FM radios. As soon as they cleared the choppers, the commanding officer dropped to his knees, grabbed a handset from one radio,

As a "Charley-Charley" command ship (top) watches on, a wave of 1st Cavalry UH-1D troop carriers descends toward a landing zone near Bong Son in January 1966.

and asked his platoon leaders for status reports. He listened a moment and then called the battalion Charley-Charley. "LZ Green," he said, which meant that no one was shooting at them.

The big guns arrived next, dangling awkwardly from slings suspended beneath six laboring CH-47 helicopters. The Chinook pilots skillfully maneuvered the 105MM howitzers onto the ground and disengaged the slings, then landed, and the artillerymen rushed out. Gunners hastily unpacked their ammunition cases and set up a table where fire direction specialists began computing a fire mission. Within a few minutes one of the howitzers fired a test shell. An airborne forward observer watched the shell explode and radioed a correction to the men at the fire direction center. The big guns zeroed in on an area a few

A CH-47 delivers an M102 105MM howitzer to men of the 2d Battalion, 320th Artillery, 101st Airborne Division.

miles away and began preparing the next landing zone by shelling it. Already jets and helicopter gunships were softening up the second landing zone for the next wave of infantry.

Ambush and escape

For all the preparation, the infantry company that landed on the second LZ immediately came under enemy fire; the commander's message to battalion Charley-Charley was "LZ Red." The company nonetheless secured the wood line, and a platoon began moving along a trail into the jungle probing for the North Vietnamese who had seemingly vanished.

Suddenly gunfire erupted all around them. The NVA troops—a battalion of them—were dug in on both sides and in front of the advancing platoon. The 1st Cav platoon was pinned down. Bunkers and foxholes and the jungle itself had shielded the enemy troops from the shells; trees and foliage were so thick that many bombs exploded high in the trees, and even napalm had burned out before reaching the ground. When the rest of the U.S. force moved up to help the beleaguered platoon, the dimensions of their plight became clear. The opposing forces were shooting at each other at nearly pointblank range, but the North Vietnamese greatly outnumbered the Americans. The U.S. company commander described the situation to the battalion and brigade commanders, but they all knew that neither bombs nor big guns could help—the enemy was too close to the "friendlies." What the commanders could and did do was seal off the battle zone by blasting the enemy's rear with bombs and artillery fire to cut off reinforcements. Then a second company was sent in amid intense enemy fire. Before long most of a U.S. battalion was in action along the jungle trail against the entrenched NVA soldiers.

The brigade commander in his Charley-Charley now decided to reinforce the battalion caught in the ambush. In the helicopter war any unit not fighting was a reserve, so a company from another battalion, already airborne and en route to another target, was diverted. Orders went out to the commanders and pilots ferrying the company. The 1st Cavalry pilots were told to look for nearby landing zones. The airborne soldiers got the first inkling of what was happening when their slicks suddenly banked and changed course. But in the haste of the midair change of plans, the assault helicopter unit headed for the wrong landing zone, one that had not been "prepped" by bombs and artillery.

Through a twist of luck, the foul-up turned into a blessing for the Americans. The reinforcing company was dumped onto a tiny clearing overgrown with tall elephant grass directly to the rear of the North Vietnamese. Enemy soldiers were so stunned to find themselves apparently flanked that some threw down their weapons and surren-

dered. No one could have anticipated that the 1st Cavalry troops would appear without a preliminary shelling of the landing zone—and of course it was an accident that they had done so.

Now that they had the initiative, the U.S. commanders moved to exploit it, ordering an attack. The Communist commander, not knowing how many Americans were behind him, had to decide whether to fight or withdraw. Neither he nor his superiors could change their battle plan significantly. The enemy lacked the capacity for flexibility, the ability to improvise a battle as it developed. The American commanders had this capacity because of their airborne Charley-Charley command posts, the elaborate, many-fingered network of communications they directed, and the mobility of their helicopter-borne troops. The North Vietnamese commander ordered a withdrawal, leaving many of his dead and wounded behind. The ambush was broken.

Other battles spurted and sputtered, quick flashes of fire in the thick jungle. The North Vietnamese attack began to unravel, in part because the Americans could react more quickly to opportunities created by chance. The enemy had more men, prepared positions, and familiarity with the terrain. But the attacking Americans were able to seize the offensive by saturating the area with small units, usually companies of 90 to 140 fighting men. In twenty-six days, Operation Paul Revere II was to claim some 800 enemy dead and a relatively high number of North Vietnamese and Vietcong soldiers captured, 118. Casualties for the 1st Cavalry Division were light, less than 100 killed. The operation blunted the North Vietnamese drive into

Moments after being dropped at their new position, men of the fire direction center of Battery B, 320th Artillery, 101st Airborne calculate firing data for the guns.

Pleiku Province and sent the enemy retreating to its sanctuaries in Cambodia.

The Charley-Charleys employed so effectively in Operation Paul Revere II illustrated a major departure in the American way of waging war. The change lay in what might be called the technology of command. Armies and navies have usually taken advantage of the most modern weapons available, but in Vietnam the U.S. deliberately applied technology to the control of military operations as well. The control systems that evolved in Vietnam came about as a result of several factors. One was the nature of the country itself, where the relatively few secure areas made control of ground and air forces difficult. Another was the increasing sophistication and interdependence of the various combat units. A third was the desire to exploit the advantage inherent in air-mobile troops along with the range and payload of modern warplanes.

Command technology

American military leaders reasoned that a mobile, flexible, and technically well-equipped command center was a "multiplier" of combat power, that it inevitably increased the impact of the various elements in an oper-

A young captain with the 1st Air Cavalry calls in his position near the A Shau Valley over a PRC-25, which became the standard small tactical radio in Vietnam.

ation—infantry, artillery, helicopter gunships, tactical air support, and the rest. It also added a quick-reaction and quick-change capability to the tremendous advantage in firepower that American forces enjoyed. As the weapons themselves became more complex and sophisticated, the means of controlling them had to improve too. It is no surprise that the funds allocated for command and control in post-Vietnam budgets exceeded the amount spent on many major weapons.

The weaknesses in command and control as they developed in Vietnam had more to do with human frailties than the mechanics of the system. The main complaint was too much centralization, especially at the lower levels of command. Since it was possible for a battalion or brigade leader to exercise minute-by-minute control he would often do so, even when it might make more sense for the leader of a smaller unit—like a company—on the ground to take charge. "It is a function of technology to centralize control and decision-making," Francis West pointed out in his study *The Lessons of Vietnam*. "As technology gets better and you can communicate, if you're in charge you're going to practice [control]." Company commanders sometimes resented what they regarded as gratuitous meddling by the majors and colonels in Charley-Charleys hovering at 2,000 feet.

The command system's voracious appetite for data was another source of disgruntlement. High-ranking officers grumbled that facts and numbers—body counts, trucks destroyed, sorties flown—often seemed to supplant any discussion of overall goals or analysis. "The computerization of management data put pressures that steered the way by what it measured," said USAF Major General Edward Lansdale, a counterinsurgency expert with experience in the Philippines and Vietnam. "Intended or not, what was fed into the computer was the report card." It was not always easy to distinguish the important from the trivial or to recognize genuine progress amid the cascade of data.

The vague definitions of the American purpose in Vietnam inevitably weakened the impact of command technology. Any system of command, however advanced, must ultimately be judged on its success in achieving its goals; if the goals are nebulous the command system is likely to bog down in confusion or to emphasize short-range tactical aims, both of which happened in Vietnam.

The goal of Operation Paul Revere II was an example of a short-range tactical objective, specifically the blunting of the North Vietnamese offensive in the central highlands. And for a limited-objective operation like that, the command system was perfect. The command ships were particularly useful because of the kind of war Vietnam was. In earlier and more conventional wars troops were normally spread along a front, and the leader moved his command post forward as the front advanced. Vietnam was largely a war without fronts; the two sides confronted each other in isolated battles scattered around the countryside. In this kind of combat, troops usually went into battle in small units, like companies, rather than maneuvering in large bodies such as brigades or divisions. For controlling such small-unit warfare, the Charley-Charley was ideal, allowing the commander to see the battlefield. Airborne command posts also made radio communication easier. And the radio console was the nerve center of every Charley-Charley.

The special radio kits assembled for Charley-Charleys could be moved from one helicopter to another if necessary and tailored to various levels of command. The console included one or more FM radios that could receive and transmit on at least two channels at a time. Some models had as many as a dozen channels controlled by a panel of buttons. Several headsets were attached to the console. A set of switches enabled the wearer of a headset to talk or listen on his various radios, simultaneously if he chose to. He could also communicate with others in the command chopper through an intercom system. The command group aboard a C&C ship ordinarily included the unit commander and key members of his staff, such as the operations officer and artillery liaison officer. All could use the console simultaneously.

Radios

The communications gear used by American ground forces in Vietnam ranged from small receivers that infantrymen clipped onto their helmets to relay satellites that enabled commanders in Vietnam to talk directly to the White House. The absence of conventional fronts meant that radio facilities had to replace much of the telephone wire system normally used for communication. The type of radio used in ground operations varied with the size of the unit: At battalion level and below it was FM; brigade and divisional commands had FM and VHF sets. The more intricate and sophisticated systems using microwave, tropospheric scattering, and satellites were needed for long-range transmissions. Pocket-sized FM receivers that infantrymen could snap onto their helmets just over the ear were designed to replace awkward and bulky walkie-talkies. Using a transmitter with a range of about a mile, a squad leader could theoretically whisper directions to his men without giving away his position. Soldiers in the heat of battle had trouble hearing the squad leader's instructions; if they turned up the volume the static between transmissions was too loud. Skeptical squad leaders shouted their orders rather than take a chance on the radios, and it was often easier to point to a tree or bush than to describe it into a microphone. Although useful in some situations, before long the squad radios, the smallest used in the war, were discharged from active duty.

The best of the small radios used by ground troops was the set designated PRC-25 and called "Prick 25" by GIs. This battery-powered radio in its backpack was the mainstay of company commanders and battalion leaders. Its chief virtues were reliability, a tuning system that enabled it to "lock" onto a frequency and stay there, and the capacity to transmit and receive on no less than 920 different frequencies. Its "line-of-sight" operating range on the ground (all military FM radios were line-of-sight and thus affected by obstructions such as hills or buildings) was three to five miles. The range of the PRC-25 could be lengthened by rigging up an antenna higher than the folding eight-foot-long aerial that came with the set. A much higher antenna consisting of several aluminum sections that could be joined to produce a twenty-foot mast increased the range to twelve or fifteen miles, but it was awkward to carry and took a long time to set up.

The one important refinement the PRC-25 lacked was a device to automatically scramble and unscramble voice transmissions. Such a device became necessary because of the lack of communications security exhibited by American units in their radio banter and the resultant ease with which the enemy intercepted and understood messages.

"Communications security was so poor that the enemy almost always knew of planned actions," Major General George Keegan complained. A program to introduce secure voice attachments to radios received high priority but slow acceptance. The PRC–25 had to be redesigned (and became the PRC–77). Spare parts were slow to arrive and the equipment reduced the radio's range.

Some tactical forces, such as air force ground liaison teams and certain army and marine units, favored AM stations because of their longer range and modest power demands, but the AM sets were often delicate and difficult to hold on frequency. At brigade and division headquarters the radios were large multi-channel VHF systems that were tied in to the even more elaborate long-range microwave and tropospheric scatter networks. Like the PRC–25s the VHFs were line-of-sight sets that had been built with traditional warfare in mind. In addition they were directional, meaning that their antennas had to be aimed at the next relay station. The twenty-four-channel VHFs were too heavy for easy mobility, so the rigs had to be either installed at secure bases or defended. Hilltops throughout Vietnam were studded with lonely VHF relay sites manned by crews of signalmen who often became the targets of enemy raids. When troops were sent to remote areas on short notice, the VHFs stayed behind. But as the battle unfolded and the need for communications became more acute, the kind of solution the army terms "field expediency" emerged: A VHF unit was stripped to twelve channels so it could be freighted by helicopter in a container as big as the bed of a three-quarter-ton truck.

A soldier operates an AN/MRC-34, the standard divisional VHF radio, with its trademark fly swatter-shaped antenna.

Longer-range microwave and tropospheric systems were part of the overall communications network the U.S. built in Southeast Asia but were not used to coordinate tactical combat operations. The tropospheric system connected distant points in Vietnam and Thailand by bouncing radio waves off the atmospheric layer known as the tropopause, which lies between five and eleven miles above the earth. This made it possible to send long-range transmissions that would otherwise be blocked by the curve of the earth. When the mobile equipment used with this system proved inadequate, the Defense Department hired contractors who built a vast $234 million tropospheric network known as Back Porch. Enormous sixty-foot-high antennas supplemented with underwater cables linked six major relay stations in Vietnam and Thailand with each other and with lines extending back to the U.S.

Vietnam was also the first combat zone with direct-dial telephone service. The military's Autovon (automatic voice) network, which connected U.S. military bases around the world, was extended to Vietnam in the late 1960s. By 1969 the fifty-four automatic exchanges in Vietnam and Thailand, funneled through nine switching centers, were handling more than a million calls a day.

The communications breakthrough in Vietnam with the most significant implications was the satellite system inaugurated in June 1966. The Vietnam War was the first in history in which a military commander several thousand miles from home could communicate instantly and directly with his civilian superiors. Each of the defense satellites had a range enfolding 8,000 miles of the earth's surface. A message from Saigon to Washington was relayed from a ground station to a satellite and then on to another, finally reaching a ground station on the East Coast.

Choppers

Leading the way into battle under the sophisticated command network was an aircraft that was to make an important contribution to the tactics of ground warfare. The helicopter was the single most important device to the U.S. soldier in Vietnam other than his personal weapon and had a greater influence on how he fought and lived than any other weapon.

The helicopter as an operational military machine was twenty years old before the first American combat unit shipped to Vietnam. The first successful helicopter was designed by Igor Sikorsky and demonstrated to the military in 1942. The armed forces immediately saw potential in the device and ordered several production machines to test their usefulness in roles such as liaison, scouting, and rescue. Some were used in theaters of war by 1944. But the early machines were short ranged, unreliable, difficult to fly, and hard to maintain. These deficiencies persisted with the second generation of helicopters used in Korea. The army's Bell H–13 and the air force's Sikorsky H–5 were underpowered, short ranged, and lacked instruments for night or foul-weather flying. While they performed feats of rescue impossible for other machines, they were very limited. The H–13 and H–5 carried wounded men by strapping them to covered pallets outside the helicopter's shell, and the larger H–5 could carry only four people—two of them pilots.

Both machines had trouble taking off in hot or humid air and were slow and low enough to present easy targets. Third-generation choppers, like the army's CH-21 Ute "Flying Banana," CH-34 Choctaw, and H-37 Mohave, were larger and more powerful but still suffered the same basic deficiencies. They were increasingly useful but still largely ancillary machines in military arsenals.

What transformed the helicopter into a true workhorse of the battlefield in Vietnam was the small gas turbine engine. Developed by Dr. Anselm Franz, a World War II German jet engine designer, the Avco Lycoming T53 was introduced in 1953. The first practical small turbine engine

corner. When it appeared in 1959, the first Huey was not yet an effective troop transport, air ambulance, or gunship. But refinements in both the frame and its T53 engine, including increased cabin space and power, soon made the B, C, and D model Hueys introduced to Vietnam in the midsixties highly practical and versatile. The turbine-powered ships could fly farther, faster, and more reliably than their predecessors. As the thumping whine of turbine-powered rotors replaced the rattling growls of piston engines, helicopters became increasingly common sights over the battlefield. For the first time in Vietnam, large numbers of troops were delivered to the battlefield by heli-

Sixty-foot-high parabolic antennas break the skyline at the Phu Lam STRATCOM site, part of the tropospheric scatter system that linked major U.S. bases in Vietnam and Thailand across hundreds of miles of contested territory.

for aircraft had what pilots craved—power and reliability—and what engineers loved—a basic soundness of design that could evolve as technology improved. The turbine engine did not vibrate like reciprocating engines, its much fewer moving parts and simple design made for greater reliability, and pound for pound turbines delivered much more horsepower than reciprocating engines. Thus the CH-34, with a 1,500-horsepower reciprocating engine, weighed almost 3,000 pounds more than the newer 1,400-horsepower turbine-engined UH-1H. The CH-34 was slower, a much larger target, and harder to maintain than the Huey, yet it had only marginally greater cargo capacity.

Air-mobile operations were conducted with lumbering CH-21s and CH-34s. But their short range and endurance and relatively low reliability and maintainability limited their tactical uses. The Bell UH-1A turned a technological

copter. The resulting "air mobility" of U.S. ground forces brought an unprecedented capacity for swiftness and flexibility to battle tactics.*

Two years after Bell unveiled the UH-1, Boeing first flew the CH-47 Chinook medium helicopter. Initially powered by two 2,200-horsepower turbines, the basic design of the Chinook proved so successful that two decades after its introduction, the CH-47D, with its engine upgraded to 3,750-horsepower, remained the army's main medium and heavy lift helicopter. Much of the tactical success of

* For more on air mobility tactics, see chapter three of *America Takes Over*, another volume in THE VIETNAM EXPERIENCE.

Huey Gunships

For optimal mobility over the hills, jungles, and paddies of Vietnam, the helicopter was the essential vehicle of the ground war. The UH-1 Iroquois, or "Huey," carried out a variety of duties, including medical evacuation and troop transport. Armed for combat as a gunship, the Huey could also bring to bear upon the enemy a wide variety of sophisticated weapons. Illustrated here is a full-fleshed UH-1B "Hog" (center) equipped for night fighting and three "ghosted" views, each highlighting a variety of armaments. Along with the AH-1G Cobra, the Huey proved a powerful addition to the U.S. arsenal in Vietnam.

Above right. *Introduced late in the war, the TOW missile system attached to this UH-1B was one of the gunship's most advanced armaments. Gunships fitted with TOWs saw limited action in 1972, most notably during the Communist Easter offensive, when helicopters used them against NVA armor. This Huey carries a three-tube launcher on each side. (For more on the TOW, see page 43.)*

Below. *This lightly armed UH-1B carries a seven-tube 2.75-inch rocket launcher on each side and an M21 7.62mm minigun in each door. The M21 and the M60 were the standard Huey door machine guns.*

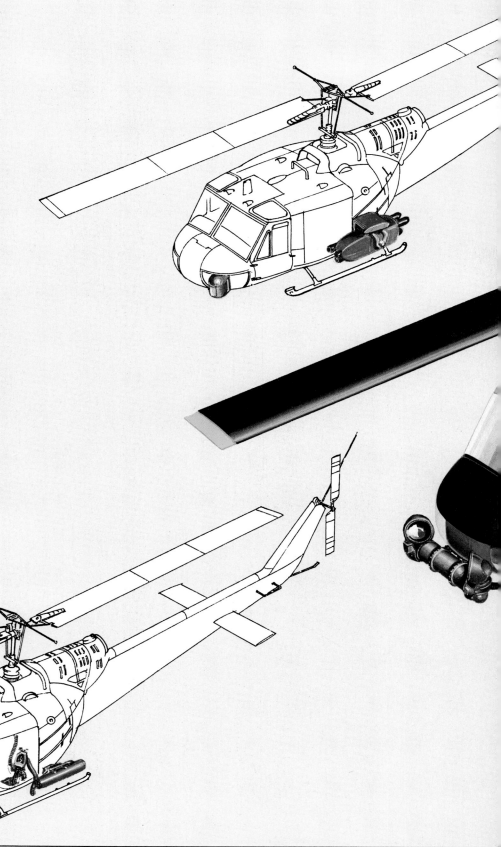

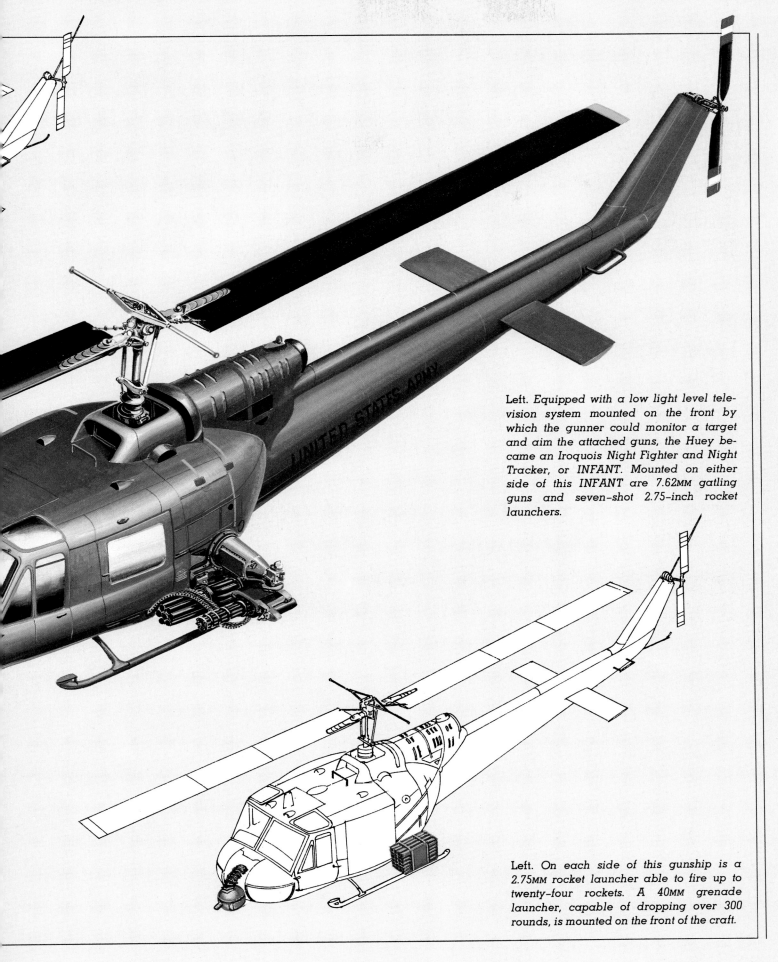

Left. *Equipped with a low light level television system mounted on the front by which the gunner could monitor a target and aim the attached guns, the Huey became an Iroquois Night Fighter and Night Tracker, or INFANT. Mounted on either side of this INFANT are 7.62MM gatling guns and seven-shot 2.75-inch rocket launchers.*

Left. *On each side of this gunship is a 2.75MM rocket launcher able to fire up to twenty-four rockets. A 40MM grenade launcher, capable of dropping over 300 rounds, is mounted on the front of the craft.*

the Huey helicopter may be attributed to the availability of the tough and capable Chinook to haul artillery, ammunition, fuel, and supplies wherever the troop-carrying Hueys took the battle.

The capacity of the enemy, whether guerrilla or NVA, to apply his doctrines of hit-and-run tactics, surprise, and mobility, could be severely cramped by the helicopter, its powers multiplied by flexible coordination of its many gunship guises (see illustration, page 36) and its other uses as troop carrier, gun tractor, supply van, scout and command ship, and medevac vehicle. Despite its myriad potential uses, the helicopter's success remained subject to the tactical sensitivity and skill of those who flew and commanded it. Consequently, air mobile tactics could become repetitive, unimaginative, and predictable, not accounting for the enemy's ability to melt into the jungle or return to his sanctuaries across the border in Cambodia, off-limits to American helicopters. Thus, while it introduced the revolutionary new dimension of air mobility to battlefield tactics, and many Vietnam air-mobile battles and campaigns are classic, the chopper, while making it hard to lose a battle, guaranteed success no more than any other piece of equipment.

Infantry arsenal

As vital as communications and air mobility were, new capabilities could not fight battles without firepower and infantrymen equipped with weapons suited to the conditions and environment that prevailed in Vietnam. American ground combatants had a wider variety of armaments than the Communist forces—and an awesome volume of firepower on call—but no single weapon that in itself proved decisive. The individual soldier had become not so much the fighting edge of the army but the focal point for a wide range of weapons. He not merely wielded his own rifle, but potentially brought to bear the big guns and aerial might behind and above him. Indeed, one expressed purpose of the infantryman on a search and destroy patrol was to serve as a kind of bait and locate the enemy by drawing his fire so that heavier firepower could be brought to bear on the Communists' then-exposed position. In the language of the electronic age the infantryman had become a "weapon system" in himself. Helicopters ferried him into battle while jets roared overhead. A dozen different guns or explosives could be mustered to help him at the flick of a switch.

The American soldier in Vietnam came to be an elaborately equipped killing machine without parallel in the annals of warfare. At the beginning of the war the infantryman was armed much like his predecessors had been in World War II and Korea. But as new equipment came into the field the resemblance ended. "A Korean War soldier would recognize the steel helmet, the pistol, the mortars, the towed howitzers, and the jerry can. The

rest of today's hardware is new," wrote John H. Hay, Jr., who commanded the 1st Infantry Division in 1967. "The lightweight M16 rifle has replaced the old M1, and the M79 grenade launcher, the light antitank weapon [LAW], and the claymore mine have increased the infantryman's firepower."

The average infantryman leaving base for an operation or a patrol of several days carried up to fifty pounds or more of gear and ammunition, food and water. The steel helmet, or "pot," was covered with a green mottled camouflage cloth. The deep pockets of the fatigue pants were filled with personal odds and ends, and over a long-sleeved fatigue shirt, army soldiers and marines were supposed to wear an armor vest known as a flak jacket. This provided protection against shrapnel and fragments from mortar rounds or booby traps, but in the steaming hot weather many soldiers preferred to risk a wound than to carry another four pounds. At the discretion of their commanders, many soldiers left their flak vests behind.

The infantryman hung on his belt, shirt, and web gear two or three canteens of water, up to four oval fragmentation hand grenades, and perhaps a smoke grenade and one or more filled with CS (tear) gas. The distinctive "pineapple" grenade of previous wars was still in use, augmented by the thin-skinned, ovoid-shaped M26 grenade, which weighed 1.7 pounds and a man could lob some forty meters. The new grenade's tightly coiled band of spring steel exploded into 1,000 fragments, effective for a "bursting radius" of five meters from the point of impact. The cylindrical, nineteen-ounce smoke grenade marked landing zones for troop and medical helicopters or established troop locations under jungle canopy for a commander loitering overhead in his helicopter. Three to four seconds after the pin was pulled, the standard hand grenade fuse ignited the caked powder filling, and dense red, white, yellow, or violet smoke poured out for fifty to ninety seconds from orifices in both ends.

Because the smoke dispersed rapidly, a smoke grenade did not produce an effective smoke screen that might permit troops to maneuver unseen by the enemy. Many troops felt that the one hand grenade that could produce a smoke screen, the M34, filled with white phosphorus, was too dangerous to carry. It weighed two pounds and a strong man could throw it only far enough not to be hit by its twenty-five-meter spray of burning phosphorus. The greater danger was its vulnerability to rupture by bullets or fragments. If the casing were punctured, the white phosphorus filling instantly ignited on exposure to air, producing agonizing, difficult to treat burns.

Bureaucracy and the M16

Of all the weapons used by Americans in the ground war, the new M16 rifle, the basic U.S. infantry weapon, probably became the most recognizable. After troops of the 1st

Cavalry Division turned back the North Vietnamese in the savage, November 1965, battle of the Ia Drang Valley, battalion commander Lieutenant Colonel Harold G. Moore lauded the new M16 rifle his troops had used in the fight. "Brave soldiers and the M16 brought this victory," he declared. To Col. Moore and other officers, the M16 was clearly the American answer to the enemy's fully automatic AK47 (see chapter four for more on the AK47 and the enemy arsenal).

Yet for all Moore's enthusiasm, the M16 rifle became a controversial weapon and had legions of detractors among U.S. troops. In the first eighteen months of its use in Vietnam, soldiers wrote letters to congressmen complaining about the rifle's malfunctions. After 160 marines were killed during a fierce battle for Hill 881 near Khe Sanh in May 1967, one veteran of the fighting wrote to Congress: "Do you know what killed most of us? Our own rifles. Practically everyone of our dead was found with his rifle torn down next to him where he was trying to fix it." Defenders of the weapon claimed that those soldiers who experienced difficulty simply failed to maintain the rifle properly. "It was admittedly a weapon that had to be cleaned meticulously," wrote General William C. Westmoreland, commander of U.S. forces. Yet the outcry was sufficient to provoke a Congressional inquiry in June 1967, which revealed the unsettling history of the rifle.

The American army has demonstrated extreme conservatism in rifle developments over the past century. Although a reliable repeating rifle had been invented by the Civil War, Union troops carried a muzzle loader into battle. The U.S. was the last of the modern armies to convert from black powder to modern smokeless powder. Although the machine gun was invented by an American in 1884, the American army was the last major armed force of the time to accept it.

After the Korean War, the Americans began an active search for a replacement to the venerable eight-shot semiautomatic M1 Garand. Many armies of the world were moving to automatic assault rifles, especially after analyses of many World War II battles showed that as many as four-fifths of the combatants never fired their rifles during battles. It was postulated that the ratio would rise if the troops were provided with automatic rifles.

The army's choice was the M14, an accurate rifle firing the 7.62MM NATO round but a heavy weapon (9.3 pounds) and awkwardly long (44.1 inches). The M14 was about the same size as the M1; it weighed three ounces less and was half an inch longer. The M14 was also semiautomatic. Although an automatic version was available, the recoil and "climb" were such that the rifle proved almost uncontrollable when fired on automatic. The semiautomatic M14 became the U.S. Army standard-issue rifle in 1957.

The Army Ordnance Corps had evinced no interest in the AR15, a light, automatic assault rifle designed by Eugene Stoner the same year. It fired a 5.56MM bullet (.22

caliber) at a high muzzle velocity (3,150 feet per second). It also acted on a tenet of "wound ballistics," showing that a small bullet that traveled quickly did more damage (had a greater "lethality") by tumbling once it made impact. A larger bullet that did not tumble tended to pass through the human body leaving minimal damage. Fully automatic, the AR15 could fire up to 700 rounds per minute without jamming. One reason for its low failure rate was that the cartridges were packed with a quick-burning gunpowder called IMR (improved military rifle). The air force tested the weapon for its special operations forces and rapidly became a proponent of the rifle. The army Special Forces began to use it. Field tests carried out in 1958 and 1959 verified that the AR15, in comparison to the M14, had more effective firepower, weighed less, handled easier, and possessed better balance, reliability, and freedom from recoil and climb on automatic. Furthermore, its failure rate was negligible; it virtually never jammed. Still the ordnance corps would not be convinced; after another series of tests, the ordnance corps concluded that "only the M14 is acceptable for general use in the U.S. Army. . . . [The AR-15] is less reliable."

As the Vietnam War expanded, the heavy M14 proved to be inadequate for jungle warfare, but the AR15 earned glowing reports from the men of the Special Forces who had used it in combat. Procurement of the AR15 began in late 1963, with 19,000 ordered for the air force and another 85,000 designated for the army Special Forces. The Army Ordnance Corps had finally accepted the AR15 design but declared it inadequately developed and ordered modifications to "militarize" it into the M16.

The degree of twist in the barrel was increased, imparting a faster spin to the bullet. This was because tests had indicated that the bullet might "wobble" when fired at minus sixty-five degrees Fahrenheit, and to enter the army arsenal a rifle had to perform as well in the Antarctic as in the Sahara. The result was a more stable bullet but one whose lethality had been reduced. A manual bolt closure was added, although its automatic mechanisms had rarely failed.

The most significant change came in the powder used in the bullet. For no clear reason, the army specified a muzzle velocity of at least 3,250 feet per second, about 100 feet per second faster than the AR15 now achieved. To increase the velocity, the IMR powder was changed to the slower burning "ball" powder. This propellant increased the muzzle velocity to 3,250 feet per second but also created other effects. It raised the cyclic rate of fire from 700 rounds per minute to nearly 1,000 rounds per minute, leading to frequent jams and breakdowns. The slower powder was still burning when the bullet passed the gas port. Ball powder also left residue in the barrel that required frequent cleaning to avoid jamming. Tests conducted by Colt in 1965 comparing the two powders found that no rifles were likely to fail using IMR but that half would fail with ball powder. M16 cartridges were nevertheless produced with ball powder.

Many of the regular army and marine units shipped to Vietnam in 1965 carried the M14 rifle, and the soldiers soon discovered that it was too bulky and uncontrollable in heavy jungle. They also found themselves being outgunned by the enemy's fully automatic AK47. Following the success of the M16 in the U.S. battle in the Ia Drang Valley, General Westmoreland sent an urgent, personal request to the Pentagon for the rifle to be issued as standard equipment for all units in Vietnam.

The ordnance corps complied with Westmoreland's request for the M16, although grudgingly. Defense officials "disregarded the urgency of my request and failed to gear American industry to meet the need," Gen. Westmoreland wrote in his memoirs. The rifle was not available to all American units until 1967, and South Vietnamese units were not fully fitted with it until long after. "The slow production of the M16 was a grave sin of omission," Westmoreland concluded, adding that it slowed U.S. operations in Vietnam and added perhaps a year to the program of Vietnamization.

Units that shipped to Vietnam with the M16 had already learned on the training field to clean the weapon, literally, as if their lives depended on it. Men issued the weapon after they reached Vietnam, as many marines were, had no such experience and were not usually told about the weapon's sensitivity to dirt, but they soon learned. Cleaning rods were often in short supply, so many soldiers resorted to a field experience common to other wars and rifles: They used their toothbrushes to clean the M16.

Following the 1967 Congressional inquiry, the ordnance corps made some adjustments to the M16. Chrome was used to line the barrel, and the mechanical "buffer" of the rifle was changed to reduce the cyclic rate of fire. These changes reduced the amount of jamming but did not restore the reliability or the lethality of the original AR15. Nor was the gunpowder ever changed from ball powder back to the more reliable IMR.

Portable firepower

One of the few completely new infantry weapons to appear during the Vietnam War, the M79 grenade launcher had no counterpart in foreign armies. Resembling a sawed-off shotgun, the M79 fired a spherical grenade only 40MM (just over an inch and a half) in diameter, yet the shell had a "kill radius" of five meters. Grooves in the barrel of the grenade launcher imparted a spiral spin to the warhead, stabilizing its flight. The spiral also caused weights in the fuse mechanism to arm the fuse after about thirty meters of flight, after which the shell detonated on impact. The warhead was thus safe from accidental detonation from a bump or fall or if struck by a bullet. With a muzzle velocity of only 250 feet per second (compared to

3,270 feet per second for an M16 rifle bullet), the shell could easily be seen in flight. Yet it had pinpoint accuracy to 150 meters and a maximum range of 350 meters, effectively covering the gap between the range of a hand grenade and the safe distance for artillery and mortar fire support. Generally two M79 grenadiers joined with eight M16 riflemen to form a squad.

Infantry companies also had the benefit of starlight scopes, which resemble large telephoto lenses. First introduced in 1965, starlight scopes permitted a sniper or guard to see in the dark by detecting faint reflections of starlight and magnifying them several times to produce an image that appeared on the eyepiece in bright green. Though their focus and detail were not sharp, the earliest models of the scopes could pick up human figures in the dark at a range of about 400 meters.

Once the technology for the starlight scope was developed, it advanced rapidly. The first starlight scopes needed three amplifying chambers to enhance the image, each chamber picking up photons of the existing light and amplifying their effect. The second-generation scope used only one stage of amplification because more efficient amplification tubes, or chambers, had become available. This allowed them to be built lighter and smaller and still produce better images—providing greater range—than the earlier devices.

Many soldiers carried a two-foot-long Fiberglas tube on a canvas shoulder strap. Called a LAW (for "light anti-tank weapon"), it was a one-shot disposable rocket launcher, a miniature bazooka, that could open up enemy bunkers. The LAW weighed just over five pounds, and soldiers did not mind carrying it since it packed a significant amount of firepower. The tube extended to thirty-five inches; a folding plastic sight and cheap trigger were built into the package. When its 66MM shaped charge exploded against a tank or bunker, it shot out a jet of hot gas and molten metal that could theoretically penetrate the thickest tank armor and spray the interior with fragments.

The LAW required considerable training to make it effective. In its first combat against Soviet-designed PT76 light tanks at Lang Vei Special Forces camp in February 1968, LAW rockets scored several direct hits with no discernible effects. One team reported hitting a North Vietnamese tank nine times and the rockets exploded with great showers of orange sparks, but the tank kept rolling.

Because the LAW was intended as an "extra" infantry weapon, troops received very little training in using it to knock out tanks or tear apart bunkers. Few soldiers fired

High-tech grunt. Wearing a flak vest beneath his shirt, this GI carries the XM148 rifle, an M16 with a 40MM grenade launcher attached beneath the barrel. An AN/TVS-2 starlight scope mounted on top gives him a daylight picture at night. Inset. A nighttime view through the starlight scope catches a soldier plugging his ears just before his gun fires.

41

The Shaped Charge

Used to penetrate armored vehicles, walls, or bunkers, shaped-charge rounds carried a punch belied by their relatively small size. The rounds had been in use since World War II; in Vietnam they were fired most often by the American M72 LAW and the Communist RPG7.

This series of diagrams shows how a shaped charge, in this case fired by an M72, magnifies the effect of a relatively small round.

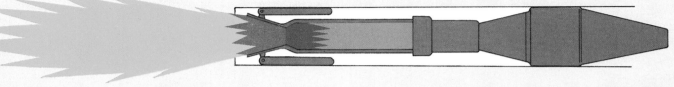

1. The round, its fins folded, is fired and emits a flame out the back of the disposable M72 tube before starting its flight.

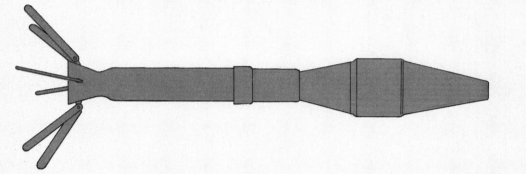

2. In flight to the target, the 66MM round's fins open to give it stability.

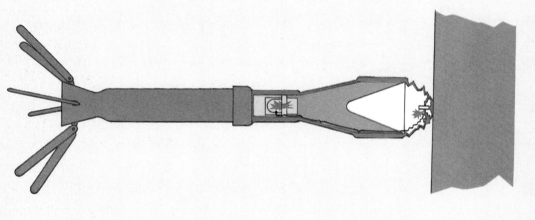

3. The round hits its target, which crumples the nose and detonates the charge (shown in orange).

4. The charge burns through the target's wall (or armor) in seconds, erupting in a huge explosion on the

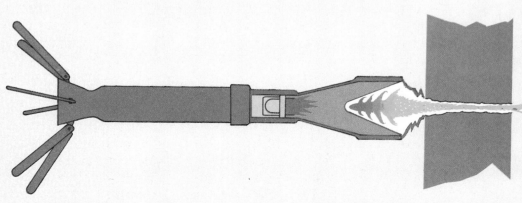

other side. The shape of the M72's charge allows it to burn through a wall several inches thick.

the weapon with accuracy. When troopers of the 173d Airborne Brigade tried LAWs against North Vietnamese bunkers on Hill 875 during the battle of Dak To in November 1967, their attacks were easily beaten back. Because of its small shaped-charge warhead, short range (325 meters maximum), and awkward sighting and firing devices, the rocket required pinpoint marksmanship that came only with training and repeated firings. ARVN soldiers received more training during the period of Vietnamization and used the LAW effectively against North Vietnamese tanks during the 1972 Easter invasion. When NVA armor rolled through Dak To in 1972, many of the LAWs that had been stored in underground bunkers failed to fire because the electrical connections had corroded. The ARVN thus fell back to Kontum to pick up a fresh supply of LAWs, hurriedly shipped in, which helped to turn the attack.

Some infantrymen on patrol also carried claymore 3.5-pound curved antipersonnel mines that came in a convenient carry bag with an electric detonator, fifty feet of wire, and a "clacker" that fired the detonator. Produced before the war and introduced into combat in Vietnam, the claymore, like the ancient Scottish broadsword for which it was named, was designed to cut a swath through the approaching enemy. Placed inches above ground on folding spike legs, the claymore fired 700 steel pellets at the height of a man in one direction to a distance of fifty meters. The claymore proved to be a perfect weapon to initiate an ambush but was used most often to protect night defensive positions. Frequently enemy soldiers sneaking up to an American bivouac bravely picked up a claymore and turned it around to face the guard position, then made some sounds to provoke the guards into detonating it.

The standard infantry company in Vietnam (at full strength 6 officers and 158 enlisted men) also carried some heavier equipment. In addition to twenty-four M79 grenade launchers and 149 M16 rifles, each infantry company was issued six M60 machine guns, three 81MM mortars, and three 90MM recoilless rifles. Every group of infantrymen always took the twenty-three-pound M60 machine gun with them on patrol. Firing a 7.62MM round (a .30-caliber bullet, also called a NATO round since it was the standard round used by all forces in the North Atlantic Treaty Organization) and operated by a two-man crew, the M60 was able to pour a heavy volume of fire against an enemy target. It proved especially useful in trying to break an ambush.

Considered by many to be too heavy to carry on the normal patrol, the 81MM mortar (132 pounds) and 90MM recoilless rifle (35 pounds, with rounds weighing 9 pounds each) were almost always left behind in the base camp and used for defensive purposes. Mortars were highly lethal at ranges up to 3,600 meters, but infantry generally patrolled under an artillery umbrella, so fire from mortars was usually considered redundant.

The 57MM recoilless cannon, usually called a rifle, made its first appearance in the Pacific during World War II. The 90MM and 106MM recoilless rifles were introduced in Vietnam. The rifle combined a relatively light weight with a relatively large, high-velocity shell propelled by gas. Unlike the normal artillery round the casing of the recoilless rifle shell is perforated with dozens of holes and it does not fit snugly into the cannon's breech. When the gun is fired, some of the propellant gases escape through the holes and fill the cavity between the shell and the walls of the breech. The gases then escape to the rear of the gun through holes machined in the back of the breech. At the same time, another portion of gas forces the projectile up and out of the barrel. The shell is then hurled out of the barrel, creating a hefty recoil that is exactly matched in force by the rocketlike blast from the breech. The projectile zips toward the target at well over 1,000 feet per second while a great blast of flame blows out the back and the gun remains stationary. Although designed to be carried by infantry soldiers especially for use against tanks and bunkers, the 90MM recoilless rifle was usually left in the base for perimeter defense, and the soldiers chose to carry the far more portable LAW.

The 106MM recoilless rifle weighed 400 pounds and was mounted on a jeep. It lacked any protective armor but was highly mobile and could be driven around a firebase or along a convoy. The 106 delivered powerful projectiles with accuracy up to 1,100 meters. Bolted to the gun was a semiautomatic .50-caliber rifle that fired a special phosphorus-filled tracer bullet with ballistic characteristics that closely matched the ballistics of the 106MM projectile. The tracer and white phosphorus filler made it easy to see where the bullet struck. The .50-caliber rifle was fired by *pulling* on a knob; *pushing* the same knob fired the main gun. The gunner could figure the range of the target, moving or still, by firing the smaller rifle until he saw a telltale puff of white smoke on target. Then he pushed the knob and the 106MM round would hit the same spot.

The TOW

One of the most advanced infantry weapons of the war found little use until very late, 1972. The TOW, a wire-guided antitank missile, was not used because the enemy, prior to his conventional 1972 Easter invasion, had very little armor. But its predecessor, the SS-11, the first wire-guided missile, arrived in Vietnam in 1965 for use against Vietcong bunkers.

As the missile flew through the air, two bobbins in its tail released fine wires connected to the launcher. The missile's flight commands traveled along the wires. The SS-11's launcher attached to the control box, which was equipped with a joystick for controlling the missile. The gunner watched the slow-moving missile through binoculars and "flew" the SS-11 to its target, gauging by eye the path of the missile and making corrections via the joystick.

Flying at 180 miles an hour, the missile had a range of 3,000 meters—the length of its control wires.

The SS-11 arrived in Vietnam with launchers that could be adapted to helicopters in place of the usual rocket pods, with the control cables leading to the copilot's seat. The missile was more powerful than the 2.75-inch rocket, typically carried by Huey helicopter gunships, and was able to penetrate an enemy bunker. But few helicopter crews had experience with the weapon, and the missiles often missed their targets. By 1971, the SS-11 had fallen into disuse.

During the Easter invasion the North Vietnamese unveiled their own wire-guided antitank missile obtained from the Soviet Union, the 9M14M Malyutka (little one), named by NATO the AT-3 Sagger. North Vietnamese gunners destroyed several American tanks during the battle for Dak To in the central highlands, but the South Vietnamese defenders noticed the missile's erratic, weaving path. The ARVN soldier soon learned of the weapon's weaknesses.

The slow-moving Sagger was easily visible as it flew through the air and it could be ducked. If the target made a sudden shift in direction toward the end of the missile's flight, the far-off gunner usually did not have time to make an accurate course correction. In addition, the gunner directing the missile had to expose himself for up to twenty-one seconds—the time a Sagger took to reach its maximum range of 3,000 meters. If the gunner were distracted or were forced to duck under enemy fire, he would likely lose control of the missile, causing it to miss the target.

The United States had solved some of the Sagger's weaknesses and improved on its own SS-11 when it in-

Below. *Sergeant John Rogers of the 4th Battalion, 12th Infantry, 199th Light Infantry Brigade fires his 90MM recoilless rifle at enemy bunkers near Saigon.* Right. *A marine moves toward the larger 106MM recoilless rifle during action in Hue during the Tet offensive in 1968.*

XM546 Beehive Projectile

Although artillery guns traditionally fire high explosive rounds, gunners also use "canister" ammunition, including the beehive, for close-range attacks against massed enemy troops. First fired in the Middle Ages, the canister ammunition used in World War II, Korea, and in the first years of the Vietnam War was usually packed with thousands of small cylindrical metal pellets or steel balls. In Vietnam, a new type of canister was introduced that used "fléchettes," small, arrowlike projectiles. The fléchettes flying through the air create a frightening buzzing noise, hence the name "beehive." When fired, the projectile leaves the gun barrel. The fuse then detonates the base charge, blasting off the forward shell case and releasing the fléchettes.

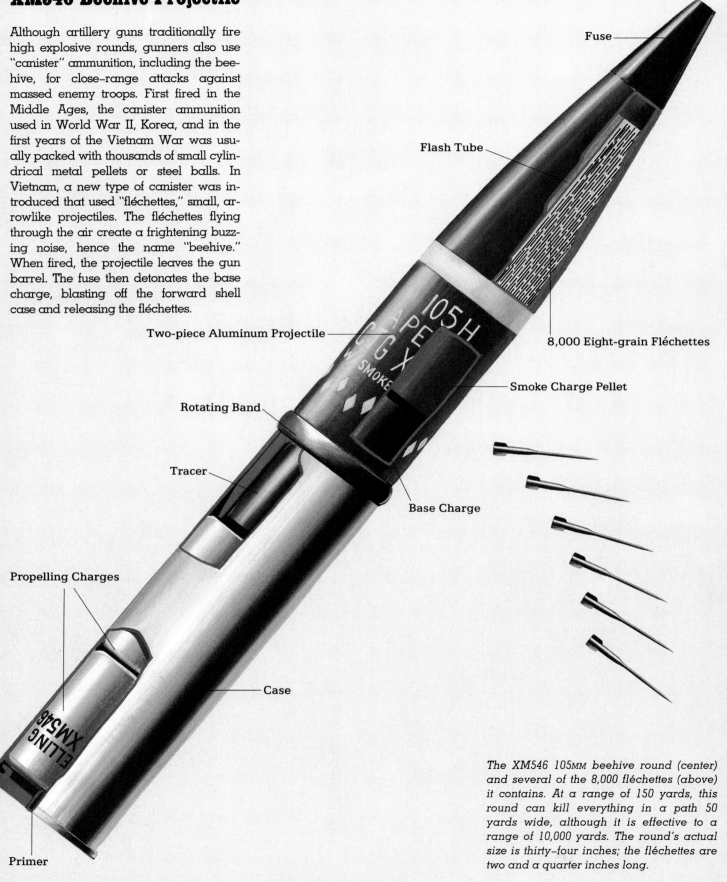

Fuse

Flash Tube

8,000 Eight-grain Fléchettes

Two-piece Aluminum Projectile

Smoke Charge Pellet

Rotating Band

Base Charge

Tracer

Propelling Charges

Case

Primer

The XM546 105MM beehive round (center) and several of the 8,000 fléchettes (above) it contains. At a range of 150 yards, this round can kill everything in a path 50 yards wide, although it is effective to a range of 10,000 yards. The round's actual size is thirty-four inches; the fléchettes are two and a quarter inches long.

troduced the TOW, originally designed to replace the 106MM recoilless rifle. The forty-three-pound TOW—for tube-launched, optically tracked, wire-guided—made a dramatic combat debut during the successful battle for Kontum City in May 1972. Their launchers mounted in helicopters, TOWs knocked out twenty-four tanks in addition to APCs, machine guns, and other targets, contributing to the defense of Kontum.

Like the SS-11 and Sagger, the TOW trailed control wires, but the TOW's wires connected to a sighting and tracking mechanism that consisted of a computer and two telescopes. One thirteen-power telescope, with cross hairs for the gunner, could magnify a tank 1,000 meters distant so that its image nearly filled the scope; the second telescope had an array of infrared sensors instead of an eyepiece. The missile was launched by a motor; at a safe distance from the gunner, a sustainer motor ignited, and simultaneously a bright flare in the tail also ignited. The infrared telescope tracked the bright flare and with the computer's assistance kept the missile on line. As long as the gunner kept the cross hairs on his target, the computer guided the missile with deadly accuracy. The six-inch diameter warhead would strike within four inches of the aiming point as much as 3,300 meters away. The TOW was not foolproof. If the gunner moved the sight abruptly, by ducking enemy fire for example, the computer might lose the image of the missile. The gunner might also lose a target if it moved too fast.

But the concept of an optically tracked, wire-guided missile, introduced for the first time to the battlefield by the SS-11, Sagger, and TOW, initiated a new approach to antitank tactics. After the war, the MGM-71 TOW, with an increased range of 4,500 meters, entered the U.S. arsenal as one of the most effective weapons of its kind in the world. TOW developments continued in the early 1980s, and although the missile saw limited use in Vietnam, in 1981 the U.S. armed forces employed more than 20,000 TOW launchers. Another weapon first used in Vietnam, the beehive artillery round, also proved effective enough to remain in the arsenal after the war.

Bird and the beehive

Firebase Bird perched atop a scrawny curved ridge in the western hills of Binh Dinh Province, in the middle of an area of several radial valleys called the "Crow's Foot," in

Soldiers lay M14 mines. Used in base defense, the plastic mine could blow off a man's foot.

which the 1st Air Cavalry Division had previously clashed with the NVA in March 1966, during Operation Masher/White Wing. The 100-odd 1st Cav troops stationed there included two artillery batteries, an understrength rifle company, and a small helicopter refueling and rearming detachment. The rain-swollen Kim Son River flowed by an all but abandoned village in the valley at the base of the ridge. In December 1966, just before the Christmas truce, having discovered it and realizing that its isolation made it vulnerable, the enemy marked Bird for destruction.

First Cavalry Division officers at headquarters in An Khe tensed for an attack but had received no information telling them how to prepare a defense. The infantry company defending the 600-meter perimeter around the base was already down to two platoons; a third platoon had recently been ordered out to conduct ambush patrols south of the river. The officers sent no reinforcements, and the men at Firebase Bird were advised merely to "be alert." Another problem was that security outposts had been placed too high in the surrounding hills to see the routes along which the enemy would most likely attack. Firebase Bird was, in short, a sitting duck.

The 22d NVA Regiment was to attack Bird while the 18th was assigned to pin down the defenders at the other firebase, Pony, twelve kilometers away, and to silence its artillery. Fortunately for the Americans, the 18th failed to move against the other base, but soon after nightfall on December 26, two battalions from the 22d moved quietly along the trails that snaked through the hills. An NVA heavy weapons company set up 82MM mortars and recoilless rifles on a low ridge 900 meters northeast of the base. Because of their careful preliminary reconnaissance the enemy gunners were able to set their weapons for the right distance in the darkness. The infantry battalion selected to make the first assault worked to within thirty meters of the wire marking Bird's perimeter without being detected. The attackers were even able to string field telephones along their assault line.

A deadly volley suddenly came from the mortars and recoilless rifles. It demolished Bird's command post and most of its artillery fire direction center in one stroke, cutting nearly all communication with the outside. Only half of the men at Bird were on alert. The rest were asleep. NVA troops swarmed across the perimeter wires and fell on the gun pits at the northern end of the base before most of the slumbering GIs realized what was happening. The defenders scrambled for the bunkers and gun sites on the southern edge of the base in a desperate attempt to hold on. By the eerie light of tracer fire they could see more than 100 North Vietnamese storming a 155MM gun emplacement. "Yankee, you die tonight," some NVA troops yelled. "What do you do now, GI?" Staff Sergeant Douglas MacArthur Graham, pinned down with six others in a drainage ditch fifteen meters away, realized that the invaders were preparing for a final charge.

Lieutenant John D. Piper thought about Bird's recently issued beehive artillery shells as soon as the attack started. The division's artillery colonel had touted the beehive for precisely this kind of situation, when the enemy was threatening to overrun a position. It was a weapon for a close-range fight with a swarming foe. Designed to be fired from a 105MM howitzer, the shell contained 8,500 fléchettes, inch-long metal arrows that resembled finishing nails with fins. When the shell exploded, the fléchettes spread out in a thirty-degree cone of fire with an effective range of 300 meters. The beehive was exactly what they needed, Piper thought, but he could not remember where the rounds were. He and several other men began a frantic search of their ammunition stores by flashlight and they found two beehive shells.

Piper set the time fuse on the shell for pointblank range and aimed his howitzer northeast, where the enemy infantrymen were thickest. Lacking a green flare to warn Graham and the other GIs in his line of fire, he and his crew men shouted "Beehive, Beehive" at the top of their lungs. Ten seconds later he fired. Immediately on leaving the gun, the shell burst open and a hurricane of tiny arrows screamed toward the North Vietnamese. Piper heard a crackling sound. Graham, 140 meters dead ahead of him, heard the fléchettes pass directly over his head "sounding like a million whips being cracked."

The crackling cone of fléchettes cut down every North Vietnamese soldier in its path. Firing from the northeast abruptly stopped. The shouts and threats were replaced by agonized screams and then a strange stillness. Dead and wounded littered the ground around the 155MM gun pit. In some cases the arrows had pinned weapons to the attacking troops' hands and bodies. Enemy soldiers who had escaped paused, fearful of the monstrous humming cloud that had decimated their assault wave. Graham peered over the rim of his ditch and saw survivors dragging their dead back toward the perimeter.

Piper called for another Beehive round. He aimed the second round a little to the left, where the remaining NVA were clustered, and let fly again. Once more the fléchettes mowed down dozens of the enemy. Now American infantrymen rushed forward and artillery men moved up to reclaim their guns. The enemy assault was broken. The base commander finally found a PRC-25 radio and called for artillery support from Firebase Pony, twelve kilometers distant. The big guns quickly zeroed in on the North Viet-

namese mortars and knocked them out. The 22d Regiment began a slow and clumsy withdrawal with allied troops in pursuit. Over the next several days the NVA regiment lost twice as many men as had fallen in the beehive-punctured fight at Firebase Bird. The 22d lost 266 men in all, the 1st Cav less than a quarter as many.

News of the beehive's awesome battlefield debut traveled quickly through American bases in Vietnam. Before long there were beehive adaptations for both light and medium howitzers, for the 2.75-inch rockets carried by helicopter gunships, for 90 and 106MM recoilless rifles, and for tanks. The artillery shells could be set to detonate anywhere up to the howitzer's maximum range of thirteen to sixteen kilometers; the infantry and gunship versions exploded at a preset distance from the launcher. As with most weapons there were ways to minimize its effects—crawling underneath the path of the darts was one—but the beehive had a sting that the enemy never forgot. Beehive rounds, such as the XM494 and XM546, proved successful enough during the war that the army continued to use and develop them afterward.

Artillery

While the beehive introduced a new twist to firepower, the guns and tanks that fired it in Vietnam were relatively "low tech." Except for advances in siting, experimental devices for night operations, new alloys to make the barrels more durable, and other small innovations, the artillery pieces and tracked vehicles used by the U.S. in Vietnam made no radical contributions to modern warfare. American infantrymen in Vietnam, however, cared little whether or not the guns were high or low tech. To troops in contact with the enemy, artillery was every bit as important as the helicopter or any other weapons system. U.S. ground troops' reliance on the firepower of artillery had grown steadily through World War II and Korea. In Korea it was the great equalizer and allowed many thin lines of infantry foxholes to hold off the human wave assaults of the Chinese. In Vietnam, as it had been in Korea and World War II, it was quite effective. Far more enemy were killed or wounded from artillery fire than from all other ground weapons combined. Yet artillery became progressively more inefficient in terms of enemy casualties inflicted per shell fired. In Vietnam, an estimated 340 shells were fired for every enemy casualty, compared to 300 rounds in Korea and 200 at Anzio in World War II.

Artillery was the constant companion of the infantryman and the security blanket for the camps, firebases, and outposts. Americans fired their artillery around the clock. During the night, if there was nothing specific to shoot at, they fired masses of shells for "harassment and interdiction"—"H&I." An embattled soldier in the field seldom had long to wait for the soft, comforting crump of artillery in the distance. The low ratio of shells fired to enemy killed was due in part to H&I practices unconstrained by ammunition scarcity. When used in support of tactical maneuvers, artillery was astonishingly responsive, flexible, and deadly. The keys to its effectiveness were several: weapons design, organizational design, and logistics.

Like most other major weapons in the ground forces' inventories, artillery was designed with front lines in mind. Within the range limitations of the gun, it was expected to support a slice of the front line, being able to fire on top and in front of the lines from positions relatively safe in the rear. Guns were generally designed to swing enough to the left and right to cover a reasonable sector of a front line and to adjust up and down to change the firing distance. Different amounts of propellant powder also resulted in different firing distances. By the end of World War II and Korea, the American army and marines had standardized three major caliber howitzers, the 105MM, 155MM, and the highly accurate eight-inch (203MM). The latter two came in self-propelled versions. Shortly before Vietnam, a new gun was introduced, the M107 175MM self-propelled artillery piece.

The standard divisional artillery piece was the World War II vintage M101 105MM howitzer with the split box "trail" design common to most artillery, including the M114 155MM gun. Clamped together, the trails formed the tow bar for the gun. To go into action, the trails were spread apart and planted firmly in the ground by shovel-like blades fixed at their ends. The trails served to give the gun a firm base and transfer to the earth the tremendous recoil of firing. Once the "spades" were well set in the ground, the gun would hardly shift in firing; only the barrel would recoil as hydro-pneumatic absorbers cushioned the shock of firing while transmitting the recoil energy to the gun carriage. This was the key to an artillery piece's capability to fire rapidly and accurately at a distant, unseen target. The only disadvantage of split-trail design was that to make a significant change—more than twenty-five degrees—in the direction of fire, the crew had to dig up the spades and manhandle the several ton gun to the new direction and replant the spades. In a war without fronts, when attack might come from several angles, this could cause problems.

The M102 105MM howitzer, designed for airborne and air mobile units, was much lighter and could pivot to cover a full 360-degree traverse. Instead of using split trails, it

---

Battery B, 1st Battalion, 83d Artillery blasts targets near the A Shau from Firebase Bastogne in 1968 with an M107 175MM gun. The M107 had a range of thirty-three kilometers, giving it the longest reach of any gun in the war.

49

used a single one, ending not in a spade but a soft rubber tire. The gun was jacked up for action on a broad steel disk that served as a pedestal. When the gun fired, the recoil was transmitted partly through the pedestal and partly down the trail to the rubber tire and then to the ground. It was fully as stable as the M101, and by merely pushing the trail around on its tire the gun could be turned about its jack stand to any direction. Where the heavy M101 had to be carried by a CH-47, the M102, 1,500 pounds lighter, could be lifted by the Huey.

The various calibers of gun had advantages and disadvantages. Because the shell is easily handled by one man and it fires "semifixed" ammunition, the lightweight 105 is fast to load and fire. A battery of six guns could dump forty-eight thirty-three-pound shells on a target in one minute. The calculated number of powder bags are loaded into a brass or steel cartridge case and the shell is fitted into the end beforehand. This allows the loading of the shell and propellant to be done in one motion. The weaknesses of the 105 lie in its relatively short range of 11,000 meters (almost eight miles) and in the fact that its thirty-three-pound shell is often not powerful enough to penetrate thick jungle canopy or destroy bunkers.

The 155MM howitzer hurls a shell almost three times as powerful although not much farther. As with larger guns, the shell is loaded first, then the correct number and size of powder bags are stuffed in, and a small firing cartridge is inserted in the breech. The three-step loading means a slower rate of fire.

The eight-inch and the 175MM self-propelled guns are loaded the same way. However, the shells are too heavy for men to load alone and the guns are equipped with hydraulic loaders. Two crewmen place one of the projectiles on the loading tray and it is then hydraulically loaded into the breech. The rest of the loading sequence is manual. The advantages of the big guns lie in the destructive power of the huge shells and in their much greater range. The 175MM gun was designed mainly to attack targets well behind enemy lines and has a range of 38,000 meters, more than twenty-three miles. However, the tremendous blast of powder required to launch the 175-pound shell quickly wears out the barrel which then must be replaced. A 105MM howitzer barrel has an expected useful life of over 20,000 firings, the 175MM gun barrel a life of only 400 full charge firings.

The organization

Artillery is designed to be fired at targets the gunners cannot see. This is accomplished by calculating, as finely as possible, the exact distance and direction the shells must fly to hit the target. Greater accuracy is gained by knowing in detail the conditions—temperature, pressure, humidity, and winds—that affect the flight of a shell.

Typically, artillery is organized into four- or six-gun

batteries. A battery's guns were normally placed in a circular or star formation that would form the basic patterns of the shells when they fell, as all guns would usually use the same "firing data." The data for each gun could be calculated separately to cause the shells to fall closer together or all in a line or in any other pattern, but this was more time consuming. In order to provide continuous artillery support, commanders did not like to move artillery unless necessary. Because it was a no-front war, each artillery position had to be self-defending, hence the development of fire support bases. The approach generally adopted was to dot the countryside with the bases, each within the range of the guns of one or two others.

Firebases and supported infantry (and advisers) were tied together by webs of radio communications. Immediate artillery fire could be called for by virtually anyone with a radio. Normally and most efficiently, it was called by trained artillery forward observers accompanying infantry or flying in scout or command helicopters. Directly, or by relay, the request for fire reached a fire direction center (FDC). Using plotting boards with pencils, protractors and rulers, slide rule calculators, and books of firing tables, the FDC translated the request into firing data for the guns. It was seldom more than five minutes between the time a soldier called for fire and the first round exploded. Although every battery included an FDC, one FDC could plot for more than one battery in such a way that a target could be attacked simultaneously by guns of all calibers in range. During the siege of Khe Sanh in 1968, 175MM, 155MM, 105MM, and even 4.2-inch mortars all had firing data and times calculated and controlled so that dozens of shells of various calibers fired from different locations exploded simultaneously over the same area. Although such coordinated fires could not be calculated instantly, in emergencies it took only a few minutes.

The redundant web of radios and capabilities of the FDCs made U.S. artillery the most flexible heavy firepower of any kind. In 1967, the army introduced a true artillery computer—the FADAC. But at first it worked no faster than human calculators because men used to slide rules had trouble with the typewriter-style console and made mistakes. Consequently, safety-conscious fire direction centers double-checked the computers with human slide rule operators. The FADAC also broke down often because of heat and erratic power generators. Their primary value in Vietnam was in planning very complex missions, such as those at Khe Sanh, when the time element was not critical.

Vietnam tracks

Tracked vehicles used in Vietnam—armored personnel carriers (APCs), tanks, and other specialized vehicles—did not share the newer Vietnam-era weaponry's luster of advanced technology. In fact, the newer M551 Sheridan

Private First Class Kerry Nelson peers through the main sight of his M48 tank's 90mm cannon.

proved less fit for action in Vietnam than its older cousin, the M48. Many tracked vehicles did, however, prove equal to the tasks set before them, and some adapted well to the character of the country and the nature of the war (see picture essay, page 56). The standard U.S. Army APC used when America entered the war was the M113, developed in the late 1950s. Though rugged, reliable, and versatile (it could be equipped with a variety of weapons), the M113 had several flaws as a combat vehicle that immediately became apparent in Vietnam. One was its reliance on gasoline: The fuel tanks between its armor and the troop compartment turned it into a rolling bomb if it was hit by an enemy shell. This was fixed by installing new engines powered by nonexplosive diesel fuel. In addition, the APC's inch-thick aluminum armor was designed to protect troops only from weapons smaller than .50-caliber, not from greater firepower used by the enemy in Vietnam. And, it was uncomfortably hot in warm, humid weather since it had no ventilation to speak of. Finally, the APC was highly susceptible to large mines. Because of these features, soldiers in Vietnam invariably rode atop APCs rather than inside them.

Mines, often placed in seemingly random patterns in Vietnam, were the main danger to APCs. APC crewmen made a variety of adaptions, known in army lingo as "field expedients," to protect themselves from the mines. The first expedient was to pile a couple of layers of sandbags on the floor. This worked but added so much weight that the engines began to give out. The soldiers then tried dirt-filled ammunition boxes and a layer of flak vests. This was equally effective and easier on the engines. Eventually the army contracted for the manufacture of APC armor kits, which included a plate of reinforcing armor that was bolted on the bottom.

Though Vietnam is not usually thought of as a battleground for tanks, there were in fact several armor engagements, including the Laotian invasion of 1970, Lam Son 719, in which the opposing forces' tanks and other armored vehicles played a major role. The principal American tank used in the war was the M48A3 Patton, introduced in 1953. Also used was the newer, lighter Sheridan M551 originally designated an armored reconnaissance airborne assault vehicle. It was armed with a 152mm gun, the largest tank gun in the world at that time, and came equipped with the latest in nocturnal aids, like starlight scopes and infrared-filtered searchlights. The Sheridan was fast and mobile but more likely to become mired in Vietnam's terrain than the "jungle crunching" Patton. It was also dangerous and unreliable. The Sheridan was hulled in light aluminum so it could be air dropped, which made it highly vulnerable to enemy shells.

North of Saigon, men of the 3d Squadron, 11th Armored Cavalry aboard a fifty-two-ton M48 tank advance toward suspected headquarters of the 101st NVA Regiment.

A task force of the 1st Battalion, 5th Infantry (Mechanized), operates an armored vehicle-launched bridge near Khe Sanh in 1969. The mobile bridge could cover spans of up to sixty feet and bear the weight of sixty tons.

Also, special combustible shell casings designed to self-destruct when the 152MM gun was fired proved equally combustible when a mine splintered the aluminum hull. In addition, the tank was fragile mechanically; one company with fifteen Sheridans experienced sixteen major equipment failures, twenty-five engine replacements, and forty-one misfires during a single thirty-day period.

The first Sheridans arrived in Vietnam in January 1969 and made a disheartening combat debut. On February 15, an M551 of the 3d Squadron, 4th Cavalry, rolled over a twenty-five-pound pressure-detonated mine. The mine burst the hull and detonated the Sheridan's ammunition, destroying the tank and killing the driver. By comparison, an M48 hitting the same mine would have lost a wheel or two, while an M113 ACAV would have been damaged, but injuries to its passengers and crew would have been minor. Other Sheridans had better luck, and the vehicle remained in service throughout the war with mixed results. But its drawbacks made it unreliable, while its main advantage—its powerful antitank guns—proved irrelevant until NVA armor reached South Vietnam in 1972.

The workhorse Patton meanwhile won its only head-on confrontation with the smaller Soviet-designed T54, whose 100MM gun was no more effective than the M48's 90MM. Patton companies were also called in to finish jobs started by the infantry. In Binh Dinh Province in the spring of 1967, a U.S. armored company attacked an NVA infantry battalion that had U.S. troops pinned down on the plain near the coast. The tanks roared in at such close range that NVA soldiers could not accurately fire their rocket grenades from their bunkers. When they emerged to fire, they were cut down by the Pattons' 90MM gun and 7.62MM machine guns and the infantrymen's weapons. Retreating back to the bunkers, the NVA troops were overrun by the fifty-two-ton tanks. When it was over the NVA battalion had suffered a casualty rate of 98 percent.

The tropical vegetation that bulged against the roadside in Vietnam provided cover for Vietcong ambush squads and command-detonated mines. Using infantry to secure the roads was costly, both in manpower and time. Instead, the U.S. decided to try and clear the jungle back from the roads a distance of 400 meters on either side. The problem was finding a mechanical behemoth strong enough for the large land-clearing job. Plowing up the trees and underbrush along a single ten-kilometer stretch of road, for example, meant clearing about 2,000 acres or three square miles.

The army's first candidate for this brutish task was a huge tractor called the transphibian tactical tree crusher. The ninety-seven-ton crusher knocked over trees with a heavy pusher bar and leveled debris with its cleated steel drums. Although it could clear ten acres of forest in an hour, the tanklike crusher turned out to be too difficult to maintain. A heavy chain (fifty pounds per foot) stretched between two bulldozers was also used, with a fourteen-foot steel ball set in the middle of the chain for added muscle, but the bulldozers broke down under the strain. The machine relied on most heavily for jungle clearing, however, was the Rome plow, a 4,600-pound angled bulldozer blade specially designed for cutting trees. Attached to the powerful Caterpillar D7E bulldozer, the plow could slash through all but the heaviest timber. Its driver rode in an armored cab with thick steel bars for protection against both enemy bullets and falling trees. Rome plows did their jobs well, mashing seventy-eight square miles of vegetation adjoining roads and firebases between 1967 and 1969. As a result the number of troops required for road security declined by three-quarters.

Weapons and will

America's weapons in Vietnam added up, ounce for ounce, to one of the most formidable ground arsenals ever fielded. With the added might of tactical air support only a radio call away for even the smallest unit, U.S. troops were able to withstand all but the fiercest, best-planned enemy attacks. As long as it was manned by Americans, the umbrella of U.S. firepower also protected South Vietnam from the Communist storm. Yet, for all its firepower,

the U.S. ground war machine was never able to drive the Communists permanently from the field and convince them their cause was futile. This was not the fault of the weapons, which, with notable exceptions, performed at least as well as expected. Success or failure for the U.S. in Vietnam, as for any force in any war, was more a matter of politics, strategy, and tactics, and of the will and weaponry of the opposing forces.

Short of defeating the enemy, however, the U.S. ground arsenal achieved impressive results, countering the Communist offensives of Tet 1968 and Easter 1972, forcing the enemy from the field in most other battles, and allowing ground patrols to exact heavy enemy casualties while taking comparatively few of their own. Equally impressive was the work of American medical men and women in Vietnam who treated the wounded with a speed and effectiveness unprecedented in warfare.

Engineers of the 27th Engineer Battalion (Combat) build roads near the A Shau Valley in April 1969. Where possible, American road builders used culverts instead of bridges (as shown at center) because they were easier to build and harder to destroy.

Over Hill and Dale

Americans and their South Vietnamese comrades–at–arms had, in addition to the helicopter, a wide variety of vehicles to carry them into battle and support them once they got there. Although the helicopter was faster and not affected by terrain, trucks still carried troops and gear where there were roads. Where the roads ended, armored personnel carriers took over to lift men through jungle and across water. And for patrolling Vietnam's thousands of miles of inland waterways, the U.S. imported its own "brown water navy."

While helicopter gunships and other aircraft provided the bulk of the firepower that supported embattled troops, tanks still played an important role in Vietnam, especially later in the war when North Vietnamese armor rolled south. Tanks used in Vietnam included the older M41, which U.S. tank crews had found cramped but seemed well suited to the smaller South Vietnamese; the M67 used by the Marine Corps; and the M48 Patton, the standard tank in the U.S. arsenal. Vietnam also witnessed the debut of a high–tech tank, the M551 Sheridan. The illustration on the facing page shows the Sheridan's interior.

As in all tanks, the Sheridan's four crewmen crammed themselves into a claustrophobia–inducing space cluttered with an impressive array of equipment and, often, the refuse of previous crews. To make matters worse, the heat in Vietnam could cause the temperature of a tank's interior to climb well above 100 degrees, often making crewmen risk enemy fire by riding outside.

The Sheridan's driver sat in the front of the hull, while the other crewmen occupied the turret. (See next page for an external view of the M551.) To the left of the gun (1), was the loader (4), who fed ammunition into the 152MM gun. To the right of the main gun was the gunner (3), and tank commander (2). The gunner aimed the main gun through a telescopic or periscopic sight. His controls allowed him to elevate or depress the gun, or swivel the turret left or right by means of electric

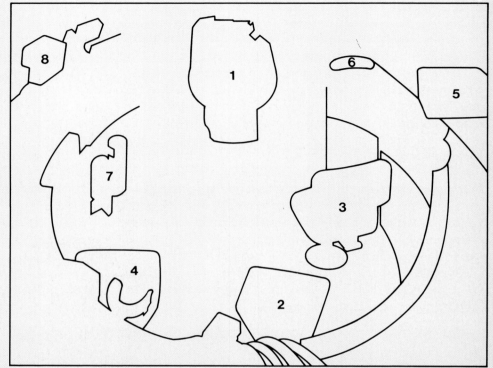

power drives. The tank commander's responsibilities included directing the tank in battle by providing instructions for the driver and gunner over the vehicle's intercom system. The commander had a special vision cupola over his head, allowing him a 360-degree vista from within the tank. The cupola also had an externally mounted .50-caliber machine gun, not evident in this view, to supplement the main gun.

An artist's view of an M551 Sheridan turret, shown from the rear of the tank looking forward and down into the turret as if its top has been lifted away. The numbers on the above sketch correspond to the turret's important features, illustrated at right.

1. 152MM gun/missile breech. In this view, the breech is open and ready for loading.

2. The tank commander's seat. Directly over this seat was the main turret hatch and vision cupola (shown next page).

3. The gunner's seat. The gunner in U.S. tanks is traditionally positioned in front of the tank commander on the right side.

4. The loader's seat. The loader has more room to maneuver than the other turret crewmen because the ammunition, which can weigh fifty pounds, is difficult to handle in cramped conditions.

5. The tank commander's controls. The tank commander can override the gunner's controls and point the turret at a target he has spotted through the cupola.

6. The gunner's controls. The gunner has hand controls to elevate and depress the gun and traverse the turret from side to side. He may also have a high-powered telescopic sight and a periscopic sight for a wider view of the scene.

7. Ammunition stowage. Ammunition is stowed in the turret and in the hull on either side of the driver. In Vietnam, very little 152MM ammunition was carried, usually only a few beehive rounds. Instead, Sheridans carried more ammunition for the vehicle's two or more machine guns.

8. The intercom control box. Since a tank is so noisy in combat, for communication each crewman has a helmet with built-in headphones.

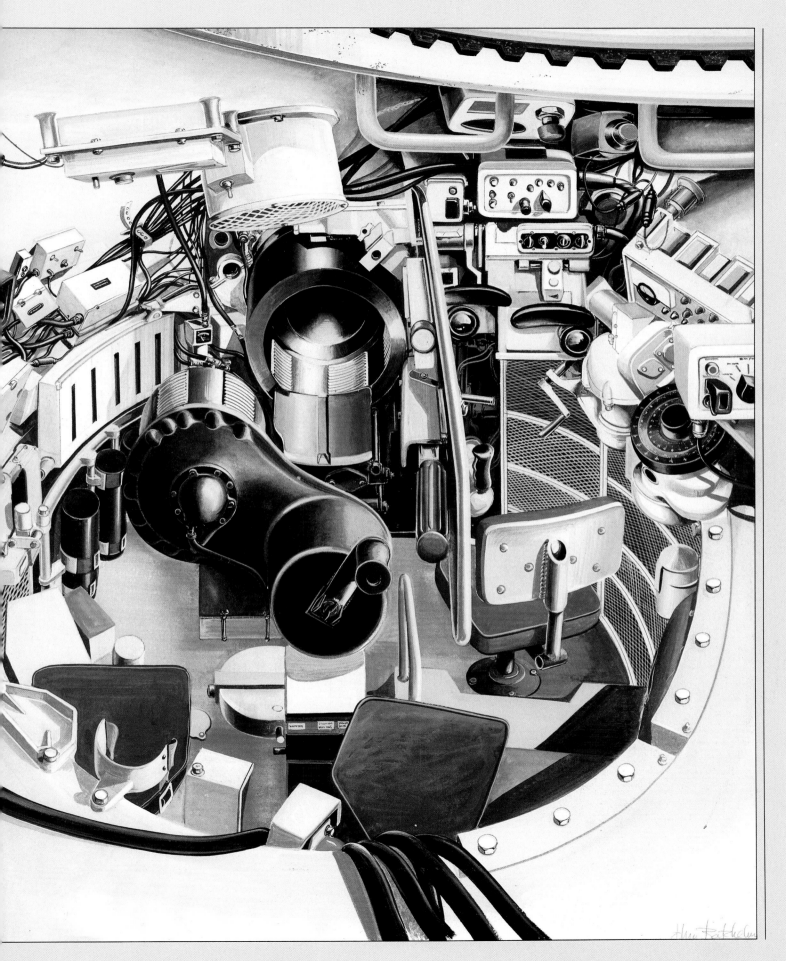

Tanks in Vietnam

Although tanks have been the dominant weapon in land warfare since the end of World War I, their utility is to some extent dependent on terrain. Vietnam did not prove well suited to European-style tank warfare, yet tanks were used early in the war to provide additional close-range fire support to infantry units. Later, they were used against the NVA armor attacks of 1972 and 1975. The most successful combination was undoubtedly the M48A3 Patton tank (right) working in concert with the M113A1 ACAV (shown next page). The M48A3 provided the firepower, while the M113, with its infantry, provided the flexibility to attack in nearly all terrain conditions. During the rare encounters between U.S. and NVA tanks, the NVA tanks were usually overcome because their crews were poorly trained. Encounters between NVA and ARVN tanks increased in the final years of the war. The ARVN tankers were better trained than their NVA opponents, but by the final campaigns, ARVN tanks were heavily outnumbered and overwhelmed.

Right. *The M551 Sheridan was a fifteen-ton, air-portable tank developed in the 1960s to replace the M41. It was armed with a complicated 152mm Shillelagh gun/missile, which made it the most powerfully armed light tank ever built. Its deployment in Vietnam, however, was not particularly successful, and it was withdrawn from most army units by the early 1980s.*

The M48A3 Patton main battle tank was the Vietnam-era descendant of the highly successful family of Patton tanks that traces its lineage to the M26 tank of 1944. The heavily armored M48A3 weighed forty-seven tons and was equipped with a 90MM gun. Reliable even under the harsh climatic and terrain conditions of South Vietnam, it proved more than capable of handling the best tanks in NVA service, like the Soviet T54. In the final years of the war, M48s were supplied to the ARVN.

Left. The M41A3 Walker Bulldog light tank was the standard U.S. Army scout tank from the early 1950s into the 1960s. Armed with a 76MM gun, it was crewed by four men. Not used by U.S. forces in Vietnam, the M41 formed the staple of ARVN armored cavalry squadrons. It proved reliable and effective in ARVN hands and saw considerable action from 1968 on.

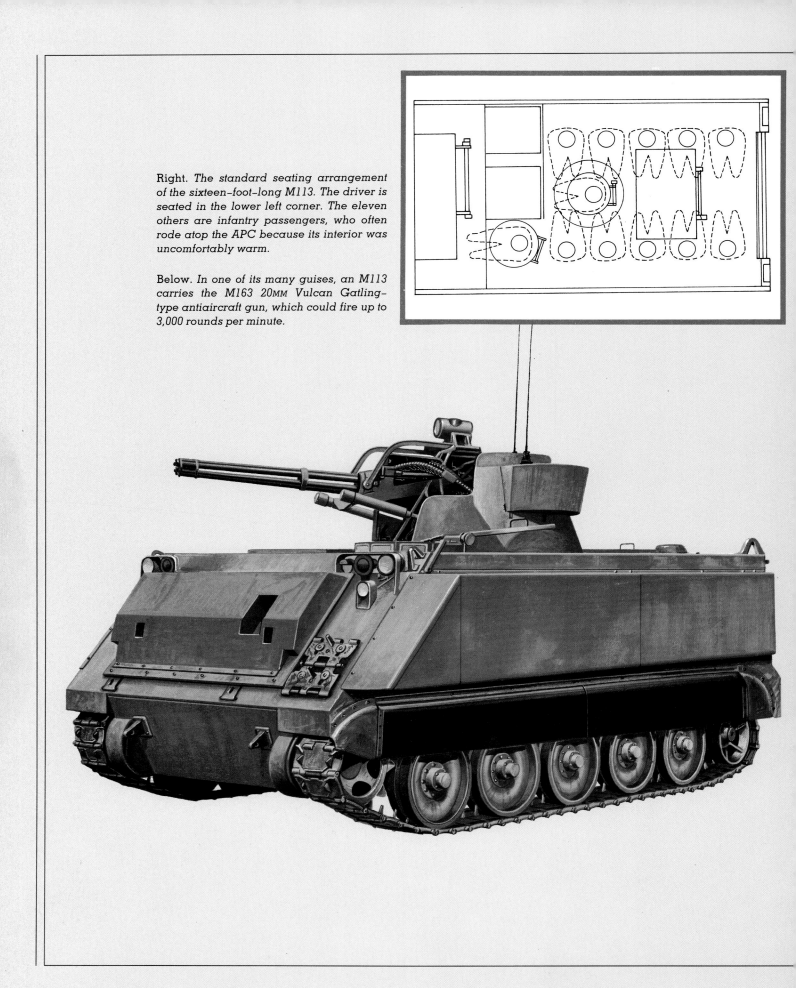

Right. *The standard seating arrangement of the sixteen–foot–long M113. The driver is seated in the lower left corner. The eleven others are infantry passengers, who often rode atop the APC because its interior was uncomfortably warm.*

Below. *In one of its many guises, an M113 carries the M163 20MM Vulcan Gatling–type antiaircraft gun, which could fire up to 3,000 rounds per minute.*

M113 Armored Personnel Carrier

The M113 armored personnel carrier has become the most widely used APC in the western world and over 30,000 have been built since it was introduced in 1961. It owes its success to its simplicity, reliability, flexibility, and easy maintenance. It is used as a gun or mortar carriage, troop carrier, fighting vehicle, ambulance, command post, ammunition carrier, flame thrower, and scout vehicle.

To fill the requirement that the M113 be air transportable, designers chose for it lightweight aluminum armor. While it protects the crew from small arms and shell splinters, the properties of the metal tend to amplify the effects of mines and shaped charges. Another weakness resulted from army planners insisting that the amphibious APCs had no function on a battlefield except to carry the troops to it. At the battle's edge, they would dismount to attack on foot. It was thus equipped originally with only a .50-caliber machine gun.

Despite these drawbacks, troops in the field, together with designers, discovered the M113's variety of uses. They added equipment to the vehicle, including armaments and armor, and replaced the original gasoline powered engine with another that burned less volatile diesel fuel. Shown here are two of the many adaptations made to the APC in Vietnam.

Below. *The M113 configured as an ACAV (armored cavalry) with armored gun shields and two M60 machine guns. With a weight of twelve tons, the ACAV could travel at 42 miles per hour and had a range of up to 300 miles.*

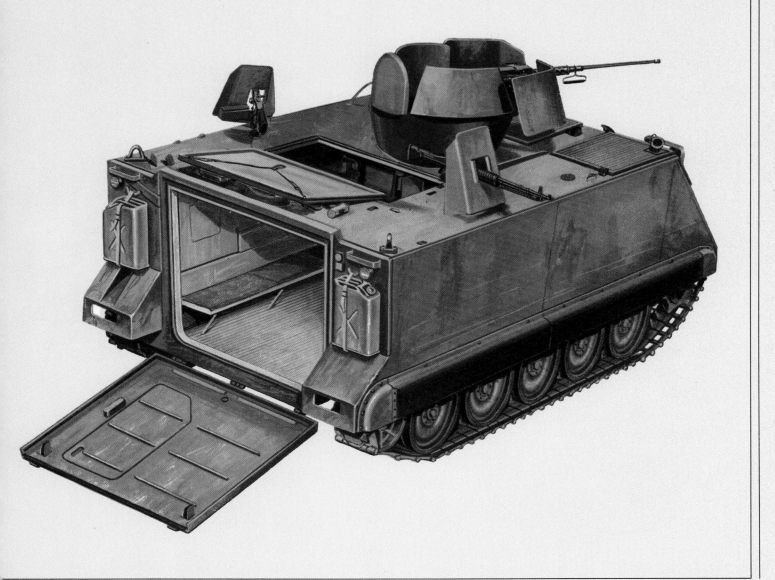

Riverine Craft

Forces tailored for river and coastal warfare had been used only rarely by America since the Civil War. When U.S. forces arrived in Vietnam, they had no suitable vessels for the purpose. By 1967, though, the American Mobile Riverine Force had been equipped with an entire river navy, much of it drawn from converted boats formerly sitting in mothball fleets. Among those vessels was the Monitor, which, with its pill box turret, was reminiscent of its Civil War ancestors. Less successful were the modern high-speed air cushion vehicles, three of which were introduced in Vietnam. Although they "flew" on a cushion of air across the surfaces of rivers, paddies, and bogs, these hovercraft saw little use because they were too noisy and too temperamental for waterborne counterinsurgency.

The greyhound of the brown water navy, the SK5 air cushion vehicle had a top speed of seventy-five knots. Crewed by four men and armed with two .50-caliber machine guns and a 40MM grenade launcher, the ACV could carry twenty troops.

The LCM Monitor was the the waterborne equivalent of the tank, with its heavy armor and armaments and its eleven-man crew. Sixty feet long and seventeen-and-a-half feet wide, it displaced sixty tons when loaded and could travel at eight knots. This Monitor is armed with a 40MM cannon in the bow turret. The aft turret (top) carries a 20MM cannon and its two side turrets, one .50-caliber machine gun each. Amidships is an 81MM mortar gun. The grillwork of steel bars gives it additional protection from enemy shells.

Below. The patrol boat river (PBR) Mark II was a standard riverine craft. Monitoring the waterways with a small radar set (top), the thirty-two-foot-long boat defended itself with twin .50-caliber machine guns forward and one machine gun aft. The PBR had a top speed of twenty-five knots.

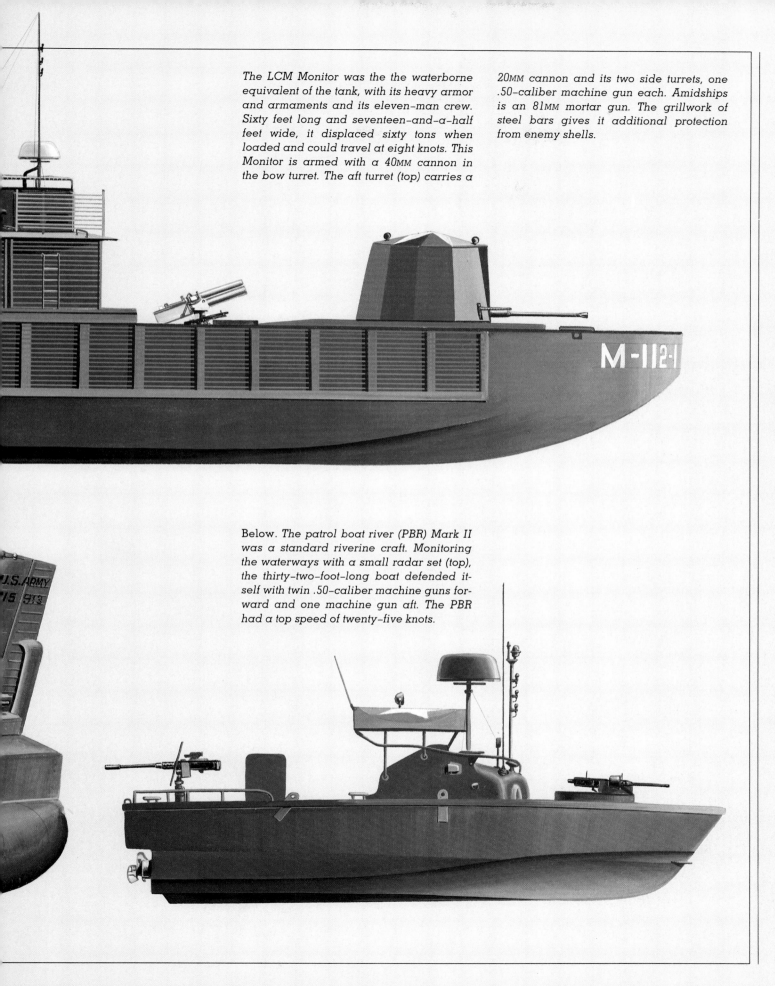

The Medicine Men

The heat was stifling. The hilltop's thick cover of dry brushwood, with stalks ten feet high, gave it the baked and brittle look of late summer. Six injured men at the edge of the landing zone next to the brush were drenched in sweat. The men, members of Charlie Company, 2d Battalion, 12th Cavalry, 1st Air Cavalry Division, had been wounded after their UH-1D "slick" helicopter had dropped them into the Bong Son area of Binh Dinh Province as part of an air mobile assault called Operation Thayer II in September 1966.

The chopper, also hit as it deposited the men, had gone down in a jade-green valley at the base of the hill. The valley was dense with jungle, and fenced along the clearings with tall stands of bamboo and large-leafed plants. The crippled helicopter was in a small clearing that had once been a rice field. A platoon from Charlie Company, sent down the hill to secure the copter, moved warily toward the craft. The enemy, as usual, could be sensed but not seen.

Violet smoke guides a medevac helicopter to a tiny LZ near Truc Vinh in June 1967 while (below) a man on the ground radios the condition of the wounded soldier to the approaching dustoff.

The men heard the UH-1 medevac helicopter first and then saw it coming in from the east, along the edge of the great crescent plain of Bong Son in central Vietnam. As he neared the hilltop, the pilot reported laconically that he was receiving 12.7MM antiaircraft fire; he would try an approach from the north instead. Moments later the pilot radioed that he was taking fire on his northerly approach and was swinging around to the south. But now a layer of dark clouds was moving in: Rain would soon arrive. The southern approach would not work here either, and his chopper's fuel was running low. The injured men, some

Preceding page. *Using mouth-to-mouth resuscitation, a GI helps a buddy wounded on Hamburger Hill in May 1969.*

with broken bones and others with severe sprains, would have to wait.

One of the men moving through the jungle toward the downed helicopter suddenly screamed. He had tripped a booby trap, and a slender spear, hurled by a bent bamboo whip, had pierced his thigh and stomach.

Then the rest of the platoon slogged toward the chopper, the rain came down in heavy sheets, puddling the valley floor. A soldier cried out in pain, then another, as they stepped on low punjis hidden in the short grass now under water. As a man's boot hit the stake, the carefully split base of the punji spread apart, increasing its resistance until its fire-hardened point penetrated both boot and foot.

The platoon leader relayed word of the injuries to the commander on the hilltop, who immediately radioed an urgent request for another medevac. Within minutes they heard the thwacking sound of rotor blades as another chopper felt its way over the cloud-quilted hills, protected from the antiaircraft guns by the overcast. The men on the ground directed the pilot, an army Medical Service Corps officer, by sound. When he popped out of the clouds he was just north of the hilltop, but they waved him off the landing zone—the men in the valley, hidden by still another cloud layer, were more seriously wounded: Several appeared to be dying.

Guided by the platoon leader below, the copter pilot dropped down into the murk between the hills and broke out almost directly over the downed slick. The seven wounded men were hastily loaded into the aerial ambulance, but the real test for the Huey was just beginning. The helicopter's Avco-Lycoming turbine engine was not designed to lift seven passengers and a four-man crew straight up through several hundred feet of sodden air. Even with six passengers, the Hueys usually needed to fly diagonally to gain altitude.

But now the turbine screamed as the pilot lifted off. The copter shuddered and climbed, its familiar whump-whump sounding more like a thunderous hammering in the air, and quickly disappeared into the clouds. Twenty minutes later the wounded men were in a hospital at Qui Nhon. Some were later transferred to the 6th Convalescent Center at Cam Ranh Bay, while others recovered in Japan and Hawaii. All seven returned to duty within two months.

Charlie Company's experience with the courageous and highly skilled professionals who manned the medevac copters was similar to that of hundreds of other U.S. units in Vietnam. The men on the ground developed a faith in the medevac helicopters and their pilots that statistics clearly justified. More than 900,000 American and allied sick and wounded were evacuated between 1964 and 1973. The average elapsed time between an injury and surgery was an hour and forty minutes, as compared with about ten hours in World War II and nine hours in Korea. An even more significant set of figures is the percentages

On board a UH-1 in III Corps, a medic evaluates the injury of a wounded Vietnamese soldier, 1966. The chopper often could take a patient directly to the facility best equipped for his type of wound.

of men hit who eventually died: 33 percent in the Civil War, 29.3 in World War II, 26.3 in Korea, and 19 percent in Vietnam. The main reason for the difference was the medevac choppers.

The percentage of copters hit on medevac missions was higher than those hit on all other types of flights combined. The aerial ambulances were downed by hostile fire more than three times as often as other copters, half again as often as those on combat missions. Nearly a third of the 1,400 army officers who flew medevacs in Vietnam were killed or wounded as a result of hostile fire or accidents, usually either at night or in bad weather. Many pilots performed feats of singular bravery. Major Patrick Brady of the 54th Medical Detachment (Helicopter Ambulance) was awarded the Medal of Honor for his daring evacuation of fifty-one men near Chu Lai in January 1968. On one occasion the gunfire was so intense that he turned the tail of his craft toward the enemy and used it as a shield while loading the wounded aboard.

The helicopter's potential as an aerial ambulance was recognized almost immediately after the craft was first demonstrated by Igor Sikorsky in 1942. The first medical evacuation by copter took place in Burma during the latter stages of World War II. But the early helicopters had a variety of limitations that persisted with the second generation of military helicopters employed in Korea. The army's Korean-vintage Bell OH-13 and the air force's Sikorsky H-5, were both powered by conventional reciprocating engines, could fly only short distances, and only during the day in good weather. Patients aboard the H-13 were strapped on litters outside the cockpit bubble, while the air force H-5 could carry only four people including the two pilots.

Both choppers had trouble taking off in "heavy" or hot, humid air and their slow flights provided hostile gunners easy targets. Despite these handicaps the copters used in Korea evacuated more than 28,000 men between 1950 and 1953. During the same years the French forces in Vietnam transported about 5,000 patients by helicopter.

The Avco Lycoming T53 gas turbine engine, introduced in 1953, transformed helicopters from fragile, pokey vessels on the fringe of the action to the effective, reliable vehicles needed for the myriad tasks planners had in mind for them. Also in 1953, the army Surgeon General's office issued its criteria for a suitable aerial ambulance. Such a craft, the medical men said, had to be highly maneuverable, capable of a 100-mile-an-hour cruising speed, able to hover at high altitudes with a full load, and to take off and land from small landing zones. It also had to be able to carry a crew of four and four patients. The first Bell UH-1A air ambulances that appeared in 1962 fell short of most of the standards. The UH-1As lacked the lift capacity, speed, and number of litters called for in their original specifications. But they were still far better than any previous craft, and they were promptly recruited by the army.

Refinements in both the copters and the T53 engine, including more cabin space and increased power capacity, would eventually bring the Hueys more closely in line with the Surgeon General's criteria; but in the meantime they would become as common as clouds in the Vietnamese sky. The Hueys turned a technological corner. Their instruments enabled them to fly at night and in rough weather. They could maneuver in and out of tight places like some mechanical cat. And they could fly farther, faster, and more dependably than any previous helicopters.

Air ambulance units in Vietnam were assigned to army divisions or to area support commands. They were controlled through a communications system that permitted only one use for its channels: Like the medevac copters themselves, the medical communications bands could not be preempted for other purposes. In practice, the radio net resembled the operation of a police dispatcher. It permitted an exchange of information that facilitated quick decisions on the nature of wounds, the locations of clearing stations and hospitals, where to take the injured men, whether to pick up a surgeon en route to a hospital, and other questions. This often resulted in a speedy trip to the right facility and thus a better chance for survival.

In the view of some commanders, the medevac operation was almost too effective. When a helicopter could evacuate a wounded man within minutes from almost anyplace in the country, it was difficult to resist the temptation to call one, even if doing so might delay a troop movement. The existence of a highly developed rescue technology made the commander's decision more difficult. A single booby trap could derail an operation for hours while a landing zone was found and secured, a medevac

At the Rock Pile, a Marine Corps doctor performs an emergency tracheotomy on a man with face and head wounds.

helicopter summoned, and the wounded man lifted out. Advances would frequently halt while the wounded were evacuated to safety.

Complaining that the time spent in recovering casualties often led to still more casualties, Lieutenant Colonel Harold G. Moore of the 1st Air Cavalry Division cautioned that "troops must not get so concerned with casualties that they forget the enemy and their mission." Certainly the delay involved in medevacking the wounded often impeded a unit's ability to pursue the enemy swiftly. Frequently, the enemy seized the opportunity to harass medevac helicopters or to set up ambushes and mortar strikes against stalled American units. For commanders, therefore, the technological improvement of the medevac helicopter solved one combat problem but created another. They constantly had to weigh the tactical hindrances that medevacking posed to their mission against their professional and personal concern for the swift evacuation of casualties.

When the medevac pilot's job took him over enemy-controlled territory, the character of the operation changed dramatically. Since the Hueys lacked the range for travel over long distances, larger HH-43 and HH-53 helicopters were used, sometimes with midair refueling. The helicopters flew as part of a rescue task force that often included a second chopper, a fighter escort, and a control plane. The Kaman HH-43 and Sikorsky HH-53 could be equipped with power hoists (all U.S. Air Force search-and-rescue helicopters but not all army or marine evacuation helicopters had them) that enabled them to reel in a downed pilot, and they carried machine guns in case of enemy resistance. Escorting fighters, usually heavily armed A-1 Skyraiders, went along to keep enemy ground troops at bay.

Different weapons, different wounds

Medevac helicopters were both the most visible and the most dramatic illustration of the technological advances that improved a soldier's chance of survival in Vietnam. But there were other innovations in medical techniques and capability that were almost equally important. The system of medical care that the U.S. Army brought to Vietnam was the most effective in military history. The medical corps in Vietnam employed new portable field hospitals, new surgical techniques, and new methods of disease prevention, all of which saved lives and minimized the long-term effect of injuries.

The statistics that show the effectiveness of the American medical support network—the lower percentage of deaths among the wounded, for example—ignore the immeasurable but equally significant results: the number of limbs saved by quick evacuations and prompt surgery, the potentially permanent handicaps that became only temporary setbacks. Statistics do demonstrate that the average length of a soldier's hospital stay declined from eighty days in World War II to seventy-five in Korea and sixty-three in Vietnam. They also show that the ratio of mandays lost to disease as compared to battle injuries dropped from 3.76 to 1 in World War II to 0.47 to 1 in Vietnam, a reflection of improved disease prevention methods. And the statistics reveal another difference between Vietnam and earlier wars: Death in combat was more likely to come from small arms (51 percent as against 33 percent in Korea) and from mines and booby traps (11 percent versus 4 percent). This difference also resulted in more complicated wounds that were far more difficult to treat and a need for more sophisticated medical techniques.

The major killers in twentieth century wars were frag-

Vietcong Survival Kit

While many U.S. troops relied on medical corpsmen for immediate attention in the field, each Vietcong guerrilla carried his own survival kit with a variety of medicinal herbs and supplies. The kit shown here, captured from a guerrilla in the late sixties, includes tea (orange and blue packages), antiseptic (top left corner), a plasma kit (next to tea), scissors, tape, a syringe, Chinese antiseptic (in blue box), a variety of spices and herbs (in plastic bags), and rolls of gauze (bottom left corner).

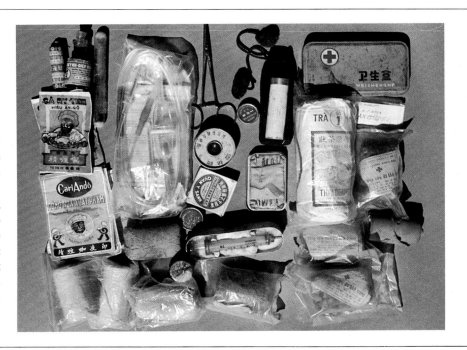

mentation weapons such as artillery and mortars. In Vietnam, however, widespread use of mines and booby traps that exploded close to their victims meant more lower body injuries and more dirt and debris in the wounds. Vietnam was also the first war in which claymore mines, with their clusters of steel pellets, were widely used; the Vietcong variations often included nails, glass, and bolts. Punji traps like those that ambushed Charlie Company near Bong Son Plain inflicted deep wounds highly prone to infection.

The rifles used by both sides in Vietnam were fully automatic weapons that fired smaller, higher-velocity bullets than their predecessors. The bullets used were also more apt to tumble and fragment inside their victim's body, driving pieces of flesh and bone outward and often drawing dirt into the resultant vacuum. The flesh fragments propelled into motion by the bullet became missiles that could cause further wounds. The bulkier and slower bullets of earlier wars, by contrast, generally passed through the body more cleanly without causing as much secondary damage.

The fact that the enemy's AK47 rifle, like the U.S. Army's M16, was fully automatic meant in addition that multiple wounds were more likely. An enemy rifleman could set his weapon so that it could fire up to thirty shots before he had to reload; the magazine of semiautomatic rifles used in World War II and Korea could hold only five to eight bullets, meaning the rifles had to be reloaded more frequently and could not fire as fast. The combination of the smaller, high-velocity bullets and rapid-fire rifles resulted in multiple, untidy wounds that were often difficult to repair. In this context the higher survival rate of the GIs wounded in Vietnam becomes even more remarkable. Much of the credit belongs to the human commitment of medics, nurses, and doctors, and to the array of medical technology at their disposal in field hospitals and rear base surgical wards.

From battlefield to recovery room

When an American soldier was struck by a bullet, hit by shrapnel, or injured by a mine or a booby trap, the field medics gave him their first medical attention. With their small green bag of emergency first aid supplies, the medics often meant the difference between life and death for soldiers downed in combat. Sergeant Mitch Daughtry, shot during an attack by Communist forces near Chu Lai in 1969, recalled: "If the medic had passed me up, I don't know if I would have been here today. He got me patched up pretty fast."

Field medics had one primary objective: keeping the wounded alive for quick evacuation out of combat. Other specially trained medics aboard helicopters applied emergency treatment to those with life-threatening wounds. They frequently performed tracheotomies to help the wounded breathe, administered plasma and blood, and gave mouth-to-mouth resuscitation.

Medics, of course, were not new to the U.S. military in South Vietnam, but they had more sophisticated training and acquired more medical expertise than their predecessors in World War II and Korea. U.S. Army medics during the Vietnam War, for example, spent ten weeks at the Medical Training Center at Fort Sam Houston, Texas, studying physiology, pharmacology, and anatomy. In addition to mouth-to-mouth resuscitation, medic trainees also learned the more advanced techniques of heart massage and the application of pressure bandages. The 10,000 medics who served in Vietnam after graduating from the center faced a special challenge. Said Colonel Charles Pixley, the center's commanding officer, "We are striving for a quality of training that will materially reduce the 21.7 per thousand death rate from all combat causes in Vietnam. . . . I believe it can be lowered by giving the combat medic more skills, more equipment and greater depth of knowledge concerning emergency medical procedure."

The medics performed only the first phase of the military's well-orchestrated operation to move wounded soldiers successfully from the battlefield to the recovery room. The second phase involved the nurses and doctors. The Army Nurse Corps served in South Vietnam from 1962 to 1972. Over that period, their Vietnam contingent rose from 13 to a high of 900 in January 1969.

Most nurses were assigned to hospitals and to the 6th Convalescent Center at Cam Ranh Bay. Nurses, like doctors, came to Vietnam skilled in the most up-to-date, innovative medical techniques available in the United States. They worked on thoracic, orthopedic, neurosurgical, maxillofacial, neuropsychiatric, renal, and other specialized medical teams. The principles of sound nursing remained unchanged in Vietnam, but ingenuity and adaptiveness were necessary to maintain high standards of care. The U.S. Army history of the Medical Corps in Vietnam noted that "nurses used their resourcefulness to overcome a lack of certain equipment. Stones in a Red Cross ditty bag made weights for traction, a piece of Levin's tube would be used as a drinking straw, plastic dressing wrappers were sewed as colostomy bags, soap and intravenous bottles were used as chest drainage bottles and items of equipment not authorized by the Tables of Equipment were designed and constructed from scrap lumber and other materials."

Although most U.S. medical facilities were located on bases in relatively secure areas, nurses and doctors occasionally had to operate under the most nightmarish conditions. The army's 3d Surgical Hospital at Dong Tam withstood thirteen separate attacks in 1969. During one two-day barrage, the hospital headquarters was leveled, the intensive care and postoperative wards were nearly destroyed, and the dental clinic, X-ray facility, laboratory, supply building, and nurses' quarters were all damaged.

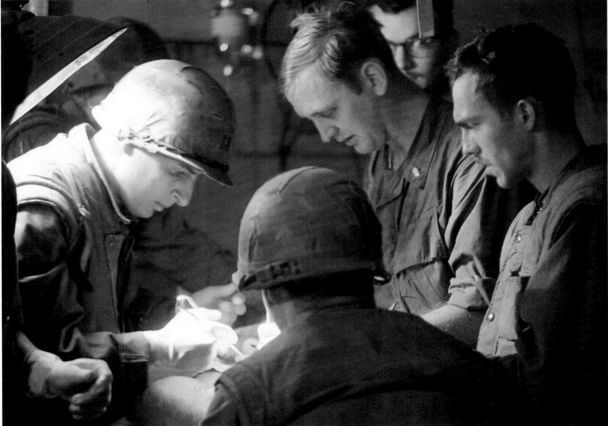

Under siege at Khe Sanh, 1968. Above. A wounded marine is carried into the field hospital. Left. Wearing flak vests and helmets to protect themselves from the constant shelling, doctors operate on a patient.

First Lieutenant Sharon Anne Jane, Army Nurse Corps, was killed by enemy fire on June 8, 1969, while on duty at the 312th Evacuation Hospital at Chu Lai.

Doctor John Parrish's duty station was a field hospital at Phu Bai. Assigned to the 3d Medical Battalion, 3d Division, he was helping to repair a marine with neck wounds one day when enemy artillery shells began exploding close to the hospital. Parrish was pumping blood while two other surgeons stitched up the marine's blood vessels. Two shells shook the operating room, sending the anesthesiologist sprawling. From his position on his back, he continued to operate the breathing bag from the floor. Dr. Parrish knelt on the floor and continued to pump blood. Another shell just outside the wall sent shrapnel through the walls and ceiling and put the lights out, the only remaining light coming through holes in the ceiling. Then another shell hit and the holes filled up with dirt that then fell into the operating room. After a long moment, emergency generators cut in and the lights came back on, even though shells continued to hit and more dirt sifted in. The wounded marine was moved to the floor. Lying on either side of him on their bellies, the doctors continued to operate until the shelling stopped. Once peace reigned again, they put the marine back on the operating table, rescrubbed, and finished their work.

Better surgical techniques

The doctors who labored in Vietnam hospitals employed both better tools and better techniques than their battlefield predecessors. Vascular surgery, the repair and restoration of damaged blood vessels, was a prime example. In World War II, the surgeons in the field customarily tied off an affected vein or artery; 36 percent of the patients with major artery damage lost a limb through amputation. In Korea, vascular surgery was performed at only the few hospitals with qualified physicians, but even so the amputation rate after suture repair to major arteries declined to 13 percent. In Vietnam, there were doctors at every forward medical facility who were capable of complex vascular surgery. As a result, the rate of amputation after blood vessel repairs was below 5 percent. Quicker evacuation helped, of course, but so did increased medical confidence, mainly the result of improved training and better techniques.

When amputation was unavoidable, new techniques and contrivances facilitated treatment and hastened healing. The development of a "total-fit" plastic socket permitted the fitting of skin grafts to an amputee's stump, which had previously been all but impossible. The application of a split-thickness skin to the stump allowed grafts to take hold quickly, often healing within two weeks. Faster healing enabled artificial limbs to be applied sooner, which in turn improved the amputee's chances for resuming a more normal life.

The exploratory operation known as a laparotomy, an incision in the abdomen performed to let a surgeon probe for internal damage, had traditionally been used sparingly because of the high risk of infection. In Vietnam, such operations were done routinely "on suspicion" of internal damage, hunches that proved to be correct about one-quarter of the time. Doctors felt free to go ahead because of better training, improved facilities, and more effective environmental control in operating rooms. The result was often the early detection of potentially fatal internal injuries and infections.

Wounds were normally left open longer in battle-zone hospitals than they are in stateside facilities, primarily because of the weapons used in Vietnam. Smaller, high-velocity bullets and booby traps produced dirty wounds; the resulting infection could spread over a large part of the body and potentially prove fatal. To minimize the spread of infections, wounds were commonly "débrided"—cleansed of loose tissue, blood clots, bone fragments, and foreign particles—drained, covered with mesh gauze, and left open for four or five days. This reduced the danger of a wound becoming badly infected after it was closed and increased a soldier's chance of survival.

Débridement and delayed closure of wounds were not new techniques. In fact, they were first introduced in the 1780s by French surgeon Pierre Desault. But since these techniques were not ordinarily used in civilian surgery, doctors in Vietnam had to relearn them.

Severely wounded patients were sometimes squeezed into tight-fitting gravity suits—or G-suits—worn by airmen in an effort to maintain their blood pressure artificially. G-suits contain built-in tubes that put pressure in the lower body to keep blood circulating throughout the body during high-velocity turns that could otherwise cause the pilot to pass out. Medical men in Vietnam turned to them in desperation to help save soldiers who had suffered severe, potentially fatal injuries to the legs and pelvis in mine explosions. In effect, the suits supplied the pressure on the circulatory system that the wounds drained away. This improvised expedient was credited with saving the lives of several patients with no measurable blood pressure and at least one who was without a pulse as well.

American doctors in Vietnam were somewhat better equipped to treat shock in the seriously wounded than their predecessors in earlier wars had been. Recognizing shock as the failure of the microcirculation of fluid in body tissue due to excessive bleeding, they pumped a saline solution through the blood stream when they spotted the symptoms. At the same time, they made sure that enough air moved in and out of the lungs and that oxygen reached the affected tissue. A patient in shock could appear to be breathing normally while loss of blood was actually cutting off his oxygen supply, with pulmonary failure a common result. The prompt replacement of lost fluid was critical. Development of the technology to measure blood gas

A Delicate Operation

Extraordinary luck saves the life of a South Vietnamese soldier, whose wound was almost as dangerous to his American surgeons as it was to him. ARVN Private Nguyen Van Long, 22, survived a direct hit by a 60MM mortar shell that failed to explode. The live shell went through his shoulder and ended up in his chest, leaving the doctors a very sensitive piece of surgery. Knowing that a tiny jolt to the fuse could still detonate the shell, surgeons operated on Long from behind sandbags. Patient and physicians had luck on their side. The shell did not explode and, after it was removed, Long recovered.

Right. *Long, his chest bulging from the shell, lies in the U.S. Army hospital at Da Nang on October 2, 1966.* Below. *An X-ray shows the shell clearly.*

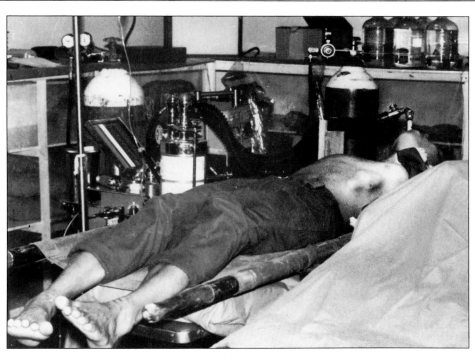

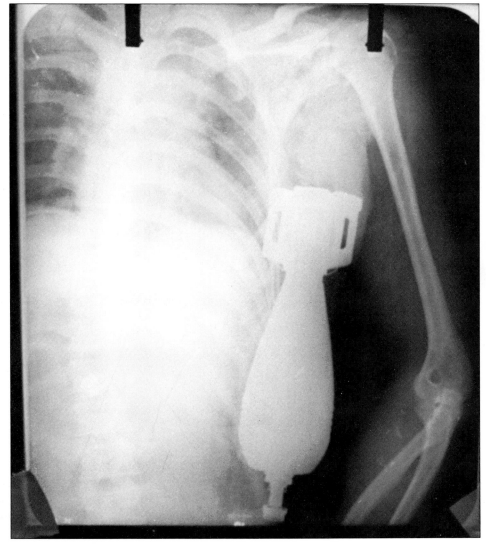

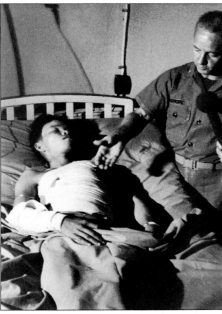

Above. *Captain Harry Dinsmore, U.S. Army Medical Corps, checks his patient after successfully removing the mortar round from his chest.*

rapidly enabled doctors in forward hospitals to spot a patient in shock.

A formidable number of lifesaving techniques and devices were pioneered in Vietnam. The routine use of tubes to control fluid levels in the chest began in Vietnam. Sophisticated heart-lung resuscitators and heart by-pass pumps were available for the first time, as were simple inflatable splints and sprays to control kidney and liver bleeding. If these innovations had emerged in earlier wars, their effects would probably have been limited: Many of the gravely wounded men who benefited from them would not have reached the hospital alive. Fast evacuation, of course, was the crucial difference. Access to a plentiful supply of blood for transfusions helped too.

In the early stages of the war, the vital supplies of blood and plasma were stored in containers called Hollinger boxes. These boxes weighed 115 pounds, had a capacity of twenty-four units of blood, and could keep the blood cool for only twenty-four hours. A more effective storage method was critical because most of the blood used for transfusions in Vietnam had to be collected outside the country. The plague vaccine administered to all American and South Vietnamese military personnel contained a catalyst that made their blood unsuitable for transfusions. As a result, blood was gathered from donors in the U.S. and the Pacific and was flown to Vietnam. In 1966 and 1967 blood was transported weekly from America; after 1967 the blood airlift flew daily. The imported blood was ferried to six depots around the country, which in turn supplied the hospitals. The problem was the blood in cold storage has a useful life of only twenty-one days. It often took as much as half that time for the blood to reach the hospitals.

A better system was needed, and Major William S. Collins, director of the blood bank at the 406th Mobile Medical Laboratory in Saigon, devised it in late 1965. Collins fashioned a Styrofoam insert that could fit inside light cardboard shipping containers instead of the larger and heavier Hollinger boxes then in use. This new insert permitted blood to be shipped at the required temperature regardless of outside temperatures. The Collins box, as it was named, needed only three cubic feet of space to store eighteen units of whole blood and ice (as opposed to eight for the Hollinger box). And it weighed just 40 pounds when full, compared to 115 pounds for the Hollinger box. Its Styrofoam insert also enabled it to keep blood cool for forty-eight hours, twice as long as the Hollinger box. Within weeks, the Collins box had become familiar in Vietnam.

Hospitals in a war of no fronts

The swift evacuation of the wounded and the superb medical care available to them would have been far less effective if the design and location of military hospitals in South Vietnam had not been adapted to a war of no fronts. American medical facilities in previous wars had been located and operated in accordance with principles laid down in the Civil War by Major Jonathan Letterman, the medical director of the Union Army of the Potomac. Dr. Letterman emphasized rapid evacuation to close-in "clearing stations" where lifesaving treatment was available, transportation of the wounded no farther from the front than the severity of their wounds required, and division of the injured into three categories that determined the priority of treatment: those not likely to survive, the

Dr. Letterman's Hospital

Dr. Jonathan Letterman organized the medical care system used by the Union army during the Civil War, and his principles guided U.S. military treatment through the Vietnam War, albeit with some revisions. These Civil War photographs show the Union field hospital on Otto Smith's farm near Sharpsburg, Maryland. There, Dr. Letterman's system received its first test on America's bloodiest day, the Battle of Antietam on September 17, 1862, when over 22,000 Americans, Union and Confederate, were killed or wounded.

Union army field hospital, Sharpsburg, Maryland, September 1862.

badly wounded who could still be saved, and those with relatively minor wounds. Under Letterman's guidelines, the larger and better-equipped hospitals to which the more seriously wounded were sent were farther from the battle zone.

But Letterman's rules were revised in Vietnam, where the country-wide "combat zone" left no true rear areas for layering facilities of greater capability or specialization. When the U.S. became involved, the nearest American hospital outside the combat area was 1,000 miles away in the Philippines, the closest fully equipped hospital in Japan, more than 2,500 miles away. In Vietnam, there would have to be major facilities in the war zone itself. All hospitals had to offer first-class medical care. Though Letterman's categories for medical care centers, such as clearing stations and evacuation hospitals, were still honored in name, they were all ultimately upgraded to the equivalent of a 400-bed hospital.

Instead of moving with the battlefront, as they had in Korea and Europe, field hospitals in Vietnam grew larger and more elaborate while remaining in place. Many were eventually as well equipped as most stateside hospitals, boasting everything from air conditioning and x-ray equipment to intricate electronic gear. Marine Lieutenant Colonel Robert Leaver, a neurosurgeon who served as a medical consultant to the U.S. Army in South Vietnam, discovered that all the "traditional equipment seen in neurosurgical centers throughout the United States" was available in Vietnam military hospitals. "Other than the physical deficiencies of a hospital in a combat area," he said, "there is little that would distinguish our neurosurgical wards from those hospitals in America."

While most hospitals remained in place throughout the war, a new inflatable hospital first used in Vietnam could be moved. Called the MUST, for Medical Unit, Self-contained, Transportable, the inflatable ward was designed to move as the scene of battle moved. When fully inflated by its attached power unit, the rubberized ward swelled into an enclosed room twenty feet wide, ten feet high, and fifty-two feet long. Accompanying it was an expandable solid-walled unit containing operating tables and other surgical equipment. In theory, six men could inflate the ward, set up the expandable operating room, and hook up the power in thirty minutes. The operating tables rested on a cushion of air and could be adjusted to nine different positions. Portable sinks contained heating units that produced instant hot water.

The MUST seemed like a "must" indeed for the modern mobile army. When it was first demonstrated in 1965 alongside a standard evacuation hospital tent, the inflatable unit looked irresistible. Nurses sloshed through inch-deep mud between beds in the drafty tent while everyone in the enclosed MUST remained warm, dry, and clean. The rubber floor was easily hosed clean of blood and dirt.

But when MUST units went on duty in Vietnam (by 1969 the U.S. Army had deployed five of them) they proved disappointing. The controlled environment and surgical theaters won praise, but the power unit proved to be both unreliable and a fuel guzzler; one unit burned 5,000 gallons of jet fuel every three days. On the occasions when mobility was necessary, MUST units could be dismantled and reerected at a new site in three or four days; other hospitals took weeks or months because they were no longer housed by tents. But the rubberized walls had a regrettable tendency to deflate when pierced by mortar or

rocket fragments and eventually had to be shored up with ribs, which reduced the unit's mobility.

The old-fashioned tent hospital that had suffered so by comparison in a 1965 test looked better in the field. Eventually refined into air-conditioned wood and metal buildings with concrete floors, the traditional field evacuation hospitals proved to have more practical value than the elaborate but unreliable MUSTs.

Healing hearts and minds

Although the U.S. Medical Corps' top priority in South Vietnam was meeting the needs of American soldiers, it devoted much attention to providing assistance to Vietnamese civilians. During the build-up of U.S. combat troops in 1965, Secretary of Defense Robert McNamara directed the medical command in South Vietnam to organize a health program for Vietnamese civilians. MACV called it the Military Provisional Health Assistance Pro-

gram (MILPHAP). The first MILPHAP teams began operating in November 1965. Each team included three physicians, one medical administrative officer, and twelve health technicians. In early 1966, six MILPHAP teams were working at six provincial centers, and at the end of 1970 a total of twenty-five army, navy, and air force MILPHAP teams were assigned to twenty-five of the country's forty-four provinces.

MILPHAP units noticeably raised the quality of medical care in provincial civilian hospitals and district health dispensaries. They assisted Vietnamese medical staffs ham-

The first inflatable MUST hospital in Vietnam is erected by the 45th Surgical Hospital west of Tay Ninh in November, 1966. Right. The MUST rises as a power unit in the background pumps in air. Below. *Hoses from a gas turbine power unit (right)* supply the MUST with light, heat, air conditioning, hot water, refrigeration, compressed air, and suction.

pered by a shortage of trained personnel and equipment and helped improve clinical and surgical services. Members of MILPHAP also designed and supported a variety of local public health programs. In coordination with the South Vietnamese government and the American military command, they established a program for evacuating critically ill patients to medical installations with a capacity for extended treatment.

An additional goal of MILPHAP was the improvement of Vietnamese medical skills. In many ways, the South Vietnamese medical establishment, while it had improved greatly after 1954, had neither the educational resources nor the instructed personnel to absorb and use advanced American methods and technology. MILPHAP, therefore, instituted training courses for Vietnamese doctors, health workers, and nurses.

The best known of the U.S. military's medical programs for Vietnamese civilians was the Medical Civic Action Program (MEDCAP). Initiated in 1965, MEDCAP's principal objective was to extend outpatient care and basic medical services to Vietnamese civilians in rural villages. MEDCAP teams, composed of several navy corpsmen escorted by an armed marine squad, periodically visited hamlets and villages. With the aid of Vietnamese medical technicians, they set up a series of rural health stations.

In contrast to MILPHAP, MEDCAP teams dispensed only relatively rudimentary medical care: inoculations, vitamins, antibiotics, and pain killers. They also treated minor ailments. Patients requiring more extensive treatment were usually referred to the nearest civilian hospital facilities. For many peasants, the basic care supplied by MEDCAP exceeded what they could normally expect from the overstretched, undermanned medical programs of the South Vietnamese government. Compared, moreover, to the herbal potions and magic cures prescribed by the traditional village "doctor" they often had to rely on, MEDCAP represented a medical revolution. As a result, rural villagers responded enthusiastically to MEDCAP "sick calls." From December 1967 to March 1968, MEDCAP handled a monthly average of 188,441 civilian patients. By 1970, the monthly average jumped to 225,000.

The combined medical campaign of MILPHAP and MEDCAP, however, could only partially satisfy civilian demand. When the fighting across South Vietnam accelerated in 1967, the number of civilian casualties rose dramatically. U.S. authorities estimated 50,000 such casualties per year and feared, according to Major General Spurgeon Neel, that "existing Vietnamese medical resources would be overwhelmed in providing care for these victims." In response, the U.S. Defense Department ordered MACV to construct additional civilian hospitals. In addition, MACV opened its military medical facilities to civilians. By 1967, the U.S. Army had allocated 400 beds to civilian patients. Because of the surge in civilian casualties during the 1968 Tet offensive, the U.S. military assumed

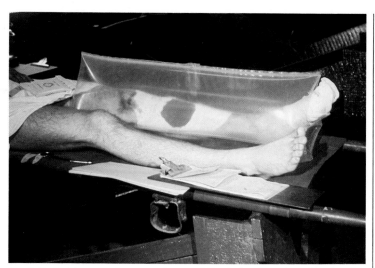

An inflatable splint supports a soldier's broken leg. Easier for field medics to carry and use, it cushioned and immobilized the injured limb without heavier, time-consuming bandages.

the highest civilian case load it could without diminishing the quality of care accorded American troops.

Throughout the war, the need of civilians for medical care of all kinds continually outpaced the ability of the U.S. Medical Corps to accommodate them. As a U.S. Army history acknowledged, "The task of substantially improving health care in an underdeveloped nation was difficult enough. Compounded by civil strife and guerilla warfare, it became impossible."

Prevention pays off

Vietnam could easily have been an enormous pestilential sinkhole for the American forces. Indeed, many of the danger signs, conditions for the presence of epidemic diseases were there: a hot and soggy climate, dense jungle vegetation in much of the country, primitive sanitary facilities. Malaria, cholera, the plague, and other tropical diseases and fevers could easily afflict soldiers new to the environment. In the long history of warfare, disease has killed many more men than battle has; of the 360,000 Union soldiers who died in the American Civil War, for example, two-thirds of them succumbed to disease.

The story was different in Vietnam. Despite the climate, the malaria-carrying mosquitoes, and rats skittering through the trash dumps, American troops remained free of serious diseases to a remarkable degree. The death rate as a result of disease was 0.35 per thousand men (in Korea, it was 0.39); only 620 of the 56,869 American fighting men who lost their lives in the Vietnam War were victims of disease.

The Vietnam conflict was the first in American military history in which preventive measures such as hygiene programs were enforced from the outset and this emphasis paid off. Mosquito control campaigns designed to avert malaria, for example, were rigorously carried out wher-

An ounce of prevention. A soldier of the U.S. Army Preventive Medicine Unit sprays insecticide to kill fleas and other disease "vectors" at Bien Hoa.

ever U.S. troops lived and worked. The only significant outbreaks of malaria occurred in areas like the central highlands, where enemy domination precluded pest control efforts. Other endemic diseases such as rabies and the plague were almost unknown to Americans there. Spraying, vaccination programs, rat control, and an efficient reporting system helped protect GIs.

Malaria has traditionally been lethal to armies fighting in a tropical zone, but in Vietnam only 117 Americans died of malaria, most of whom contracted the disease in the central highlands. Early in the war, it appeared that an epidemic might be imminent: The equivalent of two battalions of the 1st Air Cavalry Division were in effect knocked out of action by malaria during the Ia Drang Valley campaign of November 1965, and in some units the incidence level reached 60 percent. The drug dapsone was eventually found to be effective against the strain of malaria found in the highlands, and its widespread use prevented an epidemic.

Fresh food, clean water, showers, and waste control helped to head off many of the serious diseases—typhoid, cholera, hepatitis, and others—that often afflict armies in the field. "Vector control officers" were responsible for the elimination of rats and other disease-carrying pests. To avoid the danger of water contamination, there were no pits beneath army latrines. The waste was collected in cutoff fifty-five-gallon drums partially filled with fuel oil. When a drum was full, a detachment of troopers or Vietnamese hired by them burned its contents. In contrast to their normal role in other wars as breeding grounds of disease, the military camps were clean and healthy.

The afflictions that most often sent men on sick call were all relatively minor: jungle rot and other skin diseases, particularly foot irritations; the traditional military malady of venereal disease; and the infection the army called "FUO," for "Fever of Unknown Origin." The fever—whose cause was difficult to diagnose—felled an average of 58 out of every 1,000 troops and kept them out of action for four to five days each. Skin diseases were responsible for the highest number of outpatient visits; in some instances they reduced a unit's strength by as much as 30 percent.

The most common foot aggravations, sometimes serious enough to impair walking, were caused by sloshing through wet terrain like that in the Mekong Delta. Among the men of the U.S. 9th Division, which operated in the delta, half the "man-days" lost in the twelve months beginning in July 1968 were the result of skin ailments such as "warm water immersion foot" and its close relative, "tropical immersion foot." Countermeasures included improved boots, quick-drying nylon socks, and the application of silicon ointment. Experience caused infantry boots to be made with drainage holes at the base, and uppers were made of nylon instead of leather.

On one score, the Vietnam record was bad. Venereal disease afflicted more soldiers in Vietnam than in any previous American war. From 1965 to the end of the war, VD was the most common ailment diagnosed; 260 out of every 1,000 men contracted it every year, as against 43 per 1,000 in World War II and 184 in Korea. Rarely debilitating, it was commonly treated with penicillin and other antibiotics. In coping with more wasting epidemic diseases, however, the U.S. military in Vietnam had compiled a record of unparalleled excellence.

Nonmedical factors

Are there lessons from the Vietnam experience that will save more lives and limbs if another war is fought? There were two main keys to the success of medicine in Vietnam: the dethroning of disease as a wartime killer through prevention and the shortening of the interval between the time of injury and the application of the best of medical care in fully equipped facilities. But these strategies were in turn dependent on two factors: a vast logistical support system more than capable of meeting all the demands of war and virtually unrestrained air access to the battlefront. In swift and short campaigns, such as Grenada, these factors will be present. In a more intense and protracted campaign, as might occur in Europe, the air would be as dangerous as any battlefield, there would be much less security in the rear areas, and the logistical system might be saturated, if not overwhelmed, by the more basic appetites for food, ammunition, fuel, and repair parts. Even though we can expect continuous improvements in technologies applicable to the wounds of war, how available they will be will depend in large part on nonmedical factors.

A soldier uses a mosquito head net to protect against malaria-carrying mosquitoes.

From Punji Stakes to Guided Missiles

In the summer of 1970, as protest over the Cambodian incursion drew thousands of young Americans into the streets, a group of ROTC students watched from bleachers as a man in black pajamas made his way through the "hamlet" of Dong Xai, just east of Harrisburg, Pennsylvania. While the officers-to-be listened to an army lecturer, the "guerrilla" emerged from the woods near the hamlet, carrying a larger mortar round. Apparently exhausted, the man made his way slowly along a circuitous route to a mortar concealed just outside the hamlet. Handing the shell to a mortarman with obvious relief he gasped, "Comrade—from Hanoi." The "Vietcong" gunner promptly fired the round as the students waited to see what would happen next. Then he turned to the drooping man in pajamas and said, "Well, don't just stand there. Go back and get another one." The ROTC boys roared with laughter.

The image that scene conveyed—of a primitive,

labor-intensive enemy compensating for his poverty of means by an almost magic wiliness and superhuman determination—had been nurtured during the early years of the war before the introduction of large numbers of American ground troops. By 1970 it was an image that only partially conformed to reality. It was true that Vietcong guerrillas often fought with weapons that seemed primitive, with bamboo spikes and homemade mines and vine-sprung booby traps. It was also true that they often used people and animals to do what a modern army did with machinery. Yet after 1965 the VC carried the same modern assault rifles that Soviet-bloc armies used. Their NVA allies first fielded tanks in 1968, launching them against the Special Forces camp at Lang Vei in 1968. The same year, they bombarded Khe Sanh with heavy artillery. They blew holes in allied tanks with powerful rockets fired from portable launchers and shot American planes from the sky with an array of potent antiaircraft weapons including SAM missiles.

This dichotomy of vision persisted largely because the United States faced in Vietnam not one, but two armies—the Vietcong of the South and the North Vietnamese Army—each with its own resources and strategic goals. At the same time, until the NVA became a fully conventional army conducting the mechanized invasion in 1972, the value of "primitive" weapons did not decrease just because regular units became better equipped. Thus American soldiers, confronted by constantly more sophisticated weapons in the hands of Main Force units, never escaped the dangers of homemade mines and booby traps.

The paradox of the punji stake and the guided missile, however, was not as strange as it seemed. It represented a pragmatic adaptation of military means to political ends, a recognition of the strengths and weaknesses of the opposing sides, and a determined application of revolutionary doctrine to the task of defeating a force more numerous and powerful than the Communists could muster.

Fundamental to Communist thinking in Vietnam was a strategy of revolutionary warfare propounded by General

Graffiti drawn by North Vietnamese children shows a surface-to-air missile launching at U.S. aircraft while one plane falls in flames.

Vo Nguyen Giap in his 1960 *People's War, People's Army*. According to Douglas Pike, a prominent American student of Vietnamese revolutionary doctrine, such conflict proceeds through three main stages. In the first stage the revolutionaries are on the defensive, their primary goal survival. Using hit-and-run attacks, avoiding pitched battles, keeping their small units intact, guerrilla forces concentrate on building an organizational base and winning the support of the people. The success of such efforts leads eventually to the second stage in which an initial military equilibrium is achieved. As enemy troops become more defensive, the guerrillas become more offensive-minded. A structured liberation army mounts a series of carefully prepared, integrated campaigns employing larger units and relying upon more conventional tactics. Political goals continue to be paramount as the insurgents labor to break the enemy's physical and psychological hold on the population. The third stage is reached when the revolutionary forces, now organized at brigade and division level, openly challenge the enemy. "Here the struggle loses much of its ideological cast," writes Pike, "and becomes less a war of issues and more a matter of pure military force."

Two aspects of this revolutionary strategy were particularly important: the gradual movement from small-scale guerrilla forays to large, mobile operations and the primacy of political, rather than military, goals in all but the final stage. Thus doctrine, and not only circumstance, dictated a preference for sudden ambush and rapid withdrawal, emphasized camouflage and concealment, and placed a premium on speed, precision, and planning. A highly mobile hit-and-run style also meant that, at least initially, tanks and heavy artillery were less useful than rifles, machine guns, mortars, mines, and rockets.

More than anything else, revolutionary doctrine insisted upon a careful calculation of the strengths and weaknesses of the opposing sides and the necessity of forcing the enemy as much as possible to fight in ways that were to the insurgents' advantage. What emerged was what Colonel Harry Summers has called "a kind of economy of force operation" that bought the time the North Vietnamese and Vietcong needed to demoralize U.S. military forces and influence American public opinion. In a speech before the 1967 COSVN Congress, NVA Major General

Nguyen Van Vinh outlined succinctly the dilemma and opportunity that presented themselves to Hanoi. To achieve victory over the Americans, declared Vinh, did not mean "total" victory but "decisive" victory. "In a war of position they can defeat us. But with our present tactics we will win and they will be defeated. It is the same as if we force them to eat rice with chopsticks. If we eat rice with spoons and forks like them, we will be defeated; if chopsticks are used, they are no match for us."

In the years to follow, the Communist command would not always heed Vinh's advice. Neither would Communist attempts to tailor their technology to their needs by any means insure victory on the field of battle. But their use and choice of weapons did prove exceedingly pragmatic. Whether "primitive" or "sophisticated," they were well suited to political objectives at any given time and generally reflected an acute appreciation of both their own strengths and the weaknesses of their opponent.

Digging in

That dichotomy was nowhere more apparent than in the intricate network of bunker complexes and tunnels that honeycombed the battlefields of the South. The Vietnamese had been going underground to escape superior military force since the nineteenth century, but the tunnel system they built in the 1950s and 1960s was far more elaborate than anything attempted previously. The famous underground complex at Cu Chi, only 30 kilometers from Saigon, had more than 250 kilometers of tunnels on two or three levels as much as ten meters below the surface with subterranean chambers linked by passageways two feet square, easily negotiable for the slight Vietnamese. The multilayered maze reminded some soldiers of the New York subway.

Hamlets in North Vietnam were linked by tunnels that extended dozens of kilometers. In some parts of the South, villagers lived underground for weeks at a time. American infantrymen occasionally happened on complexes. The one the 1st Battalion, 8th Cavalry, 1st Cavalry Division, found in the Nui Mieu Mountains in 1967 included five vertical shafts three to fifteen meters deep connected by horizontal corridors. By the end of 1970, American troops throughout Vietnam had discovered no fewer than 4,800 tunnels, many of them stocked with food and water and at least 1 serving as an underground hospital with its own electricity.

The enemy's reliance on tunnels also had its disadvantages. Moving troops from one tunnel complex to the next ate up valuable time, dictated rigid planning, and consumed vast amounts of labor. The hard labor of dig-

Early in the war, in August 1965, a Vietcong guerrilla in an observation post high in a tree northwest of Saigon keeps watch for enemy aircraft.

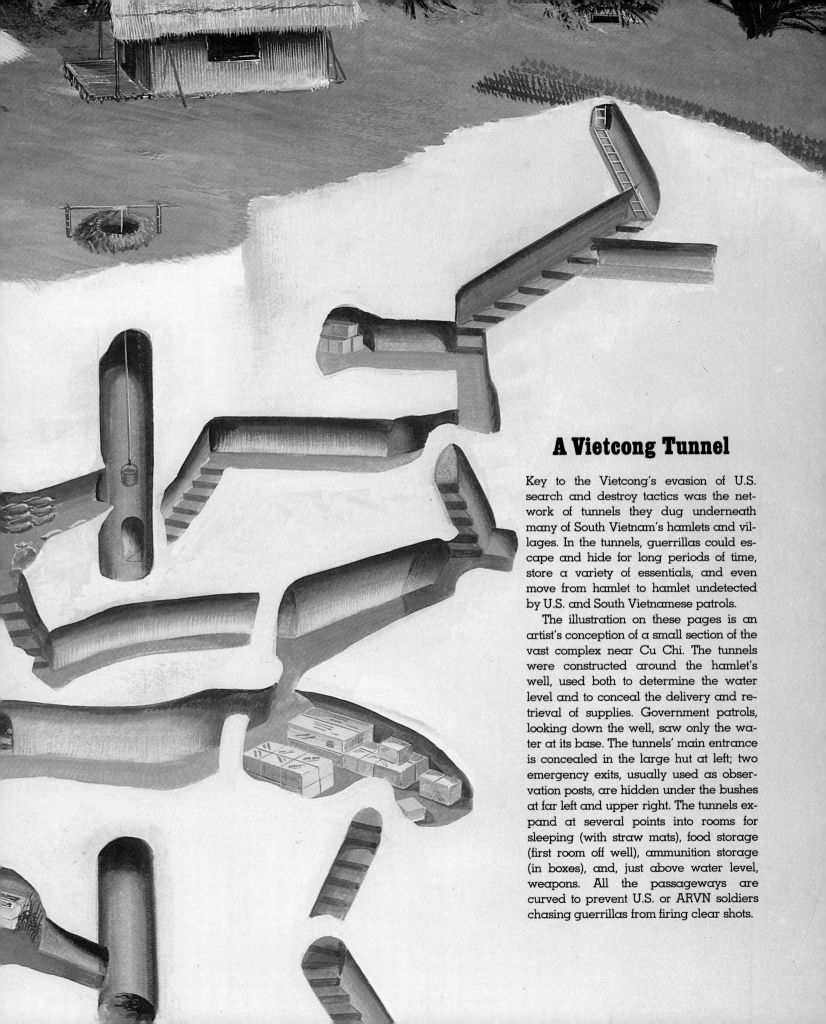

A Vietcong Tunnel

Key to the Vietcong's evasion of U.S. search and destroy tactics was the network of tunnels they dug underneath many of South Vietnam's hamlets and villages. In the tunnels, guerrillas could escape and hide for long periods of time, store a variety of essentials, and even move from hamlet to hamlet undetected by U.S. and South Vietnamese patrols.

The illustration on these pages is an artist's conception of a small section of the vast complex near Cu Chi. The tunnels were constructed around the hamlet's well, used both to determine the water level and to conceal the delivery and retrieval of supplies. Government patrols, looking down the well, saw only the water at its base. The tunnels' main entrance is concealed in the large hut at left; two emergency exits, usually used as observation posts, are hidden under the bushes at far left and upper right. The tunnels expand at several points into rooms for sleeping (with straw mats), food storage (first room off well), ammunition storage (in boxes), and, just above water level, weapons. All the passageways are curved to prevent U.S. or ARVN soldiers chasing guerrillas from firing clear shots.

ging often fell to teams of young men and women expected to excavate three meters of earth a day. They worked bucket-brigade fashion, passing the dirt back in sandbags and baskets to "disposal exits" at intervals of thirty or sixty meters. They tried to choose areas with cohesive soils and good root networks to minimize the need for shoring, which was done with bamboo. Tunnels widened into living rooms and storage chambers filled with baskets of rice and water stored in inner tubes. Bamboo-pole air shafts connected the underground rooms with the surface. Some tunnels could be entered only by swimming underwater, while other entrances were covered with camouflaged trap doors. Sharp turns every three meters or so reduced the impact of explosives dropped in the booby-trapped entrances. A tunnel at a depth of three to six meters could survive almost anything short of a direct hit by a large bomb.

Digging was an unending but tactically vital chore. "We literally dug for thirty years," a man from Cu Chi told a journalist after the war, "usually in the dark, squatting down. We carved out about a meter every eight hours, and women distributed the earth on the surface hiding it under fallen leaves. We always moved in the dark, saving our candles and torches for emergencies. Our amputees lay in the dark sometimes for months."

The tunnels were crucial to "the enemy's ability to survive bombing attacks, to appear and disappear at will, and to operate an efficient logistic system under primitive conditions," according to U.S. Lieutenant General John H. Hay, Jr. They enabled the VC and NVA to concentrate their forces slowly without being detected by allied intelligence, serving as safe steppingstones between their sanctuaries in Cambodia and the battlefield. A guerrilla who operated in the Iron Triangle northwest of Saigon recalled that "when we got orders to set up a secure base here the first thing we did was to start digging thirty kilometers of underground tunnels. This was one of our outposts to Saigon and our advanced command post throughout the war." No one will ever know how many kilometers of tunnels there were overall; one plausible guess is about 30,000.

The VC tried to fool the scout dogs used by U.S. troops to locate tunnels by rubbing GI mosquito repellent on the entrance doors and stashing American soap and cigarettes just inside. When a tunnel was discovered it was searched by teams of bantam-sized volunteer "tunnel rats" who used smoke grenades to spot additional entrances and cautiously explored the underground shafts. "You're always scared," one tunnel rat confessed to a reporter. "You find everything—dishes, ammo, guitars, banjos, letters to American GIs and even pictures from *Playboy*. You find mines and booby traps too." Carrying flashlights, compasses, and field telephones, the soldiers crawled through the snug passageways and mapped them. "The worst day I had was when I saw two rice bags

in a tunnel and pulled them apart," one GI remembered. "A grenade fell right in front of me—but it was a dud."

After the tunnels were searched they were usually destroyed by explosives or rendered unusable with CS (tear) gas powder. If they were very close to the surface they were crushed by heavy equipment, but the larger complexes were all but impossible to eliminate. "There isn't enough dynamite in Vietnam to blow up all of them," a captain who led a team of tunnel rats said. The Cu Chi system, in fact, was still largely intact at the end of the war and later became a museum. A Vietcong veteran who spent ten years in the Cu Chi tunnels worked there as a sightseeing guide in 1982.

Homemade warfare

One use of the tunnels was as a concealed site for making and storing a deadly variety of homemade weapons. By the time Americans arrived in Vietnam in force the manufacture of various kinds of booby traps in Vietcong-controlled villages had become a thriving cottage industry. Children and old people sharpened bamboo stakes, sometimes poisoning their tips with excrement, and removed the gunpowder from unexploded American shells so it could be reused in improvised mines. Though the methods were crude the organization was not. Weapon-making was frequently the work of forced labor, but it was also "part of the class work" for schoolchildren, a directive from the leadership said, boasting that "pupils in one school in Can Tho Province made 30,000 bamboo spikes, set forty booby traps, and laid two bamboo long-spike fields against helicopters." One "cell" of loyalists in each VC hamlet was designated "keeper of the arms," another document proclaimed. "Each hamlet is to manufacture firearms, land mines, and foot spikes." The bow-and-arrow-like "sling guns" and other homemade small arms were no longer necessary by 1966, having been replaced by modern rifles, but local production of mines and booby traps continued throughout the war.

The guerrillas used anything handy to fabricate their often ingenious traps. Punji stakes made from the abundant bamboo were the most common. Early in the war the stakes were placed in the ground at an angle in belts up to fifteen meters wide, concealed by grass. Others were hidden in camouflaged foot-sized holes and in gravelike pits covered with enough soil to support a Vietnamese villager but not a weighted-down U.S. soldier. Boards studded with iron barbs were set in shallow streambeds and paddies or sometimes arranged in a trap in such a way that they clamped a man's calf when they were sprung. Weapons from another century, like crossbows and muzzle loaders, were primed and attached to hair-trigger trip wires.

The biggest booby trap encountered in Vietnam was probably a fifteen-meter-long log attached to two trees by

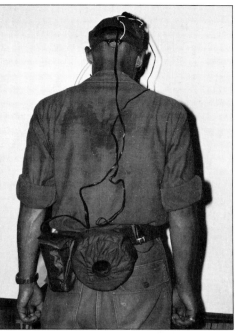

Tunnel Rat Gear

The high-risk jobs of U.S. "tunnel rats" who drew the duty of exploring VC tunnels called for special equipment. At first they were equipped with a standard .45 caliber automatic, a flashlight, a bayonet, and a field telephone, too much equipment for the tunnel rats, who usually crawled. The equipment at left was tailored to fit the task. In 1966, this tunnel rat demonstrates a miner's head lamp, a .38 caliber revolver with silencer in an easy draw holster, and a bite switch telephone headset connected to a roll of wire on his back to play out as he explores the tunnel. Tunnel rats were usually chosen from among the smallest men in a unit because the passages were barely large enough for the comparatively small Vietnamese.

Several entries to a VC tunnel complex in II corps shoot smoke and flames after men of the 101st Airborne Division set off bombs in the tunnels during Operation Seward on September 23, 1966.

a taut vine rope triggered by a trip wire. The log, known as a "Malay whip," had to be hoisted into place by a pair of elephants. When a luckless member of one particular thirteen-man ARVN patrol tripped the wire in a jungle clearing, the huge log whipped wildly through a ninety-degree arc one meter above the ground and took out the entire patrol.

The 1966 *Handbook for U.S. Forces in Vietnam* described to uninitiated American GIs an intimidating inventory of makeshift VC weapons. One was a bullet buried straight up with its firing pin on a bamboo stub; it was activated when a trespasser stepped on the bullet's tip. Another was a hollowed-out coconut filled with gunpowder and triggered by a trip wire attached to a friction fuse. Soldiers were warned to beware of opening wooden gates, which were often wired to hidden grenades. Crude bridges were cut most of the way through so they would collapse when anyone crossed; a row of punji stakes lay underwater beneath many of them. Miniforests of bamboo stakes connected to grenades were planted at helicopter landing sites; other antihelicopter mines could be tripped by a chopper's rotor wash. Eight-centimeter-long stakes lurked in the grass on the banks of narrow gullies men would normally jump across. Artillery and mortar shells were made into mines and hidden on branches overhanging a trail where they were command-detonated.

An article in a 1967 issue of a U.S. military magazine warned newcomers to Vietnam to be wary of anything that did not look right—"weapons left in the open, aban-

Vietcong booby traps. Left. *Bamboo pyramids mark punji traps for the people of a Mekong Delta village. When U.S. troops approach, the pyramids will be removed. The undisturbed camouflage under the markers contrasts with the areas of traffic, however, providing alert soldiers a clue to the traps' locations.* Below. *Villagers emplace punji stakes in a landing zone as a threat to troops jumping from helicopters. The tall stakes endanger rotor blades.*

School for Terror

At its Mines, Booby Traps and Tunnel Training Center in Vietnam, the 25th Infantry Division taught soldiers a healthy respect for the Communists' macabre tools of terror. In addition to showing their students a variety of mines and booby traps, telling them how they worked, and teaching them how they could avoid the traps, instructors put their charges through a harrowing training course. Before a group of fresh trainees entered the course, often they would hear an anguished cry from a man part way through the test who would then be carried by them, apparently bleeding and in severe pain. The "casualty" was, of course, a "plant" placed by instructors for dramatic effect. But the students did not know that, and the drama gave them the motivation they needed to approach their training—and their later patrols through trap-laden territory—seriously.

Right. *At the training center, men peer down a typical punji trap which has had its camouflaged ground-level covering removed.*

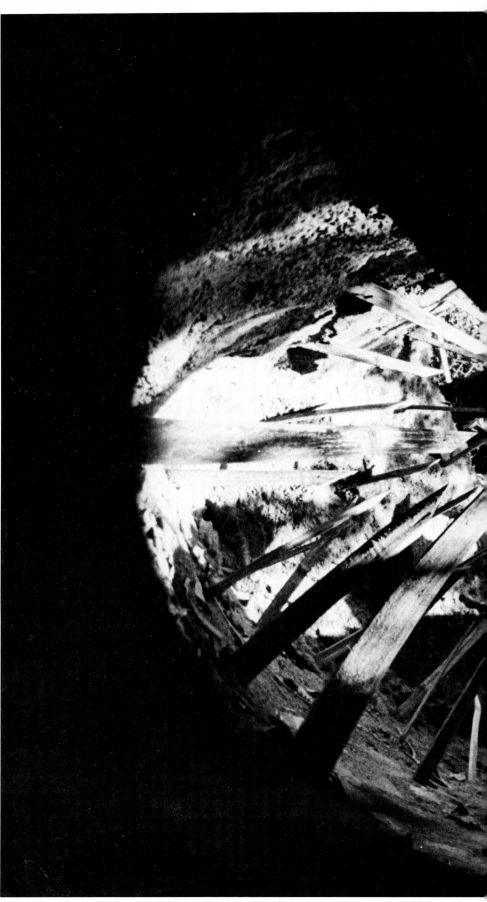

Two sample traps. Top. *A hand gre-nade attached to a trip wire. Above. A spiked "dead fall" concealed in a tree plunges earthward when a wire slung across the trail below is tugged. (The sash marking the trip wire would not be present on a real trap in the field.)*

doned equipment, foxholes, tunnels, wires, or cords either on the ground or strung between objects, and especially unusual marks left to attract attention." Soft drink and C-ration cans were often transformed into mines. American medics found that even the bodies of their dead comrades were sometimes booby-trapped.

The Vietcong employed mines and booby traps as much for their psychological impact as the physical damage they did; they counted on GI carelessness in their mining operations. Guerrillas sometimes dug dozens of holes in a road and refilled them, placing mines in only a few. A mine detection team would examine several smoothed-over sites, find no mines, and conclude the road was safe. Or the VC would smear a road with mud several nights running, forcing the mine detectors to check it daily until they decided it was no longer necessary—at which point mines would be planted. "There's no school that can tell you how to hunt for booby traps," a U.S. Marine injured by a VC trap lamented in 1967. "You only do it by experience, by some kind of sixth sense. Mine stopped working for me the other day."

VC booby traps and mines could be strikingly effective weapons. In one U.S. operation in the Iron Triangle region in 1965, 95 percent of the casualties were caused by traps and mines. Leathernecks with the 3d Marines blamed them for half their casualties in early 1967. Of the army casualties suffered between January 1965 and June 1970, 11 percent of the deaths and 17 percent of the injuries were officially attributed to booby traps and mines.

Such devices, however, were not unique—both the Germans and Japanese, among others, had employed similar measures in World War II. Nor were they infallible. Because they relied on unskilled villagers, booby traps were often poorly emplaced. The camouflage that hid them would degrade fairly rapidly, making it easier to spot them before any damage had been done. The increasing number of paved roads eliminated many possible mining sites. Better training—like the 3d Marine Division's booby-trap school the grunts called "Punji Palace"—reduced their effectiveness, as did the Americans' huge Rome plows and dogs specially trained to ferret them out. Moreover, their maintenance depended upon an organized guerrilla network. After 1968, when the back of the Vietcong guerrilla movement was broken, the "homemade" arsenal became far less of a problem than it had been earlier in the war.

Nonetheless, from a grunt's eye view the traps were terrifying. Marine Medical Corpsman Douglas Anderson had to cope with the rippling effects of a single booby trap on a patrol in 1967:

There was a slope into a ravine that we had to go down, and the VC knew that when we got to this slope we would slide down because the dirt was loose. So they rigged a trip wire where it would catch us as we slid down—it was one of the damndest things I'd ever seen. This little bitty skinny guy from somewhere

in the South tripped it. It didn't do him too much harm, but it took off part of his calf. The blast made one of the grenades on his belt start to hiss. I knew that the fuse was five seconds, so I was probably going to die, but nevertheless I struggled to get the damn thing off. It probably took me a whole minute to get it off and throw the whole belt away. Fortunately the grenade didn't go off.

In 1966, marine rifleman John Muir saw the results when the VC inherited a bonanza: 36,000 U.S.-made "Bouncing Betty" mines. The guerrillas simply took them from a camp abandoned by ARVN troops and put them to work. "All you had to do was pull the pin and bury them," Muir recalled.

You could rig them up sixteen different ways. Step on them and they usually go off waist-high. It's a sixty-millimeter mortar round. Everybody would hit them. They were up in trees, they were all over. The VC had a picnic, just like decorating a Christmas tree. It was the only time they ever had enough to spare. They put them everywhere, scattered them around like snowflakes. We had one guy who got a whole load of it in the cheeks of his behind. He was joking about his million-dollar wound, about how he'd be chasing the nurses by tomorrow afternoon. They put him on the helicopter and he went into shock and died on the way to the hospital ship.

Ground weaponry

As lethal as the homemade weapons could be, they were only a small, and scarcely the most deadly, part of the arsenal the enemy brought to bear against American and South Vietnamese troops. A battalion of Main Force VC or NVA infantrymen carried roughly the same amount of firepower as an equivalent U.S. or South Vietnamese unit. The difference was in the extra muscle the two sides could summon if they had to: allied outfits could bring in artillery, helicopter gunships, and tactical air strikes when a fight began; an enemy battalion was normally self-contained—it fought with what it carried. As a result the Communists were partial to lightweight, multipurpose weapons, even if this sometimes meant sacrificing power and range for portability.

The hardware that a typical enemy unit lugged into action included AK47 assault rifles, light machine guns that used the same 7.62MM bullets as the rifles, heavy 12.7MM machine guns used primarily as antiaircraft guns, recoilless rifles and various mortars, and long-range 107MM rockets. Communist unit commanders coordinated their firepower with field telephones and radios along with messengers and sound signals.

The Chinese-made AK47s were comparable to U.S. M16s in accuracy, slightly heavier and less likely to jam when dirty. Their 7.62MM bullet was not as easily deflected by leaves and grass as the smaller 5.56MM cartridge fired by the M16, although the latter was technically more lethal because its wound ballistics were more gruesome. The AK47's larger shell size also meant that a soldier could

carry less ammo. Because their ammunition reserves were limited and rapid resupply was difficult, enemy riflemen learned to spend their bullets frugally. Their officers also conserved firepower by holding onto the initiative in deciding when to start and stop a firefight.

The enemy's light machine guns, the Soviet RPD and RPK, were similar to their allied counterparts in range, power, accuracy, and reliability. The VC and NVA generally used machine guns in the traditional way, to control a patch of ground from a prepared position, while allied troops often fired them as if they were simply larger rifles. The foe's dual-purpose 12.7 heavy machine gun was mounted on a two-wheeled cart with a long tow shaft. The shaft formed one leg of a tripod when the weapon was fired at ground targets. To convert it to an antiaircraft gun the cart was tipped up and the shaft unfolded. The gunner then climbed on a small bicycle seat between the wheels. Because of their weight the 12.7s were most often used as antiaircraft guns from fixed positions.

Main Force Vietcong used a Chinese 75MM recoilless rifle as an improvised light artillery piece. Mounted on a two-wheeled carriage like the heavy machine gun, it was more accurate than a rocket and more potent than a mortar. Ordinarily the soldier firing the 75MM gun needed to see his target, which was likely to make him uncomfortably conspicuous when the gun exploded with its characteristic flash and noisy burst of smoke. To remedy this vulnerability the VC put mortar sights on the 75s. With these they could calculate the correct firing table and then blast away from behind a hill 1,350 to 1,800 meters from the target, firing "blind" as an artillery crew did. A direct hit with a 75MM shell would destroy a bunker.

Well-armed Vietcong guerrillas fire on Hue during the 1968 Tet offensive. From left to right, they fire an SKS carbine, an RPD light machine gun, and an AK47.

The VC and NVA infantry's favorite heavy weapon was the highly regarded, Russian-designed RPG7 rocket launcher. Descended from a German World War II weapon called "Panzerfaust," the RPG7 weighed in at a mere fifteen pounds and was just over a meter long. Its five-pound B41 rocket consisted of a slender motor section with folding fins that fit into the launch tube and a rounded warhead. The first stage fired within the launcher and propelled the rocket a safe distance from the gunner before the second and main stage ignited. This two-stage propulsion system gave the rocket an accurate range of 450 meters against bunkers and a maximum range of 900 meters. While its modest dimensions made it popular with enemy commanders, it was the rocket's destructive force that made believers out of allied officers. The U.S. counterpart, the M72 LAW, was smaller and less lethal.

The RPG7's shortcomings were a tendency to drift off course in wind and a fragile fuse that sometimes failed to detonate the warhead. The American answer to the RPG was the "RPG Screen," which was nothing more than sturdy chain-link fencing. U.S. armored vehicles carried it in rolls and fenced in many bunkers with it. When the B41 rocket struck the fence either it detonated, in which case it did so at a fairly safe distance, or the tip passed between the links, which dented the conical nose's side, as the round punched through, shorting out its detonator. Subsequently, when it hit the bunker or armored vehicle, it was just five pounds of high-speed junk.

Communist vs. U. S. Small Arms

Communist troops in Vietnam had Soviet-designed weapons comparable to many U.S.-produced arms. Prominent was the AK47 rifle, which was accurate, rugged, and reliable: as many as fifty million of them have been made since 1951. Its U.S. counterpart, the M16, was considered by many U.S. troops to be less reliable than the AK47. The enemy's rocket launchers, like the RPG7, were larger and heavier than their U.S. equivalents, but packed more punch. The U.S. M60 machine gun's quick-change barrel made it more capable of sustained fire than the lighter RPK. The illustrations on these two pages provide views of comparable weapons in the opposing infantry's arsenals.

The principal NVA/VC rifle, the AK47 (above) was heavier and shorter (9.5 pounds, 34.25 inches) than the American M16 (8.4 pounds, 39 inches). Both had an effective range of 400 meters, although the AK47 had a slower rate of fire (600 rounds per minute vs. 700 rpm) and muzzle velocity (2,350 feet per second vs. 3,250 fps.).

The Soviet SVD (above) and U.S. M14 (below) sniper rifles both used 7.62MM rounds and had comparable muzzle velocities (2720 fps vs. 2798 fps). But the SVD weighed 9.5 pounds, five pounds less than the M14. The SVD is shown here with a PSO-1 sniper scope, while the M14 is equipped with a Redfield 3-9X scope. Many Americans also chose the M14 over the M16 as their standard rifle.

The Soviet RPG7 (above) was an 85MM, 18.7-pound rocket launcher with a maximum effective range of 500 meters. The lighter (5.25 lb) U.S. M72 66MM LAW (below) had a shorter effective range, 300 meters. The NVA/VC had no counterpart to the highly effective U.S. M79 grenade launcher (right) which weighed 6.4 pounds and could fire a grenade up to 400 meters.

Both the Soviet RPK (below) and the U.S. M60 (left) machine guns used 7.62MM ammunition, but at 10.5 pounds, the RPK was much lighter than the 23-pound M60. The Soviet weapon was slightly shorter (41 vs. 43.75 inches), and had a range of 900 meters compared with the M60's 1,100 meters.

Artillery and armor

One of the keys to the enemy's relative success on the battlefield was his adaptability. This was as true of his use of weapons as his tactics, especially regarding artillery. U.S. artillery—expensive, logistically complex, electronically sophisticated—met American needs well. But the weapons the enemy included in his artillery arsenal—far less elaborate, far more restricted in their effectiveness by the need for careful advance planning—nonetheless largely met his requirements.

For much of the war, VC and NVA forces used rockets, mortars, and mines as a substitute for artillery. The 82MM and 120MM mortars were similar to the U.S. 81MM and 107MM (4.2 inch) mortars, although the U.S. mortars had in both cases about 1,000 meters greater effective range and the rounds they used were designed to be more destructive. Highly skilled Communist mortar crews selected firing positions and angles in advance through reconnaissance of the rarely disguised command posts and other facilities at U.S. bases. GIs who were unaware of the advance scouting often marveled at how accurately enemy gunners "walked" their mortar rounds across a base's vital installations.

To escape allied guns the mortar teams either fired and quickly vanished or they dug in. Sometimes before an attack they scraped out a narrow hole at the correct firing angle and slid a mortar tube into the shaft so it was pre-aimed at the target, concealing ammunition nearby. Later one or two men would return to the site, drop a dozen rounds in a few seconds, and then disappear. Mortar positions were similarly laid out in advance at likely helicopter landing zones. When the choppers came in the mortars unleashed a quick, accurate volley and then fell silent.

Mines also served in the place of artillery. Since local forces were ubiquitous, the capability to plant mines was too. Many mines were not activated by a vehicle or soldier but instead—especially in ambushes—were command detonated. In this case, a trip wire or pressure plate mechanism was replaced with wires up to several hundred meters long running to a concealed position. When an observer saw that the desired target was near the site, he touched the wires to a battery and blew the mine. With both trip-wired and command-detonated mines planted throughout an ambush zone, the effect could be much like a well-planned and timed barrage, only more effective because the pointblank proximity of the target rendered explosive booby traps or mines much more devastating. The counterpart to the allied gun crew was thus the Local Force village guerrilla or low-level combat guerrilla. And the counterpart to the artillery piece and the shell was the mine, often made from unexploded bombs and artillery rounds. Air bursts and shrapnel shells were duplicated by using claymore-type mines and suspending mines in the branches of trees.

The VC's answer to heavy artillery was the free-flight rocket. Three kinds were introduced in the midsixties, the 140MM, 122MM, and the 107MM rocket. Weighing ninety pounds, and just over six feet in length, the 107 carried a thirty-five-pound warhead to a maximum range of nearly 10,000 meters. By comparison, the American M102 105MM howitzer weighed slightly less than 3,300 pounds (one of the lightest big guns in the world) and fired a thirty-five-pound shell 11,000 meters.

The advantages of the rocket were that to put 1,000 pounds (about thirty rockets) of high explosive on a target, 2,600 pounds had to be transported to the firing position. For 1,000 pounds of high explosive to be put on target by a 105MM howitzer, 4,600 pounds had to be transported to the firing position, 3,300 of which comprised the gun itself. Rockets could be transported in two sections, assembled,

and fired from any kind of launcher, including a simple wooden fork rest. Thus, given time, a considerable barrage could be assembled almost anywhere. More normally, metal tubes or wooden troughs were used. The rockets were aimed by pointing the launcher and elevating it to the correct angle for the desired range. A salvo of several rockets could be fired very quickly for maximum shock effect.

Free-flight rockets such as the 107MM rocket are much less accurate than artillery, and the accuracy is not helped by simple launchers. Communist troops partly overcame this by being able to pick the time and location for the stand-off attack and by accurately surveying target and firing positions. The usual targets for these rockets—firebases and command posts—were more than large enough for the rocket's large CEP. The 107MM rockets could destroy almost any allied bunker with a direct hit. As rockets became more plentiful after 1967, allied units felt compelled to commit a percentage of available air and ground forces to constantly patrolling a wide "rocket belt" around their major bases.

In late 1967 the North Vietnamese Army wheeled true artillery on line along the DMZ, and for the first time the rockets and other substitute big guns were backed up by the real thing. The main NVA artillery piece at this time was the Soviet-designed M46 130MM field gun, a long-barreled weapon dating from 1954. It could fire a seventy-

NVA gunners pound an ARVN base near Quang Tri with an M46 130MM field gun in April 1972 during the Easter offensive. Troops on the receiving end of the Soviet-made artillery piece considered it superior to any gun in the U.S. arsenal.

four-pound shell to an effective range of 27,000 meters. The NVA added other types of 1950s-vintage Soviet big guns after the 1973 cease-fire, both truck-drawn like the M46 but smaller and shorter-ranged.

U.S. and South Vietnamese practice was to cluster batteries of six guns in a star pattern and fire them together. Soviet doctrine, taught to the North Vietnamese, was to place guns in larger masses more or less in line. However, in the artillery battles near the DMZ in 1967 and 1968, the need to hide from U.S. aircraft forced the NVA to disperse guns in scattered, deeply entrenched, and carefully camouflaged positions. To concentrate fire, separate firing instructions for each gun were computed and communicated to each weapon, usually by wire telephone, and their firing times closely coordinated.

The weapons were protected by antiaircraft artillery making it extremely difficult to pinpoint the guns or attack them. U.S. forces had some success using counterbattery radars and sound ranging and tracking units, and the air force was able to destroy gun positions with laser-guided bombs once the precise firing position had been pinned down. During the 1972 Easter offensive, NVA antiaircraft defenses were insufficient to prevent U.S. aircraft from attacking at will, and enemy artillery units suffered as badly as armor and infantry did.

North Vietnamese tanks first appeared in the South in February 1968 when three Soviet PT76s participated in the assault on Lang Vei. Comparatively lightweight (13¾ tons) and amphibious, the PT76 could travel twenty-seven miles per hour on land and seven mph in water. The comparable U.S. tank, the Sheridan M551, was heavier and faster on land but more complex to operate and maintain. The main weaknesses of the PT76 were a relatively thin armor shell, a susceptibility to fire when struck by an anti-tank round, and a tendency to sink in rough water.

Heavier and thicker-hulled T54 Soviet-made medium tanks and their Chinese copy, the Type 59, were added in 1972, but armor was never the NVA's strong suit: Tank crews were poorly trained, and their commanders proved incapable of integrating armor attacks with infantry and artillery, rendering the tanks far less effective than they might otherwise have been. Though armed with 100MM cannons, machine guns, and antiaircraft guns, the T54s were comparatively lightly armored and took a beating in clashes with ARVN M48 tanks during the Easter offensive of 1972. American Cobra gunships, exploiting the NVA tanks' vulnerability to air attack (the armor was thinnest on top), were also effective against enemy tanks during the offensive. At An Loc alone, the NVA lost 86 of the approximately 100 tanks deployed there.

Hanoi dispatched more armored vehicles to South Vietnam after the 1973 cease-fire, including Soviet BTR50 and Chinese Type 531 armored personnel carriers. Though armor was never the NVA's main weapon, its tanks proved particularly effective during the final offensive in 1975 when lack of parts and maintenance left South Vietnamese defenders with few aircraft or tanks of their own to oppose the Communist attack.

Air war in the South

Using mines and booby traps, automatic weapons and rockets, long-range artillery and tanks, the Vietcong and the NVA were able to contest with allied forces the war on the ground. When it came to the battle in the air, however, they began at a serious disadvantage. With no more than a handful of aircraft—and those of limited range and destructive capacity—they were forced to wage the war in the sky primarily from the ground. The evolution of the enemy's antiaircraft arsenal, from rifles to guided missiles and jet planes, demonstrated his ability to adapt to the threat of aerial bombardment. But it also demonstrated his dependence on outside sources of modern weaponry, as well as the limits of what he could accomplish when the arena of battle belonged to some of the most sophisticated technologies of war.

The network of antiaircraft batteries and long-range missiles built by North Vietnam was the most elaborate air defense system ever devised. General John P. McConnell, a former chief of staff of the U.S. Air Force, said flatly that it constituted "the greatest concentration of antiaircraft weapons that has ever been known in the history of air defense." By the late stages of the war the system, which included a wide range of guns, massive radar coverage, and two types of surface-to-air missiles (SAMs), covered not only all of North Vietnam but also northern and central Laos, a portion of the Gulf of Tonkin, and the northernmost sections of South Vietnam.

In the beginning, however, enemy antiaircraft measures were rudimentary at best. Vietcong guerrillas depended on clever camouflage and night maneuvers to shield them from the ubiquitous helicopters, along with an early warning system that consisted of deep foxholes and good ears. A Vietcong crouching at the bottom of a foxhole would not hear nearby surface sounds, but he could pick up a helicopter motor before those on the surface heard it. Several foxhole listeners were connected by field telephones so a warning could be passed quickly and defensive positions taken.

The Vietcong did not at first understand how lethal helicopter gunships were. Their initial reaction when they came near was to stand up and spray the Hueys with an orchestrated salvo of small-arms fire. Though this technique netted an occasional chopper, this tactic exposed the guerrillas' position and tended to bring in a barrage of U.S. firepower. As late as 1967, guerrillas in some parts of Vietnam were still innocent of the gunships' capacity for destruction. When the 1st Air Cavalry Division began operations near Duc Pho in the northern province of Quang Ngai that year, the Huey pilots were surprised to see Viet-

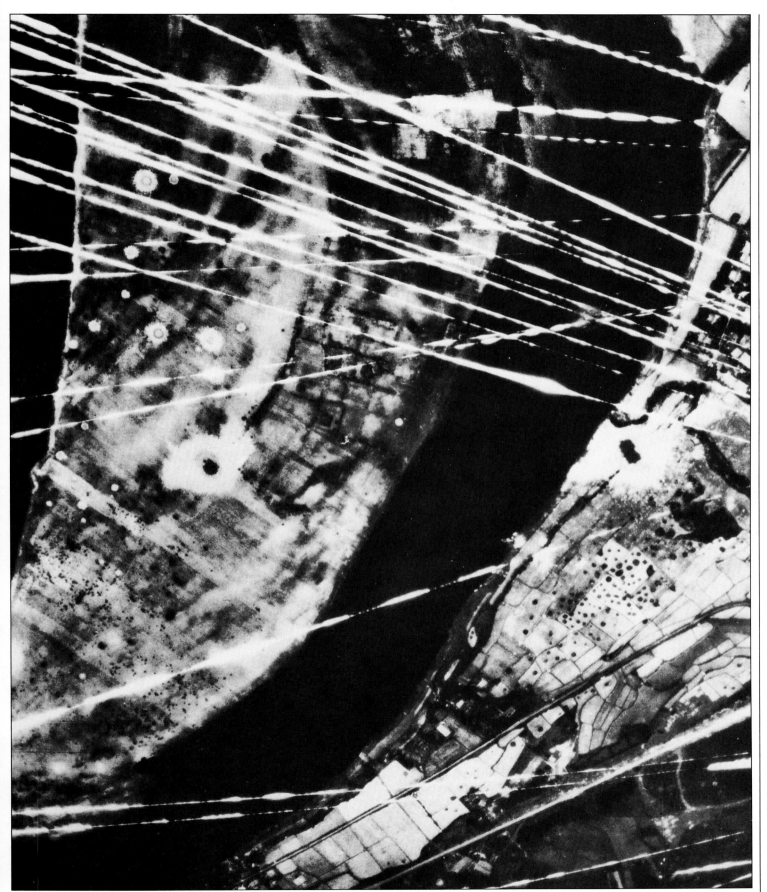

A reconnaissance photo taken by a U.S. RF-4 flying high above antiaircraft fire from an NVA staging area near Dong Hoi shows why many American pilots found the North's antiaircraft artillery more threatening than any previous air defense system.

The North's Antiaircraft Artillery

The KS19 100MM gun, the biggest of the Soviet AAA weapons used by North Vietnam, weighed twelve tons and required a crew of seven. Able to fire fifteen to twenty rounds per minute, its shells could reach as high as 45,000 feet in the air.

All the Soviet-developed antiaircraft guns used by the North Vietnamese were dual-purpose. The 100MM AA gun (below), for example, was also an antitank gun when introduced in 1949; the SU-23-2 (right) fired armor-piercing as well as high-explosive antiaircraft shells. Although these weapons were no longer used by the Soviets in the mid-1960s, their presence in North Vietnam threatened American jets to an unanticipated degree. Many guns, especially the lighter 12.7MM and 23MM, also appeared in South Vietnam and Laos.

The accuracy of the guns was in-creased when they were hooked up with target acquisition radar, although the 100MM (and the 85MM and 57MM, not shown) were rarely used without radar. A larger gun could by itself prove dangerous, but an array of guns of varied calibers and ranges, especially when coupled with surface-to-air missiles, posed a more significant threat. The net effect of the AAA network was to increase the cost of the U.S. bombing effort: in pilots' lives and downed aircraft; in additional aircraft sent aloft to protect the bombers; and in bombs dropped awry of their targets by aircraft evading AA fire.

Above. Operated by a crew of four, the SU–23–2 twin 23MM gun could fire 1,000 rounds per minute from each barrel. The 23MM was usually used with the 37MM gun (not shown); the two guns could hit aircraft at altitudes of up to 10,000 feet.

Right. The DShK M1938 12.7MM dual–purpose heavy machine gun is shown here in its antiaircraft configuration. Firing up to 600 rounds per minute, it could reach aircraft flying as high above it as 3,000 feet.

cong moving in large groups in apparent disdain of the choppers. Every so often they would stand in the open and fire at the whirlybirds. During one two-week period in April the cost of their ignorance was 176 killed and 127 captured, primarily because of the gunships.

When they realized the folly of pinging with rifles at helicopters, the guerrillas switched to light machine guns, but with a range of about 450 meters these were not much of an improvement. The 12.7MM heavy machine gun, the weapon that could be tilted up and transformed into an antiaircraft gun aimed by a gunner on a bicycle seat, was different. When pilots spotted the 12.7's characteristic greenish tracers they showed their respect by climbing swiftly out of range to above 2,500 feet. The gun had a crude wire sight that the gunner used to calculate his firing angle along with data he had memorized about different types of aircraft. Early in the war this was the mightiest antiaircraft weapon encountered in South Vietnam, but when U.S. troops moved into the A Shau Valley after the Tet offensive in 1968 they discovered that the NVA and VC antiaircraft capability had expanded dramatically. The guerrillas were now peppering the copters with 14.5MM, 23MM, and 37MM guns supplied by the Soviet Union, the largest of which had a slant range of 2,460 meters.

The thorniest enemy antiaircraft thickets outside North Vietnam were along the Ho Chi Minh Trail in Laos. U.S. jet pilots and gunship crews who were part of Operation Lam Son 719 in 1970 ran a gauntlet of guns ranging from the dual-purpose 12.7 to a radar-controlled 57MM weapon with a range of 5,900 meters. This five-ton gun had a fire control computer that figured the firing angle from data on the target's speed and course recorded by tracking radar. The defenders clustered smaller-caliber guns together in groups of three or more in circular patterns, usually on high ground not far from likely landing zones. Although the U.S. Army reported its helicopter losses during the Lam Son operation as "tolerable," it was clear that the price, both in terms of risk and complexity, of conducting air-mobile operations had been raised to a new level.

In the ensuing months the weapons fielded by both sides on the Laotian section of the trail escalated in a kind of mad spiral of high-tech destructiveness. From 12.7 and 37MM antiaircraft guns the enemy upped the ante to 57s and then 100MM weapons and surface-to-air missiles on the northern spurs closest to North Vietnam and the mountain passes between the two countries. The constantly rising range of the AA guns drove the planes ever higher, in turn demanding longer-range weapons on the aircraft. By late 1971, according to a *Christian Science Monitor* report, the enemy's antiaircraft defenses on the trail in Laos were double what they had been a year earlier. Another ominous sign was the appearance of the first SAM missiles in Laos that same year.

Though North Vietnam had imported its first SAMs from Russia in 1965, the initial surface-to-air missile seen in the South did not arrive until the Easter offensive of 1972. But the weapon that the NVA introduced in that campaign was a stunning surprise—a hand-fired, transportable, thirty-two-pound, infrared-guided antiaircraft missile. This remarkable fifty-four-inch-long weapon was the SA-7 "Grail," which weighed only twenty-three pounds. With it, as with the U.S. equivalent, the FIM Redeye, an infantryman could shoot down an airplane, and during its first few weeks of operation in April and May 1972, it achieved a 33 percent rate of accuracy.

A soldier fired the Grail from his shoulder by aiming it at a target plane and squeezing the trigger partway. This activated the missile's electronics and infrared seeker. When a red light in the launcher's sight turned green it meant that the weapon's heat-seeking device had locked on to a plane's exhaust, and the gunner pressed the trigger the rest of the way to launch it. A two-stage motor boosted the missile to a velocity of about 750 miles an hour for an effective range of about a kilometer. Helicopters were more vulnerable to the Grail than jets, in part because of its small, five and one-half pound, warhead, but mostly because they were much slower than the jets. The missile trailed a telltale column of smoke behind it that pilots learned to look for and avoid. Because of such liabilities, and because the surprise of its initial use soon wore off, the Grail proved generally ineffective during the 1972 Communist offensive. A later, improved version had a much longer range—nearly five kilometers—and a mechanism better able to ignore decoy flares fired by target aircraft. One of these brought down a U.S. jet at an altitude of 11,000 feet in 1974, and others had a devastating effect during the final NVA offensive in 1975.

Air war in the North

When American bombing raids began, North Vietnam's air defense already possessed the rudiments of its deadly antiaircraft maze. But the arrival of the first SA-2 SAM missiles from the Soviet Union in June 1965 brought Hanoi to near technological parity in its efforts to combat U.S. bombers. Before the SAMs arrived, American pilots learned to fly at high altitudes, above the AAA network's range. But the SAMs were most effective at altitudes of around 20,000 feet and took away the heights from U.S. warplanes. A month after the SAMs were introduced, an American F-4C fighter-bomber became the first victim of the thirty-five-foot-long (ten-meter-long) missile U.S. airmen ruefully called "the flying telephone pole." While the number of SAMs in North Vietnam increased steadily from then on, the arsenal of big antiaircraft guns grew as well. Between 1965 and 1968 the most pervasive antiaircraft weapons were 37MM and 57MM guns, which were highly effective at the lower altitudes and clustered close to the major targets. By 1972, when U.S. planes were dropping "smart" bombs from higher altitudes, 85MM and 100MM

An SA-2 surface-to-air missile sits in a rice field north of Hanoi. By 1972, 300 such sites protected the North.

guns were common. By that time there were also some 300 SAM sites north of the DMZ.

The SA-2's 5,000-pound-bulk included a 286-pound warhead with fuses that could be set to detonate close to a target, on impact or on command. Detonation within 200 feet of an aircraft was normally sufficient to knock out the attacker. On launch a booster rocket accelerated the missile to a speed of Mach 1.5 while the firing crew kept the weapon centered in the radar tracking beam that homed in on its target, which it reached in about twenty-five seconds. The missile's range was considerable—up to thirty horizontal miles and about eleven miles up. North Vietnamese placed the SAMs in batteries of six launchers in a star pattern about fifty meters apart. Despite their tremendous weight—the launch equipment for a battery weighed about 100 tons—they were moved constantly to make it more difficult for U.S. bombers on "protective reaction" missions to find them.

The early warning radar system linked to North Vietnamese guns and missiles was so extensive that surprise was all but impossible. The radar net covered most of Laos and the Gulf of Tonkin as well as North Vietnam between the altitudes of 3,000 and 30,000 feet. Jets approaching from U.S. bases in Thailand were picked up even before they penetrated Laotian airspace. Attacking planes that came in low could avoid both radar and SAMs, which were ineffective below 1,500 feet, but they risked heavy barrages from antiaircraft guns.

For a U.S. airman who spotted a "flying telephone pole" headed his way—the missile could best be recognized by a trail of white smoke in its first stage—the best tactic was to dive toward the SAM and then veer off sharply, a maneuver the missile could not follow. Electronic jamming gear and Wild Weasel planes armed with Shrike missiles that homed in on SAM radar sets were the most potent counters to the SAMs, but there were simply too many radar stations to jam. The enemy responded by switching rapidly from one radar post to another, changing frequencies, waiting until the last possible moment to activate the radar, and by firing missiles in blind barrages—"wall to wall SAMs," in the lingo of American pilots.

Another ace in the defender's hand was the policy that limited U.S. bombing raids to certain targets and placed others off-limits. This allowed the North Vietnamese to concentrate their defenses around predictable targets while other areas could be lightly protected. The policy also forbade attacks on SAM assembly sites for fear that Russian technicians might be killed; only operational SAM batteries could be hit. SAMs remained the most daunting monster in the enemy antiaircraft lineup until the war ended. It was neither the SAMs nor the antiaircraft guns, however, that made flights over North Vietnam perilous, but the combination of the two. For many U.S. military theorists, who had relegated AA guns to the scrap heap of military technology, the mix of gun batteries guarding low-level approaches and SAMs able to reach high-flying aircraft posed entirely unanticipated problems.

Not so North Vietnam's small air force. When the U.S. involvement in Vietnam began, Hanoi's most formidable airborne weapons were their six Ilyushin light bombers. Though surface-to-air missiles were installed around critical U.S. bases to protect against them, the Ilyushins were never used, and they were shuttled to China when their main base at Phuc Yen was raided in 1967.

Soviet-made MiG fighters ranging from Korean War-era MiG-15s and MiG-17s to fast, state-of-the-art MiG-21s carried the aerial load, their numbers rising steadily as the war persisted: The North's 66 MiG fighters in 1966 increased to 206 by 1972, 93 of them MiG-21s. Since all the MiGs were designed as defensive, interceptor craft they were smaller than their U.S. counterparts and had a shorter range. But the MiG-21, dubbed the "Fishbed" by NATO, the best of the North Vietnamese planes, was a for-

midable weapon. Initially armed with 23mm and 37mm guns, each MiG-21 was eventually equipped with four Atoll heat-seeking air-to-air missiles. Compared with F-4s, their most frequent head-to-head foes, MiG-21s were slightly slower but easier to maneuver at low speeds and high altitudes. Their chief defects were relatively ill-trained pilots and a rigid ground control that limited their ability to take the initiative so crucial in a dogfight.

At first North Vietnamese fighters attacked in squadrons of up to sixteen, but as their ground control radar improved they flew in fours, then pairs. Teams of MiG-21 interceptors were guided by radar to positions behind U.S. planes where they launched their heat-seeking missiles, which locked onto the target plane's exhaust. Slower MiG-17s sometimes harassed the main body of the invading squadron at the same time. The objective was not only to shoot down the intruding craft but also to force them to jettison their bombs short of their targets and to separate the bombers from their electronically equipped escorts, thus making them vulnerable to SAMs. MiG-21s often made quick feints at the strike force to try to get the fighter-bombers to shuck their bombs. The older M-17s, possibly piloted by North Koreans, patrolled approach routes and tried to lure U.S. fighters into low-altitude dogfights where their fuel would quickly be exhausted.

Despite the intricate, well-coordinated, and potent air-defense system fashioned by the North Vietnamese, and despite the fact that there was never a concerted effort to knock it out (which allowed the system constantly to adapt to American countermeasures), the U.S. dominated the air war in Vietnam. The defenders, in the end, were unable to prevent American planes from hitting the targets they went after. Average U.S. losses in the best-defended areas seldom ran higher than four and a half planes per thousand sorties, a much lower rate than Allied aircraft suffered over Germany's Ruhr Valley in World War II.

North Vietnamese pilots receive training from Soviet instructors on MiG-21 supersonic interceptors, also provided by the Soviets, in 1966.

Under the onslaught of American air power North Vietnam suffered severe damage to its industrial plant and transportation network. But the U.S. also paid a high price for its success—in a tremendous tonnage of bombs dropped short of their targets, in planes lost, and in pilots killed or captured. Antiaircraft seldom "defeats" the enemy. It is successful to the degree to which it elevates the risks of continuing the attack or raises to unacceptable levels the attrition of irreplaceable equipment. If the North could not "win" the war in the air, neither were the Americans able to halt the infiltration of men and supplies to the South or force the enemy to submit. In the end, this proved victory enough for the Communists.

Much the same conclusion can be drawn about the enemy arsenal in general. Neither Hanoi nor the southern insurgents could have fought an American-style war even had they wanted to. In part this was because their sponsors—principally the Soviet Union—were not prepared to give them the wherewithal to do so.

Although it was "the only war in town," the Soviets did not use it as a proving ground for their latest technology. Moscow provided the North Vietnamese with weapons of sufficiency, not superiority. This "appropriate technology only" approach was cheaper for Hanoi's patrons, but it was also more suited to North Vietnam's military requirements and expertise. As a result, the technology the enemy used was probably more effectively tailored to his needs than that employed on the allied side. In most respects equipment and systems were kept fairly simple and uniform, while the failure of the NVA to integrate successfully armor, infantry, and artillery during the 1972 offensive suggested that more sophisticated systems may actually have hindered rather than helped.

Nowhere was this strategy of technological sufficiency put to work by the enemy with better results than along the dirt tracks, narrow waterways, and, eventually, paved roads that made up the Ho Chi Minh Trail. In a very real sense, the Vietnam War was a war of logistics. For North Vietnam to realize its goals it had to support operations in the South for as long as necessary. For the allies to defeat the Communists the flow of supplies had to be cut off. The outcome of that contest would be determined in large measure by the degree to which the "primitive" technology of the enemy's logistical life line could withstand some of the most sophisticated instruments of destruction and detection the world had ever seen, the high-tech U.S. aircraft used to bomb the Communists and the Igloo White sensor network strung along the trail in Laos.

A pontoon bridge swings into position across the Red River in North Vietnam in 1968. Pontoon bridges could not handle as much traffic as a fixed bridge, but they were easy to hide and repair. Some were made to float, hidden, a foot below the water.

Flying Workhorses

The United States launched into the skies over Southeast Asia nearly every jet in its arsenal. What characterized the U.S. aerial armada were its technological sophistication and its versatility. Some of the aircraft that flew against the Vietcong and North Vietnamese were used in ways never foreseen by their original designers. Other aircraft, orginally designed with flexibility in mind, improvised new roles once they joined the fray.

Of all the U.S. aircraft in Southeast Asia, by far the most versatile was the twin-seated F-4 Phantom II. The supersonic jet was originally intended for use as a fighter, but performed almost any kind of mission imaginable. One model of the Phantom flew photo reconnaissance, another was used to counter North Vietnamese radar, and others were fitted to fly a variety of bombing missions. So flexible was the F-4 that it became the first U.S. Navy jet to be accepted for use by the air force, despite the strong rivalry between the two service branches.

The U.S.A.F. F-4D shown here is equipped to perform one of the most technologically advanced jobs an aircraft could do in Vietnam: dropping a laser-guided bomb. LGBs hit their targets with pinpoint accuracy by following the reflection of a radar beam "shot" at the target from either the aircraft carrying the bomb or another aircraft equipped with a laser "designator" pod.

An F-4D equipped for a laser-guided bomb mission flies over North Vietnam. Underneath its right wing, the F-4 carries two Paveway 1 500-pound laser-guided bombs; under the left wing is another LGB and a Pave Knife "designator" which shoots a laser beam at the target. The aircraft also carries three air-to-air missiles, a pod filled with electronic equipment used to jam enemy radar, and a large centerline fuel tank.

U. S. Navy MIGCAP F-4B

The F-4's most accustomed role was as a fighter. When American bomber pilots flying over the North first encountered the Communists' MiG interceptors in 1965, air commanders realized that to protect their bomber squadrons they would have to launch fighter escorts with every mission. The Phantoms were the most popular choice for the assignment, which was called MIGCAP for MiG Combat Air Patrol. F-4s also flew most of the missions over the North intended strictly to lure MiGs into battle. During Operation Bolo on January 2, 1967, the largest anti-MiG mission to that date, fifty-six air force Phantoms flew out of U.S. bases in Thailand to down seven North Vietnamese aircraft. Of the 137 MiGs knocked out of the sky by U.S. Air Force pilots during the war, 107 were "killed" by Phantoms and their two-man crews. Navy pilots were credited with fifty-seven MiG kills, F-4 crews accounting for thirty-six of them. The only "aces" (pilots with five MiG kills) of the war flew the F-4.

The pilot of a U.S. Navy F-4B lights his afterburners and rolls inverted to chase a North Vietnamese MiG. The Phantom is equipped for its fighter mission with four AIM-9 missiles (two under each wing) with infrared guidance systems that home in on an enemy aircraft's exhaust from up to two miles away. For longer-range firing (up to ten miles), the F-4 carries four AIM-7 Sparrow radar-guided missiles under its fuselage (one of the Sparrows is hidden by the centerline fuel tank). The three fuel tanks may be jettisoned to give the aircraft more speed and maneuverability.

A-7 Mining Mission

Another of the versatile U.S. aircraft to fly in Vietnam was the A-7 Corsair II. Originally built for naval carrier operations, the A-7, like the F-4, was eventually adopted by the air force as well. Its designers had intended the subsonic Corsair to provide close air support of troops in contact with the enemy, but by the end of the war it had flown a variety of other missions. Capable in theory of carrying up to 20,000 pounds of bombs or other armaments, the A-7 hit targets in North Vietnam, attacked truck convoys traveling down the Ho Chi Minh Trail in Laos, carried mines (as shown here) for the mining of Haiphong Harbor in May 1972, and even flew in support of operations to rescue U.S. pilots knocked down over North Vietnam.

Corsairs proved highly durable, accurate bombers, in large part because of the sophisticated navigational equipment most of them carried. The all-weather navigational and bomb delivery equipment allowed an A-7 pilot to take constant evasive action throughout his bomb run while computers kept the plane headed toward the target and automatically released the bombs once it arrived there.

The Corsair's navigational equipment made it a perfect choice for flying the dangerous Operation Pocket Money, the mining of Haiphong Harbor. Because of heavy antiaircraft defenses—especially MiG-21s—around the harbor, mission planners had anticipated that 30 percent of the aircraft flying the mission would not return. Thanks to support from naval destroyers armed with surface-to-air Talos missiles, however, all six A-7s and the three A-6 Intruders that accompanied them completed their mission and returned unscathed.

In this artist's rendition, a U.S. Navy A-7 Corsair II laden with Mk-52 mines heads for Haiphong Harbor on May 8, 1972. Electronic equipment in the 2,000-pound mines allows their activation to be delayed, in this case by three days, to allow ships already in the harbor to leave.

When American pilots first entered the war in a combat role, a large part of their inventory of weapons had not been designed for the kind of war they were to fight in the skies over Southeast Asia. The Defense Department had placed high hopes on the air campaign over North Vietnam that began in March 1965, Operation Rolling Thunder, which was expected to dissuade Ho Chi Minh from continuing aggression in the South. But civilians in the department, largely in response to President Lyndon Johnson's concern that all-out bombing would bring North Vietnam's allies the Soviet Union and China into the war, placed severe limitations on the bombing. Final authority for targets rested in the Defense Department, under the close scrutiny of President Johnson. Early on, civilians also dictated tactics designed to minimize civilian casualties. Further, American pilots returned from the first Rolling Thunder missions in spring 1965 with reports of the North's highly sophisticated antiaircraft net-

work, which was to become one of the tightest in history. And, in 1967, when Defense Department reports began to reveal that the bombing was having little effect, American commanders realized that Hanoi might well be able to withstand the "graduated pressure" of Operation Rolling Thunder.

Much of the American equipment used in the air war over North Vietnam developed out of that precarious strategic situation. The need for great bombing accuracy to avoid civilian casualties, the challenge of the air defense net, the need for increased destructive capabilities (short of nuclear warheads) all resulted in technological advances to the American aerial arsenal used in Vietnam and later.

The "Thud"

Before they brought to bear new weapons in the skies over North Vietnam, however, Americans faced the challenge of adapting for Vietnam the equipment already available to them. A prime example of an old weapon in need of an overhaul for effective use in Vietnam was the B-52 (see illustration, page 128). Another was the staple of the U.S. Air Force's stock of aircraft: the Republic F-105 Thunderchief or "Thud" as it was dubbed by its pilots.

First operational in 1958, the single-seat F-105 was designed as a tactical bomber that from bases in Europe could carry nuclear bombs deep into the Soviet Union while flying too low to be detected by radar and fast enough (more than twice the speed of sound) to prove difficult targets for enemy interceptors. It was a big aircraft, heavier than many medium bombers of World War II, and on a hot day with a full load it could require a mile and a half of runway to boost its more than twenty-five tons into the air. Along with the disadvantages of its size and weight the Thud initially had little armor, which increased its range but made it vulnerable to antiaircraft fire, and a dizzying collection of dials and switches in the cockpit. All in all it appeared an unlikely candidate for a conventional war, but it was what the air force had and until a replacement was found it would have to carry the burden of air combat.

With new fuel tanks, armor for the crew and vital aircraft parts, and pylons to hold six tons of bombs under the fuselage and wings, it became a formidable fighter-bomber and gained a reputation for reliability. Its ability to absorb battle damage and still survive became legendary and it was so agile that F-105 pilots shot down twenty-nine Communist aircraft during the war over North Vietnam. The workhorse of Rolling Thunder operations, it flew 75 percent of the missions in the North. But

Preceding page. While steam issues from the deck catapult, an A-6 Intruder with its wings folded is guided into launch position on the U.S.S. Coral Sea off Vietnam in 1972.

the F-105 did not prove up to the task of hunting down trucks along the Ho Chi Minh Trail in Laos, the focus of the bombing after President Johnson halted Rolling Thunder in November 1968. As a result, the air force pulled it from bomber service in Vietnam by 1970 and replaced it with F-4s, A-7s, and, eventually, F-111s.

In addition to its conventional job as a bomber, the F-105 also played a highly renowned role in direct response to the DRV's most sophisticated attempt to counter the American air offensive—the Russian-made SA-2 surface-to-air antiaircraft missile. All the aircraft in the U.S. arsenal would do no good if they were shot down or had to jettison their bomb loads randomly in order to evade the radar-guided SAMs that flew even faster than the jet fighters. Searching out the missile sites with photo-reconnaissance flights and later returning to bomb them seldom worked as a tactic, since the mobile equipment was camouflaged and moved regularly.

The air force's answer to this problem was the Wild Weasel, which remained active in the war until 1975. Fifty two-seat F-105G trainers were rebuilt and packed with the latest electronic countermeasures (ECM) gear—radar detection and jamming equipment—and armed with missiles designed to follow a radar signal back to its source. The second seat of the F-105 Wild Weasel became the realm of the electronics warfare officer, the "Bear," one of the few back-seat aviators to share a genuine slice of the prestige and status enjoyed by fighter pilots. While his pilot cruised enemy territory, the Bear would search with his special equipment for emissions from any of the enemy's Fan Song and other radars which were used to spot targets for the SAMs. Once a SAM site switched on its radar the Wild Weasel locked onto the signal and the Bear passed the location to the pilot. The crew could then choose from a variety of options. They could render ineffective the radar beam tracking them by jamming it or attempt to destroy the SAM site by firing an antiradiation Shrike or Standard ARM missile that would follow the radar beam back to its source. Or, if the Communist gunners fired the missile, the Wild Weasel crew could jam the radar beam guiding the SAM and throw it off its target. Before attacking the SAM sites, Wild Weasels could jam or attack the Communists' long-range search radars, which generally picked them up long before they reached a SAM site.

Wild Weasel crews always sought to destroy the SAM sites that had proved dangerous from the day they were first made operational in July 1965. But the specially equipped F-105s, which usually worked in pairs, accompanied U.S. bombers primarily to prevent them from being challenged by the surface-to-air missiles. Often, the mere presence of a Wild Weasel with its antiradiation missiles was enough to prevent enemy SAM operators from turning on their radar. The SAMs could be fired without radar guidance, but this vastly diminished their threat to Ameri-

can aircraft. If a Wild Weasel was able to find, fix, and fire on a SAM site, it was usually followed by a flight of F-105s with full loads of bombs. Their mission was to destroy the missiles and their crews after the radar was disabled.

The SAM sites were far from defenseless, however. Antiaircraft guns surrounding the SAM emplacements themselves took a heavy toll of Wild Weasel aircraft and airmen, particularly in the early days of the war when crews were thrown into combat with little training and with experimental equipment. Nonetheless, the Wild Weasel helped lessen the threat to U.S. aircraft flying over the North and its tactics and equipment continued to improve. Two decades later Wild Weasel squadrons and their equivalents played active roles in the world's major air forces, although the dangerous job of baiting enemy missile defenses to make them reveal themselves had been taken over to some extent by remotely controlled, pilotless aircraft.

"Warning Star"

Enemy missiles and antiaircraft guns were not the only worries for the pilots of the bomb-laden warplanes carrying the fight to North Vietnam. While aviators concentrated on their targets, flights of radar-vectored MiGs would swoop from high altitudes or out of the clouds and

An E-2A Hawkeye prepares to take off from the U.S.S. Midway, stationed in the South China Sea in summer 1965. A carrier-based version of the EC-121, the Hawkeye tracked enemy aircraft with its huge radar dome, which was later replaced by a streamlined dome that provided more lift.

rake the American aircraft with cannon fire and air-to-air Atoll missiles. To block this threat, the U.S. Air Force called on another old warrior, the venerable EC-121 "Warning Star," a version of the commercial Lockheed Super Constellation transport airliner modified to conduct electronic warfare. First operational in 1954, the aircraft flew on four-piston engines that could keep 40,000 pounds of equipment airborne for twenty hours. The EC-121, with a range of 4,600 miles, carried a vast amount of electronic equipment with which technicians on board tracked other aircraft. Originally built to form a link in the chain of early warning posts in North America protecting the U.S. from surprise Russian attack through Arctic airspace, the aging aircraft was being phased out of front-line service when the war in Vietnam intensified.

Both above and below its fuselage the EC-121 carried large domes that housed the most powerful airborne search radar of the time and additional radar designed to gauge the speed and directional bearing of targets. To this basic load was added more equipment including

U.S.S. Enterprise

The "Big E," the largest warship built until the mid-1970s and the first nuclear powered aircraft carrier, performed several tours of duty off the coast of Vietnam during the war. Carrying 5,000 men and ninety aircraft, the *Enterprise* could cruise for four years without refueling, in theory. Below its flight deck, life's amenities coexisted with the necessities of war in hundreds of passageways and compartments, some of them shown in this artist's cutaway view. The general dining room (see number 19 in sketch at right), for example, doubled as a bomb assembly area before a mission. Aside from sailing the ship, the crew's only function was to fuel, arm, launch, and recover the aircraft on board.

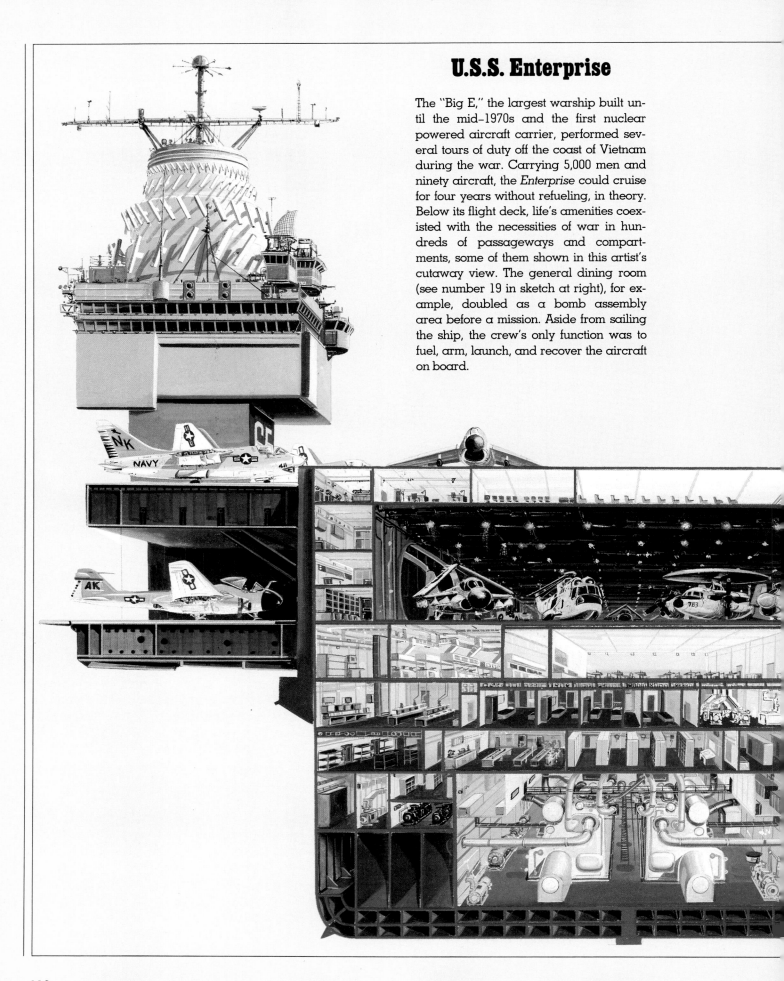

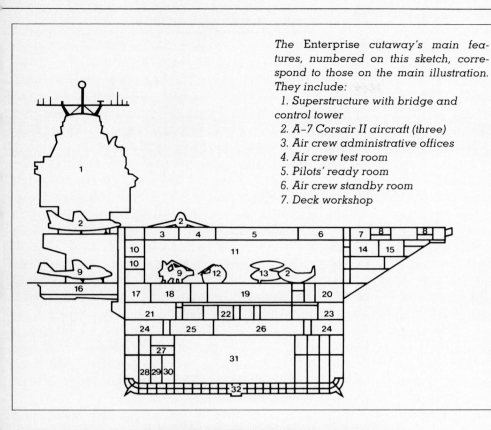

The Enterprise cutaway's main features, numbered on this sketch, correspond to those on the main illustration. They include:

1. Superstructure with bridge and control tower
2. A-7 Corsair II aircraft (three)
3. Air crew administrative offices
4. Air crew test room
5. Pilots' ready room
6. Air crew standby room
7. Deck workshop
8. Angled deck catapult cylinders for launching aircraft
9. A-6 Intruder aircraft (two)
10. Administrative offices
11. Hangar deck
12. SH-3 Sea King helicopter
13. E-2C Hawkeye aircraft
14. and 15. Administrative offices
16. Aircraft elevator
17. PX
18. Galley
19. General dining room
20. Electronic test bay computers
21. Galley stores
22. Officers quarters
23. Air conditioning plant
24. Crew quarters
25. Missile assembly room
26. Computers
27. Generators for ship's electricity
28. Domestic water (length of ship)
29. Aviation fuel (length of ship)
30. Water (length of ship)
31. Condensing plant for nuclear generators
32. Cellular double-bottom hull.

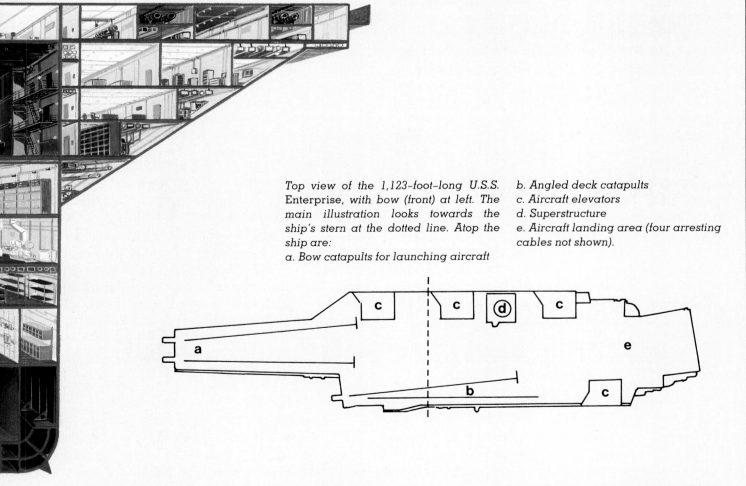

Top view of the 1,123-foot-long U.S.S. Enterprise, with bow (front) at left. The main illustration looks towards the ship's stern at the dotted line. Atop the ship are:

a. Bow catapults for launching aircraft

b. Angled deck catapults
c. Aircraft elevators
d. Superstructure
e. Aircraft landing area (four arresting cables not shown).

computers to monitor, sort out, and relay information about enemy activities to U.S. strike force commanders. The new EC-121 became an airborne battlefield command and control center (ABCCC).

ABCCC was the air force version of the U.S. Navy's radar ships that monitored navy bombing flights over North Vietnam. The radar allowed observers on the ships to warn pilots of approaching enemy flights that could be intercepted by escorting fighter aircraft. But the floating radar site could not range its beams beyond coastal North Vietnam, so air force aircraft flying out of Thailand further inland and in Laos needed their own radar coverage. Starting in mid-1965, the EC-121 provided this coverage by flying orbits along the Laotian border and the Gulf of Tonkin. All the information picked up by the aircraft's equipment was relayed to "Motel," the ground station in Da Nang that collated information from all the orbiting EC-121s and other sources and relayed it back to the orbiting command centers. The Warning Star aircraft then passed on news of enemy air activities to pilots entering unfriendly airspace. In 1972 during the Operation Linebacker bombing of North Vietnam, the navy and air force integrated their warning systems, sending all reports from ground, airborne, and shipboard sources to a controlling facility in Nakhon Phanom, Thailand, where the newly-formed "Teaball" station in turn relayed information back to the ABCCCs.

The airborne command system could pass on to the American pilots not only the location of an enemy aircraft, but also what kind of a MiG it was. Through intercepts of North Vietnamese aviation radio traffic, airborne controllers could also pass on to pilots the identity of airborne enemy pilots. And by tracking a Communist aircraft from the moment its wheels left the runway, the airborne command system could also tell if the plane was low on fuel based on its speed and time aloft. If an American pilot heard the words "black bandit," he knew the MiG chasing him was low on fuel.

While the EC-121 performed its ABCCC functions throughout the war, by 1975 another aircraft had been adapted for similar use. The air force equipped modified EC-130 transports with a modular airborne command center that could provide command and control for immediate battlefield areas, relaying target information, monitoring air strikes, processing ground requests for air strikes, and directing any required military response. EC-130s were used to coordinate airlifts during the evacuation of Saigon in May 1975. In the 1980s, with powerful and reliable turbo-prop engines, the EC-130 carried on the ABCCC role envisioned and developed during the Vietnam War. Yet another advanced descendant of the EC-121 is the E-3A airborne warning and control system (AWACS) aircraft, used by the American military in the 1980s to provide advance warning of enemy attack and to coordinate the U.S. aerial arsenal.

New tasks, new aircraft

While the U.S. Air Force and the navy's air wing were meeting the demands of war with these and other older aircraft modified for new roles, they were also hurriedly developing new aircraft to answer new challenges posed by the Vietnam conflict. One of the most advanced, and controversial, new aircraft was the General Dynamics F-111 tactical dual purpose fighter-bomber.

General Dynamics intended the F-111 to be the first aircraft designed to meet the needs of both the navy and the air force. It was also the first aircraft produced in sizable quantities to use variable sweep wings. Pivoting on two huge bolts and controlled by hydraulically powered screws, the wings could be changed from a nearly perpendicular 72.5 degrees to a radically swept back 16 degrees. This special feature allowed the heavy aircraft and its more than sixteen tons of bombs to take off from aircraft carrier decks or short (3,100-foot) ground runways and yet fly at a maximum speed of 1,650 miles per hour, two and a half times the speed of sound, at altitudes of 36,000 feet. The wings' perpendicular configuration provided maximum lift at low speeds while the backswept "delta" shape permitted efficient supersonic flight.

Originally meant to save the money that would have been spent to design two different aircraft for both forces, the F-111 was cursed with heavy cost overruns and construction defects during its development. The 582 aircraft finally ordered from General Dynamics cost $3.5 billion more than the price originally planned for the entire production run of 2,400 F-111s. In 1968 the navy cancelled its order after receiving seven prototypes; they arrived eight tons overweight, which prevented their use off of carrier decks. The navy opted to produce a fighter, the F-4 Phantom, and a bomber, the A-6 Intruder, rather than use the hybrid F-111 that did neither job as well as originally hoped.

The air force put its first eight F-111As into combat in Vietnam in March 1968. Within two weeks three of them crashed. Investigation of these, and further crashes also apparently not the result of enemy fire, uncovered a structural failure in the boxes that held the wing pivots in place. After this defect was corrected at a cost of $80 million, however, the plane originally conceived as a multiservice fighter proved itself as an excellent all-weather bomber. When the F-111's specialized electronics equipment worked correctly, the forty-four 750-pound bombs it carried could be delivered with pinpoint accuracy in any weather and at an altitude low enough to avoid detection by enemy radar.

What enabled the F-111 to fly low and fast in all weather was its terrain-following radar (TFR). This terrain radar mapped the ground ahead and detected any obstructions. When a hazard appeared the radar instantly flashed a course correction necessary to avoid it at the

plane's top speed at ground-hugging altitudes, 915 miles per hour. The TFR allowed the F-111 to settle into the job it was uniquely qualified to do—flying alone at high speed to its target at an elevation of only a few hundred feet through weather that stopped almost every other plane.

The F-111's navigation system had first gone to war in July 1965 aboard the navy's A-6A Intruder tactical bomber, built by Grumman as a state-of-the-art aerial weapon with technology that was in many cases superior to the F-111's. When the navy scrapped the idea of buying the F-111, planners concentrated on installing the most sophisticated equipment possible in the new A-6 attack aircraft. Although the carrier-based Intruder lacked the variable sweep wings and the supersonic speed of the F-111, it too had radar equipment powerful and advanced enough to make it a plane for all conditions. The Intruder's electronic equalizer was its Digital Integrated Attack Navigational Equipment.

The DIANE system's visual display screen, a radar console in the Intruder's cockpit, provided the two crewmen with a picture of the terrain in front of them regardless of weather (see illustration, next page). When the coordinates for a bombing target were fed into the plane's computer the time and distance to the target flashed on the screen. An onboard computer then calculated the course to the target and showed it on the DIANE screen as a three-dimensional line on the picture of the terrain. At the end of the line the bombs were released automatically by the computer at the correct time to hit the target.

The Intruder carried great destructive power; it could fit

The F-111, shown here with its wings extended for maximum maneuverability and lift, was the first mass-produced American aircraft with adjustable wings.

18,000 pounds of bombs beneath its wings. When two Intruders from the U.S.S. *Kitty Hawk* demolished a power plant near Haiphong in the spring of 1966 the North Vietnamese charged that the U.S. had unleashed B-52s against their cities. Later that year a squadron of A-6s scored ten direct hits on the Hai Duong Bridge west of Haiphong. The A-6 exemplified a concept central to U.S. hopes of fighting a limited war against the Communists: it could deliver great destruction against intended targets, yet do it so precisely that the danger to noncombatants nearby was lessened. Ten years after the war, the Intruder was the only Vietnam-era attack aircraft still prominent in the U.S. aerial arsenal.

Guided missiles

For the flights of fighters providing protection for the bomber squadrons over North Vietnam, the missile was a prime weapon against both enemy aircraft and land-based defenses. The air war over North Vietnam thus became a testing time for several types of air-to-air and air-to-ground missiles developed in the 1950s and 1960s. Carried by fighters, fighter-bombers, and sometimes gunships, the missiles were generally guided by either radar or infrared homing mechanisms. The record achieved by air-to-air missiles in Vietnam, the scene of their first ex-

A-6 Intruder Cockpit

The first attack aircraft designed to rely on 1960s' state-of-the-art technology entered service in Vietnam in June 1965. It was the A-6 Intruder, equipped to fly in any weather, day or night, and at low altitude with over seven tons of bombs. Its targets were spotted by radar, its bombs released by a ballistic computer. Manned by a pilot (on the left) and a bombardier/navigator (B/N), its instrument panel was understandably complex. The panel's main instruments, numbered below and shown at right, are:

1. Vertical display indicator—the pilot's primary instrument, shows what he would see if visibility were not restricted by weather or darkness.

2. Pilot's radar scope—primarily for navigating and terrain avoidance.

3. Pilot's control stick—with buttons to release ordnance.

4. Throttles.

5. Rudder pedals.

6. Bomb/gun sight.

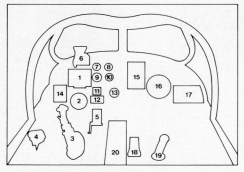

7. Air speed indicator.

8. Back-up attitude gyro.

9. Altimeter.

10. Radio navigation instruments—a back up for main navigation system.

11. Fuel gauge.

12. Master warning light panel.

13. APR-25—indicates presence of enemy radar, giving both source and type.

14. Engine instruments.

15. Armament panel.

16. B/N radar scope—primarily for target acquisition and navigation.

17. Digital display panel—displays target and flight data.

18. B/N foot controls—operate the aircraft's radios.

19. B/N slew control—directs A-6's radar.

20. Radio and environmental controls.

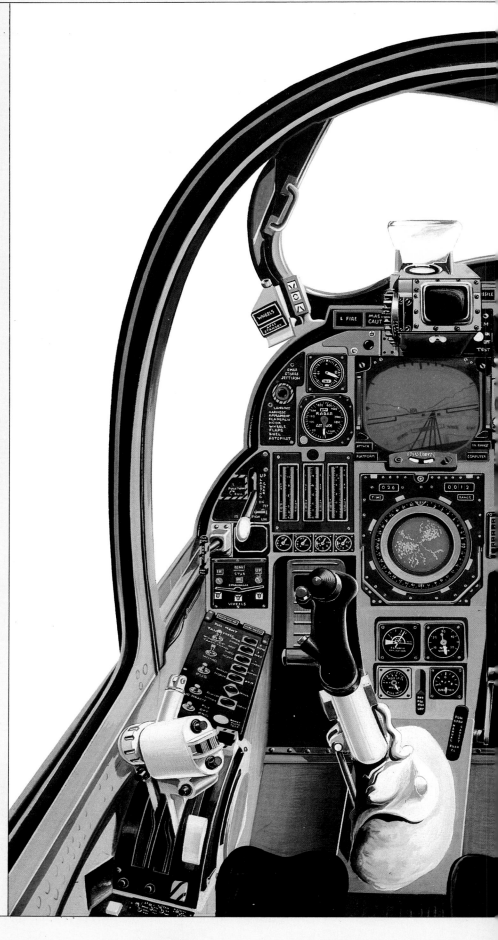

123

tended tour of combat duty, was unimpressive at first glance. Their overall "kill rate," the number of firings that resulted in successful hits, was more than ten to one. But a closer examination of the weapons and their use suggests that the low percentage of hits was caused by a combination of factors.

Radar- and infrared-guided missiles had been designed in the 1950s to be carried by fighters for only one quick intercept mission. In Vietnam, though, the F-4 Phantoms that usually carried them had to fly long distances and often landed with unfired missiles. The constant vibration from several long missions often disabled the missiles before they could be fired. Americans learned, once again, that high-technology equipment can only be used successfully in the environment for which it was designed. The demands of Vietnam were greater than had been anticipated.

Another problem was that U.S. rules of engagement required U.S. pilots to identify positively an enemy aircraft before it could engage that plane. The appearance of an unidentified blip on a radar screen was not enough; a pilot had to fly close enough to an aircraft to see it. A visual fix was only possible within five miles of the enemy plane, but the U.S. radar-guided missiles were designed, for the most part, to be fired at longer ranges of at least ten miles. They could be released closer to the target, but that left less time for the missile's radar guidance system to be set and the missile fired. Also, the missiles' guidance systems locked on to a target only after the missiles had flown several miles. When aircraft maneuvered close to each other, their angles relative to one another changed very quickly and a pilot might be in and out of the missile's "launch envelope" before he could fire the missile accurately. Thus the Americans' self-imposed rules often mitigated against effective use of the more advanced missiles.

All in all, though, the missiles performed well against North Vietnam's Soviet-made MiG interceptors, which were guided by one of the most advanced ground radar systems in existence at the time. Although the MiGs were often more maneuverable than their American counterparts, the presence of the missiles could make enemy pilots wary. If a North Vietnamese pilot saw the plume of a missile's exhaust, he could not be sure whether its guidance system had locked onto him, so he might break off the attack just in case.

The simplest and most common of the U.S. air-to-air missiles used in Vietnam was the AIM-9 Sidewinder, a 150-pound, nine-foot-long weapon whose infrared detector guided it to an enemy plane by homing in on the heat given off by the plane's engine. Intended as a short-range weapon, the original Sidewinder was effective only when fired when the fighter carrying it was directly behind an enemy aircraft. The restrictive U.S. rules of engagement thus tended not to affect the Sidewinder's performance. If fired from a long distance, the Sidewinder's grip on its target could be broken by rain, smoke, and bright sunlight. An advanced version increased the Sidewinder's original two-mile range to eleven miles, and possessed a faster turning rate and a more sensitive infrared detector that could fix onto a jet tailpipe from the side as well as from the rear, but rules of engagement made it more difficult to use. The missile, which could travel at more than twice the speed of sound, was relatively simple, demanding only a modest electronic support system. The navy made heaviest use of Sidewinders, although almost any fighter could carry them. In Vietnam navy aircraft using the AIM-9H attained an 85 percent kill-per-engagement ratio.

The radar-guided AIM-7 Sparrow missile was at 600 pounds four times the size of the Sidewinder and considerably more lethal—its 66-pound warhead exploded into 2,600 separate chunks of steel. Before firing the Sparrow, a pilot "shot" a radar beam at the enemy aircraft. Once the beam "hit" the target plane, the pilot fired the missile, which fastened on to the reflected beam and rode it to the target. Half the weapon's twelve-foot-length was filled with electronic and control devices including several antennas attached to the missile flush on their sides. The antennas picked up the reflected radar beam and held the missile on course while a computer gauged the proper lead on the aircraft being stalked. Unlike the Sidewinder, the Sparrow could attack from any angle as long as its radar locked onto the target. Later models carried solid-state electronics equipment that fit into a smaller space, allowing the missile's power source to be enlarged and increasing its range to twenty miles. F-4 fighters carrying Sparrows killed fifty MiGs with them.

If the Sparrow and the Sidewinder carried the burden of the air-to-air war, the most important antiradiation air-to-ground missiles used by the U.S. forces in Vietnam were the AGM-45 Shrike and AGM-78 Standard ARM. Radar-directed like the Sparrow, the Shrike was carried by navy and air force jets, including the Wild Weasels. Its purpose was to knock out the ground radar stations that controlled the deadly SAMs and radar-guided anti-aircraft guns. The Shrike, with a top speed of twice the speed of sound, picked up the beam of a transmitting enemy radar installation within the missile's twenty-mile range and simply followed it to its source. Antennas on the missile detected changes in the strength of a radar signal and maneuvered the projectile and its sixty-pound warhead toward the point where the signal was strongest.

In 1968, after the North Vietnamese had learned to avoid exposing SAM sites to radar detectors carried by U.S. aircraft by flicking their radars on for only a short time, the AGM-7B Standard ARM was fielded. Aircraft carrying the new missile were equipped with a new tracking device called a Target Identification and Acquisition System. The TIAS could not only identify the enemy radar signal but could also compute a trajectory for the missile in the event the target radar was turned off. The Shrike and the Standard ARM achieved success both by knocking out SAM sites and radar-guided AA guns and by keeping enemy gunners guessing. The military judged its use of antiradiation missiles in Vietnam successful, and development of the weaponry continued after the war.

"Dumb" bombs

Once the bombers and their escorts forced their way through the North's aerial obstacle course, which included bad weather, enemy fighters, missiles, and antiaircraft guns, they could deliver an awesome array of bombs and missiles. Like the aircraft, the bombs were often old ones adapted to new uses. Others were new, produced after a specific need was sent from the field back to the weapons developers.

One major development in the American aerial arsenal during Vietnam was the advancement of the cluster bomb

Ordnance men of the 33d Maintenance Squadron enclose cluster bomb submunition, or bomblets, in an SUU-41 "clamshell" casing. Inset. Three CBUs are mounted on the wing of an F-4 Phantom. The red protective covers will be removed before flight.

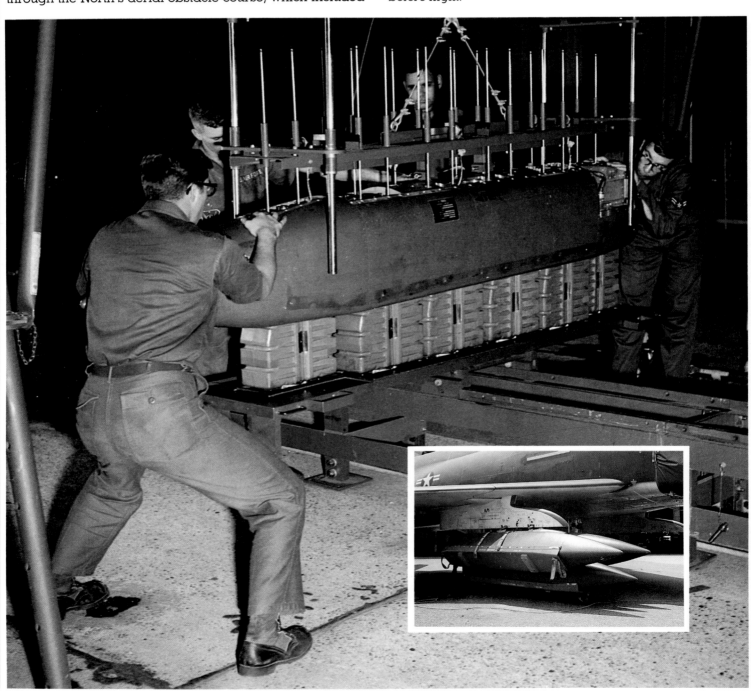

unit. The idea for the CBU originated with the "Molotov breadbasket" first employed in 1937 in the Spanish Civil War. The breadbasket was simply a container filled with small bombs; after being dropped from a plane, the container opened up, dispersing the submunitions over a wide area. Cluster bombs were intended to broaden the radius of a bomb's destruction. A standard bomb was intensely lethal in a small area, while a CBU of the same size spread its explosive power over a wider area. For use in Vietnam, several types of CBUs were developed: cluster bombs for use against personnel were the most common, followed by antitank and antimaterial bombs, containers filled with mines, and fuel air explosives. Like conventional bombs, all were dropped by aircraft.

Antipersonnel CBUs came in several varieties. One, the CBU-24, contained 600 golf-ball sized bomblets, each of which dispersed 300 steel pellets after they were released from their container. The CBU-46 bomblet, or submunition, was shaped like a small pineapple, its fins creating drag and causing the bomblets to disperse further before exploding like standard shrapnel bombs. Another submunition was the size of a baseball with grooves to impart spin; like the CBU-24, it dispersed tiny steel pellets. Antipersonnel CBUs were used over the South for close air support as well as over North Vietnam and in Laos against Ho Chi Minh Trail infiltration.

A common antitank cluster bomb was the MK-20 Rockeye, which dispersed nine-inch dart-like bomblets containing shaped-charge warheads for penetrating armor. Of the mine CBUs, two that were used in Vietnam were Dragonteeth and WAAPM (short for wide area antipersonnel munition). The Dragonteeth submunition dropped small mines powerful enough to blow off a foot but not to kill. The existence of WAAPMs was highly classified during the war. Dropped in plastic cartons resembling those used for eggs, the WAAPM units after hitting the ground shot out lengths of fine wire like a spider's legs. If a strand of wire was touched, the mine exploded. Sometimes U.S. bombers would use mine CBUs in tandem with antipersonnel bombs against AAA sites in the North. The antipersonnel cluster mines made it difficult for reinforcements to man the artillery.

The fourth type of CBU used in Vietnam was the fuel air explosive (FAE), not employed until South Vietnam's last panic-stricken days in the spring of 1975. FAEs were basically large canisters filled with a volatile gaseous explosive. Dropped like a conventional bomb, the canisters sprayed out fuel when they reached a preset altitude near the ground, forming a cloud as long as 1,000 feet. The cloud of fuel was detonated once it reached maximum volatility; the explosion's effects were to immediately burn all nearby oxygen, choking its victims and creating a huge shock wave. FAEs could also be dropped by helicopters.

Conventional "iron bombs" similar to those used in World War II were by far the most common aerial weapons in Vietnam. They differed from their predecessors in their more streamlined shape and greater weight, since the newer aircraft could carry heavier loads. The explosives they employed were also much more effective. The biggest of them was the 15,000-pound BLU-82B "Daisy Cutter," which floated earthward on a parachute and exploded twenty feet above the ground. Exploding in a huge mushroom cloud, its purpose was to level all vegetation within a radius of 100 feet in order to create an instant helicopter landing zone. A few were used as antipersonnel weapons in the final weeks of the war in 1975 as the South Vietnamese tried desperately to find a substitute for the withdrawn B-52s of the U.S. Air Force.

Napalm was another World War II weapon widely applied two decades later in Southeast Asia, especially in support of embattled ground troops in South Vietnam. The silver canisters containing 125 gallons of jellied gas ignited on impact, consuming oxygen and choking enemy troops or burning them. Most effective against entrenched infantry, napalm gave off no lethal fragments and could be used close to friendly forces without the dangers of fragmentation posed by conventional bombs. Often the fire from napalm would penetrate jungle that was immune to shrapnel. A single napalm canister spread its contents over an area a hundred yards long.

To insure accuracy, American pilots flying over both the North and South had to drop their bombs from low altitudes. But low-flying bombers risked damage because the aircraft was still directly above the bomb when it exploded. To ease this risk, the high-drag Snakeye bomb was designed. Its fins popped open on release and acted as air brakes so the bomb fell well behind the attacking plane.

"Smart" weapons

The increasing effectiveness of North Vietnamese antiaircraft defenses, and the higher demands for accuracy placed on U.S. air crews, pushed the Americans to even more striking ingenuity—the first of the so-called "smart" bombs and missiles. These bombs were designed to be dropped from relatively safe distances and were designed to home in on a target with minimal human intervention and great accuracy. With the aid of laser beams, television cameras, and computers they could almost do the job themselves: find a target, guide themselves to it, and destroy it. These weapons were a first step toward a weapon with a mind of its own, an aerial agent of destruction that could be fired with high expectations that it would hit its target precisely.

The success of the two types of "smart" weapons used in Vietnam—laser-guided bombs and computer-directed, electro-optically-guided bombs—helped to fulfill the need for greater accuracy and lethality at lower risk to aircraft and pilot. If they were not yet fully automatic they repre-

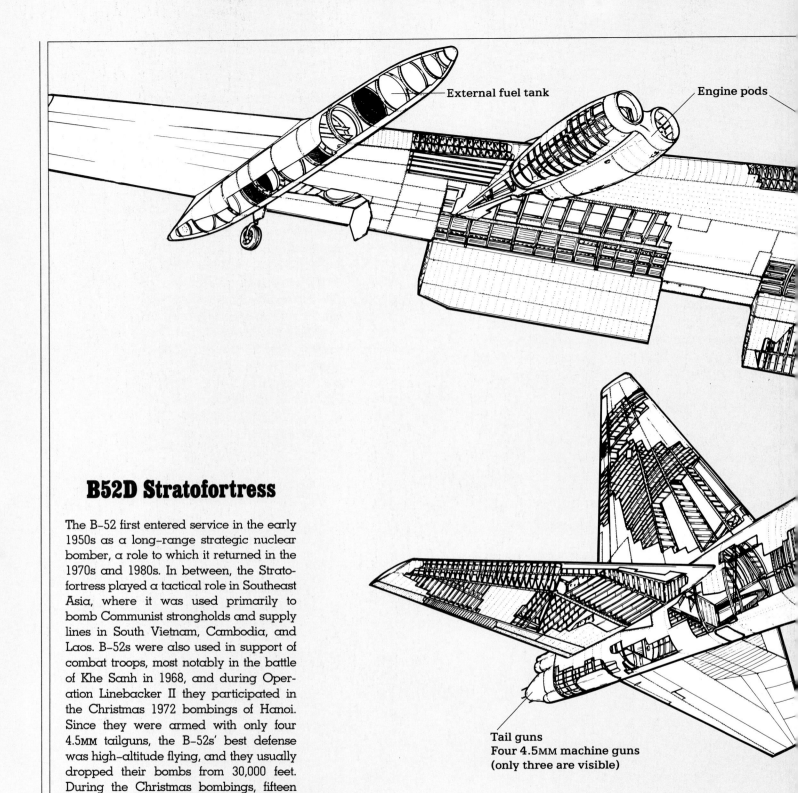

External fuel tank

Engine pods

B52D Stratofortress

The B-52 first entered service in the early 1950s as a long-range strategic nuclear bomber, a role to which it returned in the 1970s and 1980s. In between, the Stratofortress played a tactical role in Southeast Asia, where it was used primarily to bomb Communist strongholds and supply lines in South Vietnam, Cambodia, and Laos. B-52s were also used in support of combat troops, most notably in the battle of Khe Sanh in 1968, and during Operation Linebacker II they participated in the Christmas 1972 bombings of Hanoi. Since they were armed with only four 4.5MM tailguns, the B-52s' best defense was high-altitude flying, and they usually dropped their bombs from 30,000 feet. During the Christmas bombings, fifteen were shot down by enemy SAMs, although B-52 tail gunners exacted some revenge by downing two MiGs. In all, the 156-foot-long B-52s flew 126,615 sorties over Southeast Asia.

Tail guns
Four 4.5MM machine guns
(only three are visible)

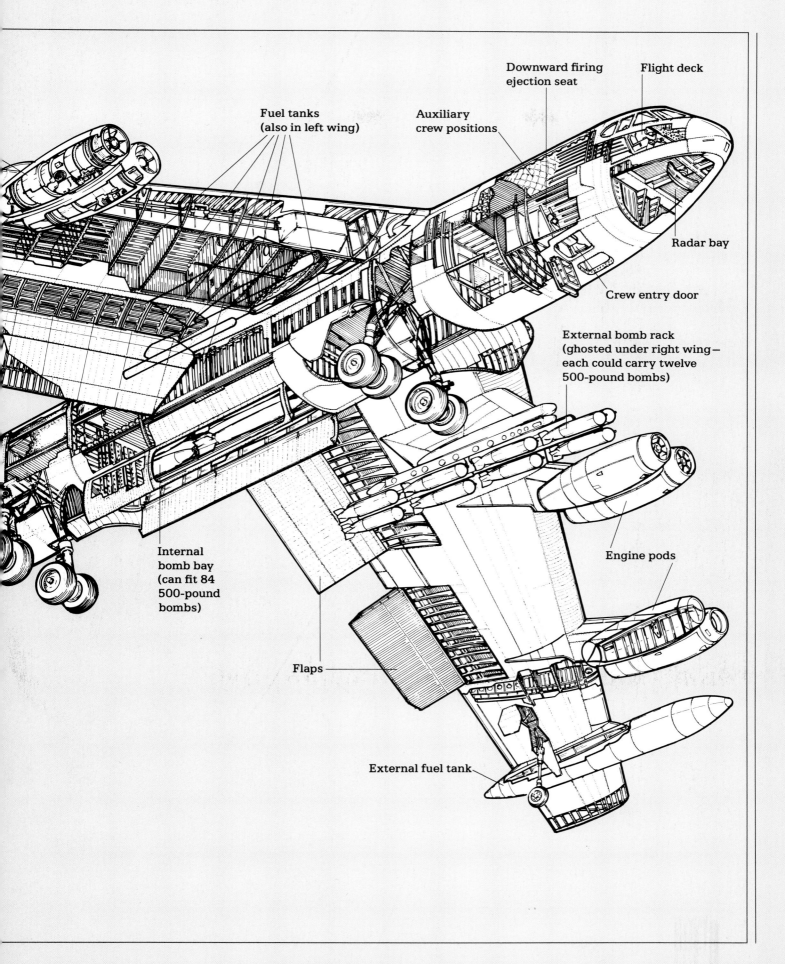

Fuel tanks
(also in left wing)

Auxiliary
crew positions

Downward firing
ejection seat

Flight deck

Radar bay

Crew entry door

External bomb rack
(ghosted under right wing—
each could carry twelve
500-pound bombs)

Engine pods

Internal
bomb bay
(can fit 84
500-pound
bombs)

Flaps

External fuel tank

sented a long jump in that direction and were stunningly accurate. A single eight-plane squadron carrying laser-guided bombs in 1972, for example, destroyed the heavily defended Thanh Hoa Bridge in North Vietnam, a target that had remained defiantly intact through no fewer than 873 previous sorties with conventional bombs and the loss of ninety-five American planes. Navy Commander Homer Smith flew the first plane to carry an electro-optically-guided Walleye bomb into combat in a 1967 mission over a North Vietnamese military barracks at Sam Son. Smith watched as the missile homed on its target with its television camera, plunged through a window of one of the barracks, and exploded. Weapons with that kind of accuracy could be used where others could not—on sites, for example, that had previously been off-limits because a strike would endanger civilians. The hydroelectric plant at Lang Chi, completed in 1972, would have been off-limits to conventional bombers because destruction of the dam next to it would have caused heavy flooding. But commanders reasoned that laser-guided bombs would be precise enough for the job. Twelve 2,000-pound bombs of this sort hit a section of the power plant some fifteen feet square, destroying the plant's generators while sparing the dam a few yards away. Similar pinpoint raids were made on the Hanoi rail yards and radio station.

Smart weapons also increased a bomber crew's chances of survival. The weapons delivery computers carried by bombers for conventional weapons could calculate a bomb's path to the ground based on wind, speed, and other factors, but the aircraft had to follow a steady course to the bomb release point, making it vulnerable to antiaircraft fire. Armed with laser-guided bombs or Walleyes the pilots could fly higher and maneuver more freely.

When the American military first attempted to apply the laser principle to warfare in the early 1960s the focus was on ground-fired antitank weapons. By 1964, however, laser technology was being developed for use in the air, and the first laser-guided "Paveway" bomb was tested two years later. The two main elements in a laser-guided bomb (LGB) system are the "designator," which directs a beam of laser light at a target, and a laser-seeking device attached to the bomb. The designator can be either on the plane carrying the bomb or on a second aircraft (see illustration, page 132).

When a target is selected its image appears on a television screen monitored by the pilot or weapons officer on the plane carrying the designator. The designator then sends out a beam that the officer aims by moving a small joystick resembling the control stick on a video game. The beam must remain centered on a target while the bomber maneuvers into position and while the bomb is falling. The bomb is equipped with a laser-seeking mechanism on its nose, a computer, and a set of movable control fins. The computer converts signals from the laser seeker into commands that move the fins to keep the bomb on target.

The laser guidance system operates as a fine tuner, holding the bomb on its course by following the laser beam emitted by the designator. Since the seeker responds only to the precise wavelength of the beam sent by the designator it cannot be confused by other light sources. One drawback of laser bombs is the need for the aircraft carrying the designator to loiter over the target in order to hold the beam on target, drawing fire until the bomb hits. But on the plus side, these new bombs could be released from safer distances, and their accuracy proved far greater than any other previous bombing technique. In raids on North Vietnam, laser-guided bombs had a circular area probability of thirty feet. This meant that 50 percent of the time the bomb landed within thirty feet of the target. Conventional "dumb" bombs in Vietnam averaged a 420-foot circular area probability.

Walleye bombs and their "electro-optical" (EO) guidance systems were more complex than LGBs and more expensive. But the Walleye could be released and left alone to guide itself. Nobody had to point the way for it. The Walleye combined a TV camera and a computer with a conventional 2,000-pound iron bomb. The Walleye camera, grafted to the front of the bomb, served as the eyes of its computer. Once the pilot aimed the camera at a target the computer took over and made a map of the pattern of lights and darks around it in its memory. It then guided the bomb to the target by locking onto the light map and steering for it. The pilot, meanwhile, could head for home.

Walleyes in use at the end of the war could glide to their targets from as far as thirty-two miles away. They could be carried by virtually any combat jet. If necessary, a crewman on the plane could replace the computer. He would see the view through the TV camera on a screen in his console and guide the bomb to the ground with radio signals. The success of the laser and EO-guided bombs in Vietnam dictated further development in the direction of true "fire and forget" weapons after the war. Subsequent research concentrated on improving the guidance sensors' ability to "see" moving targets as well as stationary objects and to discern specific objects such as tanks and hit them even as they moved. The new guidance system uses imaging infrared technology, which is far more sensitive than the optical seekers used in Vietnam.

Electronic chess

The swirl of advanced American bombers, fighters, missiles, and electronic countermeasures equipment led to a complex and deadly game of electronic detection and cover-up over North Vietnam. To some analysts, the most important military legacy of the war in Vietnam was the U.S. effort to deceive and suppress enemy radar.

American bombers heading into North Vietnam had to contend with a gauntlet of radar stations and radar-guided weapons. The system began with early warning radars that banished the possibility of surprise. Ground control intercept (GCI) stations tracked the bomber squadrons and guided MiGs to the best interception sites. Other radar installations tracked American and South Vietnamese aircraft for the countless nests of antiaircraft guns and for the formidable Soviet-built SAM missiles. Also, MiG fighters carried heat-seeking Atoll air-to-air missiles similar to U.S. Sidewinders. Finally, enemy fighters had their own tracking radar and, to add to the confusion, Communist ground sites could emit false signals to make it appear that surface-to-air missiles had been launched.

Attempts to penetrate this mighty defensive screen precipitated a series of moves and countermoves with each side probing for the decisive edge. In the 1950s and 1960s, the newly invented American electronic countermeasures devices were placed only on bombers on the theory that the bulky equipment would hinder the maneuverability of the smaller jets. It soon became obvious, however, that the fighter-bombers needed more immediate warnings of enemy threats. The air force and navy rapidly equipped fighters and fighter-bombers with ECM gear that monitored SAM radar channels and transmitted a gong-like warning over a pilot's headset when a missile radar locked onto his aircraft. Quick, high-speed turns could often take the aircraft out of the path of the radar-guided SAM, which needed five seconds to make an in-flight course change, but the best evasive action was a plunge toward the ground because the SAM had great difficulty reversing its upward motion.

American pilots and Communist antiaircraft crews frequently tried to outfox each other with feints and jabs like circling boxers. Americans soon fielded an electronic device that let the pilot know what kind of Russian radar was tracking his aircraft and therefore whether to expect to be attacked by radar-guided antiaircraft guns, missiles, or MiGs. Invariably the first to reach the target area and the last to leave it, the Wild Weasel pilots took great risks but comprised a necessary part of this airborne technological mosaic. With their help, the kill ratio for SAMs declined from 5.9 percent of missiles fired in 1965 to less than 1 percent in 1968.

American aerial tactics changed and changed again because of the enemy's bristling defenses. When the bomb raids over North Vietnam began, U.S. pilots came in low in order to elude radar detection. As soon as they encountered antiaircraft batteries, the bombers were driven up to 20,000 feet. But starting in mid-1965 the proliferation of SAMs eliminated safety at high altitudes and the attacking planes resumed operating at low levels, back in the range of enemy gunners. The result was an expanding bombing armada. Eventually, the typical bombing mission array of bombers, refueling tankers, and rescue aircraft was augmented by a fighter escort to fend off MiGs, several Wild Weasels, electronic reconnaissance aircraft, and early warning radar planes. By 1972, when the air offensive over North Vietnam resumed, U.S. countermeasures had become effective enough that SAMs were no longer the threat they had been during the Operation Rolling Thunder bombing. Desperate Communist launch crews fired missiles blindly in bunches as the B-52s of Operation Linebacker II roared over Hanoi during Christmas 1972.

Chaff

By late in the war U.S. crews had made highly effective two old techniques for electronically neutralizing enemy radar. One was the use of "chaff," strips of aluminum foil or metallic Fiberglas which when released near a radar

High-drag Snakeye bombs, their fins extended, land on their truck targets at a U.S. Navy test range.

site would overload the enemy radar with reflections. The other was jamming the Communist radar with overwhelming or confusing signals. Both methods required help from electronic intelligence in identifying the proper frequencies to disrupt.

With chaff the problem was how to store and release it in the air. The strips had to be cut to different lengths to conform to a radar beam's wave length before a mission—shorter strips for higher frequencies, becoming progressively longer for the low registers of the radar band. During World War II chaff was tossed out of bombers by hand, but on modern jets it had to be released from a pod on the outside of the aircraft. The first versions were card-

Left. Conventional iron bombs dropped by U.S. Navy A-4 Skyhawks from the carrier Oriskany *hit the Thanh Hoa Bridge in North Vietnam in November 1967. When the smoke cleared the bridge still stood; it survived over 800 bombs sorties until destroyed by laser-guided bombs in 1972.*

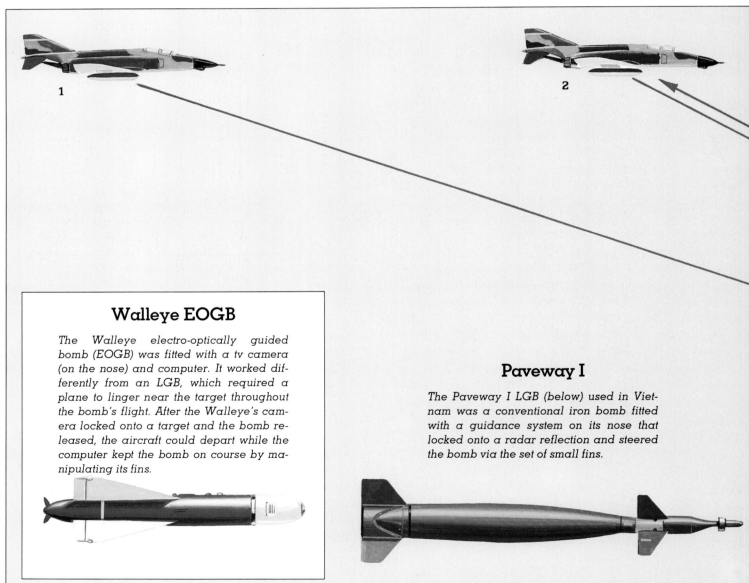

Walleye EOGB

The Walleye electro-optically guided bomb (EOGB) was fitted with a tv camera (on the nose) and computer. It worked differently from an LGB, which required a plane to linger near the target throughout the bomb's flight. After the Walleye's camera locked onto a target and the bomb released, the aircraft could depart while the computer kept the bomb on course by manipulating its fins.

Paveway I

The Paveway I LGB (below) used in Vietnam was a conventional iron bomb fitted with a guidance system on its nose that locked onto a radar reflection and steered the bomb via the set of small fins.

board containers that tore apart on release or tightly rolled balls that unraveled in the slipstream. In time a motorized eleven-foot-long pod unrolled chaff of varying lengths on a spool and set it adrift behind the aircraft.

During an operation, F-4 fighters flying ahead of the bomber group strewed chaff along the corridor the ordnance-laden planes planned to follow, but this turned out to limit the corridor too sharply and could backfire, alerting enemy radar operations to the bombers' flight paths. Blanketing a large area near the target with a cloud of chaff just as the bombers arrived proved to work better. The release point had to be precisely calculated so that the chaff would be at maximum effectiveness during the few minutes the bombers were over the target.

One plane in each group of four fighter-bombers (or, over a particularly heavily defended area, an orbiting "standoff" aircraft some distance from the target), carried jamming gear. Electronic jammers were used to drown out an enemy radar receiver with irrelevant noise or to deceive it with false signals. An attached computer stored a variety of signals in its memory bank. These false signals were then transmitted to the enemy radar, mimicking the true echo but gradually becoming stronger until the deception was "accepted," if only temporarily, by the enemy radar's circuitry. The jamming aircraft could then transmit altered signals which falsely depicted the attacking aircrafts' distance or direction from the radar receiver. A similar jamming technique could also cause radar-controlled fuses in surface-to-air missiles to detonate early. To counter this North Vietnamese missiles sometimes had two fuses, each set to a different signal.

The legacy of ECM

It is difficult to measure the impact on the war of the complicated jamming and deception schemes introduced in Vietnam by the U.S. The major aim of the air campaigns over North Vietnam had been to diminish the will and ca-

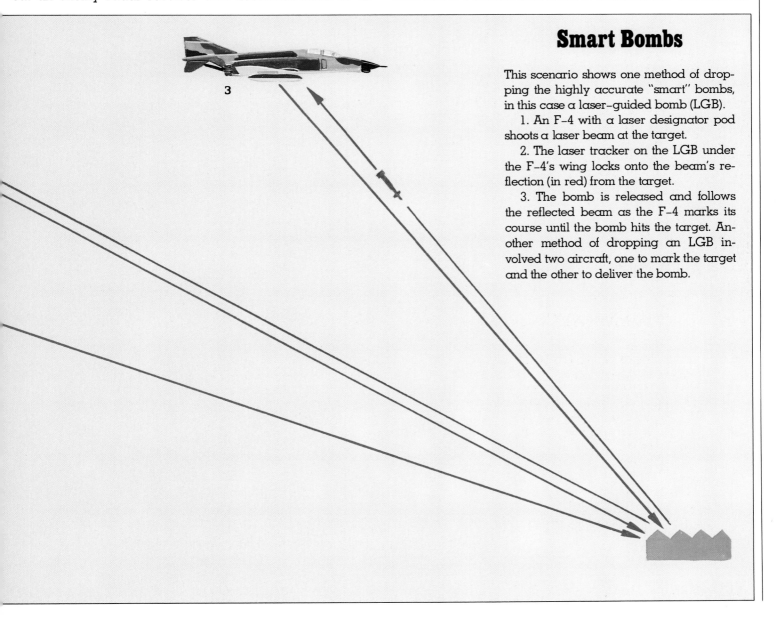

Smart Bombs

This scenario shows one method of dropping the highly accurate "smart" bombs, in this case a laser-guided bomb (LGB).

1. An F-4 with a laser designator pod shoots a laser beam at the target.

2. The laser tracker on the LGB under the F-4's wing locks onto the beam's reflection (in red) from the target.

3. The bomb is released and follows the reflected beam as the F-4 marks its course until the bomb hits the target. Another method of dropping an LGB involved two aircraft, one to mark the target and the other to deliver the bomb.

pacity of the Communists to wage war. Some argue that the large ECM effort actually detracted from the effort to reach that goal, adding planes and spending money to neutralize the enemy's defenses rather than to increase the bombing might of the American and South Vietnamese aerial armada. Given the North's tight defenses and the restrictions placed on U.S. pilots, especially during the Rolling Thunder campaign, without the countermeasures many of the bombers would never have reached their targets. Additionally, the funds spent on specialized equipment and aircraft may have saved money by preventing the loss of more U.S. aircraft. It certainly saved lives—of the pilots that might have been shot down, and of the civilians that might have been hit in an all-out effort to bombard North Vietnam's defenses.

At any rate, it became evident after the war that what had been learned in the effort to neutralize the enemy's SAM missiles and sophisticated antiaircraft defenses was a vital legacy for U.S. military air (as the counterefforts no doubt were for the Soviet Union). The experiences influenced the priorities for post-Vietnam weapons and aircraft development. The technology developed step by step, by trial and error over North Vietnam accelerated important design changes for greater effectiveness against radar. For one example, Israeli air force pilots in the Yom Kippur War in 1973 and in Lebanon in the early 1980s flew successfully through unprecedentedly thick antiaircraft defenses because their planes were equipped with devices born of the war in Vietnam.

Right. *The crew of an F-4E Phantom goes over its preflight checklist before taking off on a predawn anti-MiG combat air patrol mission from Phan Rang Air Base in South Vietnam. A Sparrow air-to-air missile is visible under the wing and a Vulcan 20MM Gatling gun bulges under the nose. Below. Inside his F-4 on the airfield at Da Nang, First Lieutenant Victor Seavers of the air force's 390th Tactical Fighter Wing awaits clearance to take off on a night mission.*

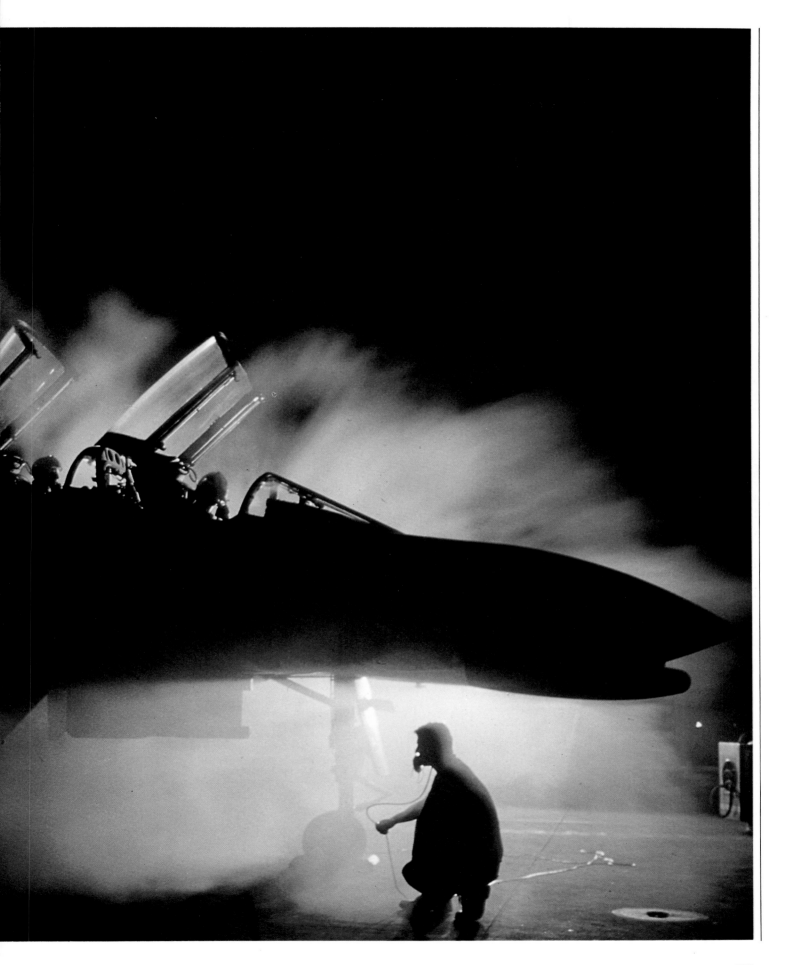

Of Blackbirds, Tom Cat, and Mohawks

General purpose aircraft met many of the challenges of the air war over Southeast Asia, but some jobs were performed by specialized aircraft suited for specific roles. Among these tasks were observing the enemy—both over North and South Vietnam—and overcoming the intricate radar system used in the North to track aircraft and direct AAA and SAM fire. For these tasks, the U.S. fielded some of the most advanced planes and equipment technology could offer.

Perhaps the most intriguing looking aircraft used in the war was the SR-71 Blackbird clandestine reconnaissance plane. Its radical shape and heat-reflective black paint allowed it to fly at three times the speed of sound sixteen miles above the Earth. A precursor to later "stealth" aircraft, the SR-71 was very difficult to detect by radar because of its shape. Equipped with a wide variety of sensors, including high-resolution cameras and side-looking radar, the SR-71 flew hundreds of reconnaissance missions over North Vietnam.

The SR-71A shown here, its afterburners lit, nears top altitude of 85,000 feet. Below is a front view of the Blackbird.

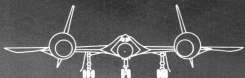

Pilotless Aircraft

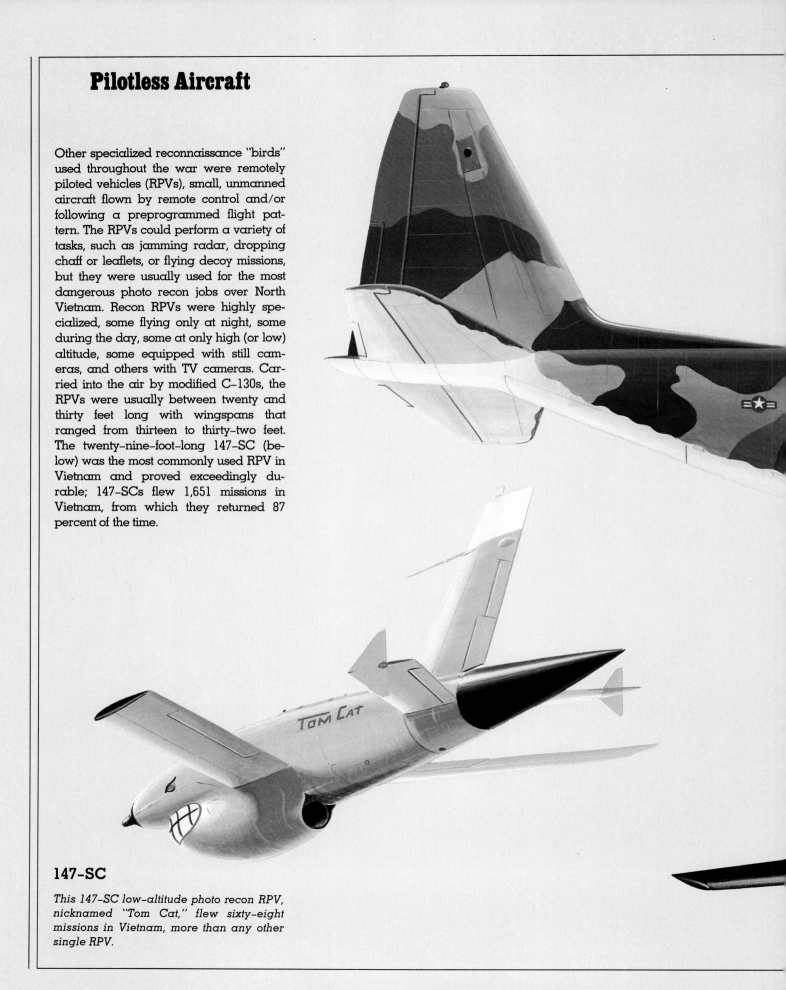

Other specialized reconnaissance "birds" used throughout the war were remotely piloted vehicles (RPVs), small, unmanned aircraft flown by remote control and/or following a preprogrammed flight pattern. The RPVs could perform a variety of tasks, such as jamming radar, dropping chaff or leaflets, or flying decoy missions, but they were usually used for the most dangerous photo recon jobs over North Vietnam. Recon RPVs were highly specialized, some flying only at night, some during the day, some at only high (or low) altitude, some equipped with still cameras, and others with TV cameras. Carried into the air by modified C–130s, the RPVs were usually between twenty and thirty feet long with wingspans that ranged from thirteen to thirty-two feet. The twenty-nine-foot-long 147–SC (below) was the most commonly used RPV in Vietnam and proved exceedingly durable; 147–SCs flew 1,651 missions in Vietnam, from which they returned 87 percent of the time.

147-SC

This 147–SC low-altitude photo recon RPV, nicknamed "Tom Cat," flew sixty-eight missions in Vietnam, more than any other single RPV.

DC-130 Drone Carrier

This DC-130 carries under each wing two 147-NA RPVs, which were equipped with ECM pods for radar jamming missions. The DC-130s would carry the RPVs toward their targets and release them near the North Vietnamese border. A "pilot" inside the DC-130 then controlled each RPV until it was snagged by a recovery helicopter at the end of its mission.

147-J

The first low-altitude daytime photo recon RPV to fly in Vietnam, the 147-J was used in 1966 and 1967 primarily to skim over North Vietnam below the rainy season's heavy overcast. The twenty-nine-foot-long "J" had a wingspan of twenty-seven feet.

Electronic Warfare and Scout Aircraft

Among the most specialized aircraft U.S. pilots flew were those used to neutralize North Vietnam's radar web. These "electronic warfare" planes included the EB-66 Raven, F-105 and F-4 Wild Weasels, and the EA-6B (below).

Since the Communists' vast air defense network stayed for the most part north of the DMZ, planes flying over South Vietnam faced other challenges, including scouting out the enemy at night and in bad weather. The answer tended to involve hooking up modern surveillance gear to existing aircraft, such as the radar pod on the OV-1 Mohawk (bottom right). This challenge was also met by one of the few planes designed specifically for use in Vietnam, a scout aircraft so quiet that it could barely be heard by enemy patrols, the YO-3A (top right).

EA-6B Prowler

The EA-6B, with specialized equipment for electronic warfare, is a derivative of the twin-seated A-6 Intruder attack aircraft. The Prowler's four-man crew consists of a pilot and three officers who operate its sensors and jamming equipment. Delivered to navy squadrons in 1971, the EA-6B was used to collect electronic intelligence, or ELINT, on the location and frequencies of North Vietnamese radars. This information was later used to protect American planes on air strikes by jamming radars and communications networks. On the pylon furthest out on each wing the Prowler shown here carries electronic countermeasures pods; atop its tail is equipment for monitoring enemy radar.

YO-3A Quiet Aircraft

Powered by a muffled 210-horsepower engine, the YO-3A was a quiet, long-range scout plane. The ball-shaped pod below its fuselage contained a night periscope and infrared illuminator for night operations, and a laser target designator.

OV-1B Mohawk

The OV-1 Mohawk was a two-man visual and photographic scout aircraft. In South Vietnam, the OV-1B, shown here, could continue to seek out the enemy in bad weather because it carried a side looking aerial radar (SLAR) pod under its fuselage.

The Automated Battlefield

The operation was known as Igloo White. Its purpose was to detect, quantify, and halt the constant movement of North Vietnamese men, weapons, and supplies south along the Ho Chi Minh Trail in Laos but without risking American lives. An early version of the system began in secrecy in late 1967. By the time the American public heard of it in 1971, Operation Igloo White had become the most comprehensive, sophisticated application of technology in Vietnam. It brought a new term to the military lexicon: the automated battlefield.

The trail, which passed through Laos and Cambodia before ending near the South Vietnamese border, had become the life line for the Communists in South Vietnam. Starting off as a rudimentary network of jungle paths and crude roads traveled chiefly by foot and bicycle, it had grown into an interconnected system of developed roads—some of them paved—able to bear the traffic of trucks and tanks. The North Viet-

namese changed and added to the route constantly in order to move more men and equipment and to elude the American aircraft that bombed the trail with increasing frequency and bomb tonnage starting in 1964.

Throughout the war, and especially after President Lyndon Johnson halted the bombing of North Vietnam in November 1968, American pilots bombarded Laos to "interdict" traffic down the trails. This forced the Communists to move only at night but stopped little of the infiltration. Despite the urgings of the Joint Chiefs of Staff and General William Westmoreland when he was commander of U.S. forces in Vietnam, home front political concerns had proscribed U.S. troops from striking in Laos early in the war. After the Cambodian incursion of June 1970, U.S. Congressional legislation passed in December of that year forbade American combatants from setting foot in Cambodia or Laos. The next year, the South Vietnamese invasion of Laos—Lam Son 719—to cut the trail ended in complete failure. To compound matters, when President Richard Nixon moved in 1969 to start turning the war back to the South Vietnamese by withdrawing U.S. forces, U.S. pilots began to return home and fewer U.S. aircraft were available for missions over Laos. Further, slowing down the Communists' Ho Chi Minh Trail life line seemed essential to buying time for Vietnamization, the training of South Vietnam's forces to continue their defense without the Americans.

As early as 1966, civilians in the Defense Department reasoned that U.S. technology could provide a critical edge in combating infiltration via Laos. That summer, Defense Secretary Robert McNamara had asked the Jason Summer Study Group, a panel of top scientists formed in 1959 to study military technology, to develop a lower-cost alternative to the Rolling Thunder bombing of North Vietnam, which, since its inception in March 1965, has seemed to have little effect on the Communists' war effort. The scientists proposed an electronic barrier across the Ho Chi Minh Trail and the more conventional "wall" across the demilitarized zone that was to become "McNamara's Line." At first the military opposed both ideas, arguing that they would not work. Also, according to Lieutenant General Kenneth Cooper (U.S. Army-Ret.), a participant in the planning, the generals feared that money would be diverted from their programs to fund the proposals.

But McNamara, growing increasingly disillusioned about the bombing of the North, approved the ideas and in September formed the Defense Communications Planning Group to develop them. A top-secret group drawn from the upper echelons of American science, the DCPG was to spend the next five years advancing military technology. Out of the DCPG, viewed by some of its members as the Manhattan Project of high-tech warfare, came a variety of new military hardware, including "people sniffers" designed to detect humans by chemically sensing their sweat and urine, the starlight scope, ground target radars, and several types of cluster bombs and aerial-dropped mines. The group made its greatest impact on the tools of unmanned warfare, which were developed for use along the Ho Chi Minh Trail in Laos. Turning to the problem of detecting infiltration without placing men on the trail, the DCPG's work led to great strides in a device that was to become the heart of Igloo White, the sensor.

Under Operation Igloo White, which the DCPG rendered fully operational by 1969, the trail was littered with tens of thousands of the sensors, electronic devices able to record a variety of signals indicating troop movement and to transmit the information to listening posts. Banks of computers far from the scene could assemble and analyze the resultant data and suggest possible bombing targets. With the technology devised by the DCPG doing much of the work and shouldering the risks, the idea eventually became irresistible even to military men: North Vietnamese convoys in Laos could be attacked without risking the life of a single American on the ground.

Here is how Operation Igloo White worked. On any given night North Vietnamese convoys reassembled shortly after sundown to continue down the trail. Within a few minutes the line of trucks would begin to bump along the road. Meanwhile, hundreds of miles away in Nakhon Phanom, Thailand, where the U.S. Air Force's Task Force Alpha commanded Igloo White, technicians studied the screens of their IBM 360-65 computers in an air-conditioned shelter. The so-called Infiltration Surveillance Center at Nakhon Phanom was housed in reputedly the largest building in Southeast Asia, partly because the comparatively crude IBM 360-65 at first demanded large amounts of space to store and process the reams of information—including every branch of the Ho Chi Minh Trail known to the Americans.

The convoy entered the Igloo White web when an Acoubuoy, an acoustic sensor dropped in a small camouflaged parachute to lodge in a trail-side tree, picked up the sound of one of the truck's engines. Soon after, another Acoubuoy farther along the trail heard the trucks. Similar to sonar mechanisms used by the navy to detect submarines, each Acoubuoy sensor contained a rugged sensitive microphone, a small radio transmitter, a battery, and a self-destruct device activated when anyone tampered with it. Most hung in trees, but some were designed to fall to the ground where they planted themselves.

The listening devices automatically transmitted their readings to a relay aircraft orbiting high above the trail, earlier in the war an air force EC-121, later a "Pave Eagle," an unmanned Beechcraft QU-22B prop-driven aircraft. Radio receivers on the aircraft picked up the

Operation Igloo White

Unmanned warfare became a reality for the first time during the Vietnam War when the U.S. seeded the Ho Chi Minh Trail in Laos with electronic sensors and monitored Communist traffic from the distant safety of Nakhon Phanom, Thailand. This schematic overview illustrates the key elements of Operation Igloo White and the Ho Chi Minh Trail's major routes.

1. North Vietnamese trucks traveling down the trail in Laos, usually at night, set off a series of seismic or acoustic sensors (here highlighted in red, but camouflaged for use in Igloo White).

2. An unmanned QU–22B Beechcraft plane picks up the sensors' signals and relays them to the Infiltration Surveillance Center at Nakhon Phanom.

3. At the ISC, computers with maps of sensor-seeded sections of the trail in their memory banks determine the location of the convoy as well as its length and speed, revealed by the number of sensors activated and the length of time they broadcast their signals.

4. Men at the ISC then relay the convoys' anticipated location to fighter–bombers, in this case an F–4 carrying cluster bombs. To destroy the trucks, the aircraft then flies over the trail and drops its bombs at the point indicated by the computer.

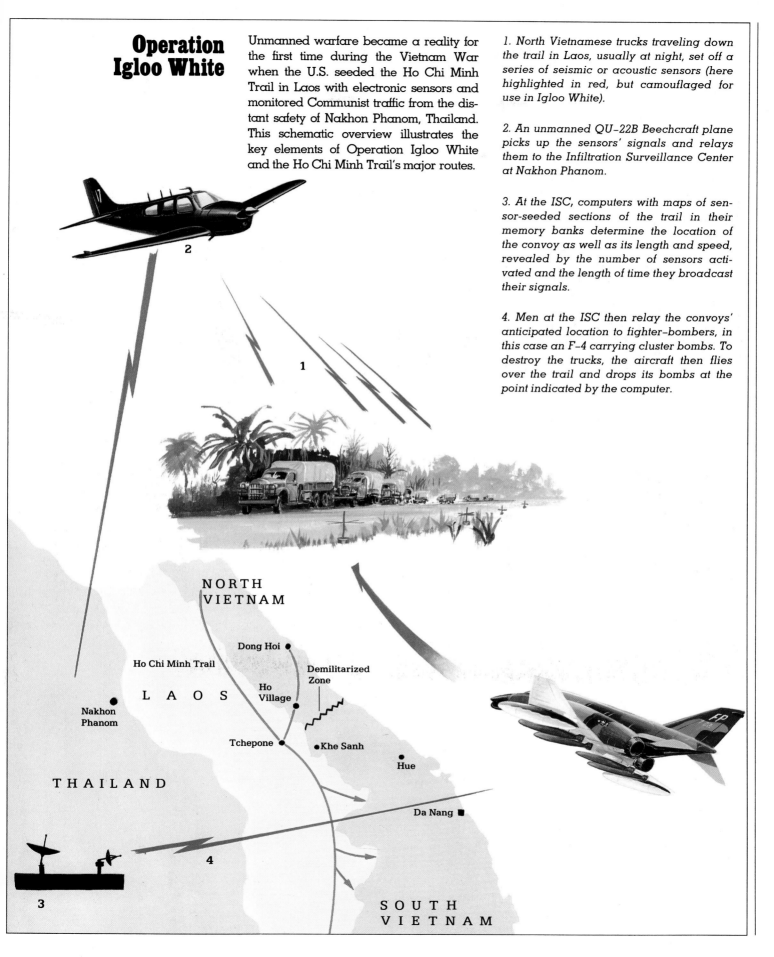

weak signals from the Acoubuoys, recognized them as different from the normal forest sounds, and relayed the signals to Thailand and the computers monitored by the airmen.

The computers at Nakhon Phanom analyzed the signals and waited for corroboration from ground sensors in the vicinity. Several different kinds of the short-lived battery-powered ground sensors were usually in place. A seismic sensor might record vibrations transmitted through the ground. A magnetic variety responded to metal in the surrounding area. Heat sensors reacted to the heat in passing bodies and vehicles. As the data from the sensors came in, the computers would calculate the location of the convoy, the direction it was traveling, its speed, and the number of trucks. Drawing on its memory of the trail network, the computer would calculate where the convoy was going.

The air force operations officer, watching intently as maps and projected route lines emerged on the screen, asked the computer to program possible interception points on the predicted route. The computer suggested several. In response to another request from the officer it then plotted an interdiction mission for one of several types of aircraft, including air force or navy or marine F-4s. Aircraft flying over the trail carried a variety of ordnance, from conventional iron bombs to "smart" bombs.

On board an AC-130 Spectre gunship, crew men scan their video sensor consoles for signs of enemy activity in the jungle below. "Joystick" controls are used to aim the sensors.

Soon afterward, bomb-laden aircraft took off from their base and headed for the point on the trail identified by the computer. As the planes approached the target the computers at Nakhon Phanom continuously updated the data as the moving convoy triggered more sensors. The planes hurtled through the night at a speed, altitude, and heading determined by the computer. A few minutes later they reached the target and the pilots released their bombs.

The bombs' blast would destroy a few of the Acoubuoys that had started it all. Others recorded the explosions and—if the bombs hit—the chain of secondary blasts. The mikes might even have picked up the cries of the injured, dispatching this information along with the rest to the still-orbiting relay aircraft, which in turn relayed it to the airmen at Nakhon Phanom. The fighter-bombers then returned home while the Communists on the ground were left to count their dead and wounded. The enemies had met, an engagement of sorts had taken place, but one side had been invisible. It had followed the script of a classical ambush, except the ambushing force consisted entirely of machines instead of men.

Pave Spectre

Key elements of the Igloo White net were the aircraft used to fly the computerized missions against the convoys. During the early going of Igloo White, F-4 Phantoms and other fast-moving jets were heavily relied on, but their very speed made them less effective at hitting the precise targets than the slower, but more accurate, B-57 Canberra. The Canberras, dropping incendiary bombs developed during the Korean War, proved to be the most effective "truck busters" until the appearance of a cumbersome-looking, maundering aircraft called "Pave Spectre." An advanced successor to the AC-47 gunship used so effectively to protect U.S. and GVN troops in South Vietnam, the AC-130 had undergone the most remarkable metamorphosis of any aircraft in Vietnam.

Spectre started off as an advanced tactical transport first flown in 1956 and still in production twenty years later. The C-130's four turbo-prop engines made it fast for a cargo ship of its weight (175,000 pounds). In the air war over Laos and Vietnam the cargo plane, transformed into the AC-130 (the A for "Attack"), found a new role as a gunship, guided by the most sophisticated electronic equipment available and firing its powerful guns against truck convoys on the Ho Chi Minh Trail in Laos. The unlikely dragon became the most effective "truck killer" of the war.

Chosen for its size and powerful engines, the C-130 was highly maneuverable, albeit at slow speeds, and very capacious. A gunship's job was to rake ground targets from low elevations with cannon and machine-gun fire. Fighters like the F-4 had traditionally drawn this duty, but when a high-speed fighter bursts in on a target it has only a fraction of a second to aim and fire. A fighter is also handicapped by the relatively light load of ammunition it can carry: The F-4 normally carried about a thousand 20MM shells, which worked out to some ten seconds of sustained firing. The gunship, by contrast, toted several thousand rounds along with miscellaneous other equipment inside its ample frame, could loiter over a target area for hours, and its slow pace, low altitude, and agility made it easier for its gunners to zero in.

Gunships maximized their potency through use of the aerial maneuver known as the pylon turn. In a pylon turn, the wings of the plane remain at the same angle to the point on the ground as if it were tethered to the spot. Guns mounted on the side, perpendicular to the fuselage, could thus fire at the same point throughout the turn. A fighter's speed made its turning radius much wider than that of the slower AC-130. The greater fuel capacity of the cargo plane also permitted it to linger over a target for hours, while a fighter could loiter only a few minutes—another plus for the more clumsy gunship. Unlike the older, twin-engined AC-47, the AC-130 had enough power to climb with a full load even with one or two engines out. Perhaps

its greatest weakness was that, despite its thick skin, its top speed of 400 miles per hour (compared to an F-4's 1,500 mph) made it more vulnerable to antiaircraft fire than jet aircraft.

Outwardly, the gunship was the antithesis of the modern air war: big, slow, and low-flying. Inside, though, Spectre looked like something out of the launch control room at Cape Canaveral. An AC-130 typically carried fourteen men, 7,000 pounds of armor plate, several tons of ammunition, two 40MM automatic cannons, two 7.62MM and two 20MM Gatling guns (or some combination of those three weapons), a flare launcher, a 1.5 million candle-power searchlight, a powerful computer, and various highly sophisticated sensor systems.

The AC-130's primary sensors, low-light level television (LLLTV) cameras and imaging infrared (IIR) devices, allowed the gunship to locate targets at night. LLLTV worked like a starlight scope with a screen instead of a small gun sight. Several chambers inside the cameralike device greatly magnified existing light, amplifying the energy of individual photons, to provide a surprisingly clear picture even under a dim moon. At the same time, IIR sensors—the AC-130 used forward looking infrared or FLIR—registered the minute thermal differences among objects on the trail and converted them to detailed images on another screen. The infrared sensors reacted to the radiated heat of truck engines, campfires, and even collections of human—or other—bodies.

Other sensors provided clues to help guide the LLLTV and IIR sensors. These included a moving target indicator, a new radar device used to pick up movement on the ground, and the top-secret "Black Crow" ignition detector, able to pick up static from a truck engine as far as ten miles away. The gunship's searchlight and flares were used to support the electronic sensors and fix on targets once they had been located.

Each sensor was monitored via a screen by a crewman aboard the aircraft, who zeroed in on targets and fed data into the targeting computer. When a target was identified, the computer calculated the pylon turn necessary for the best firing angle. To the pilot's left was his "heads-up display" gun sights, which showed him a set of cross hairs. The computer then showed him on his panel another set of cross hairs representing the target. He would then maneuver the plane to line up the two sets of cross hairs. Once they intersected, the ship's guns were aimed at the target and it was ready to fire. Its Gatling guns then spat out cartridges that were fed into the weapons in long belts. The larger 40MM cannons, adapted from a navy antiaircraft weapon used by the army and navy, were hand-loaded with four-round clips. Trucks were the gunship's prime target, but it was often difficult to confirm a hit on a truck unless it was afire. To aid confirmation and to increase the round's destructive capabilities, a more flammable 40MM ammunition was developed. The new ammo

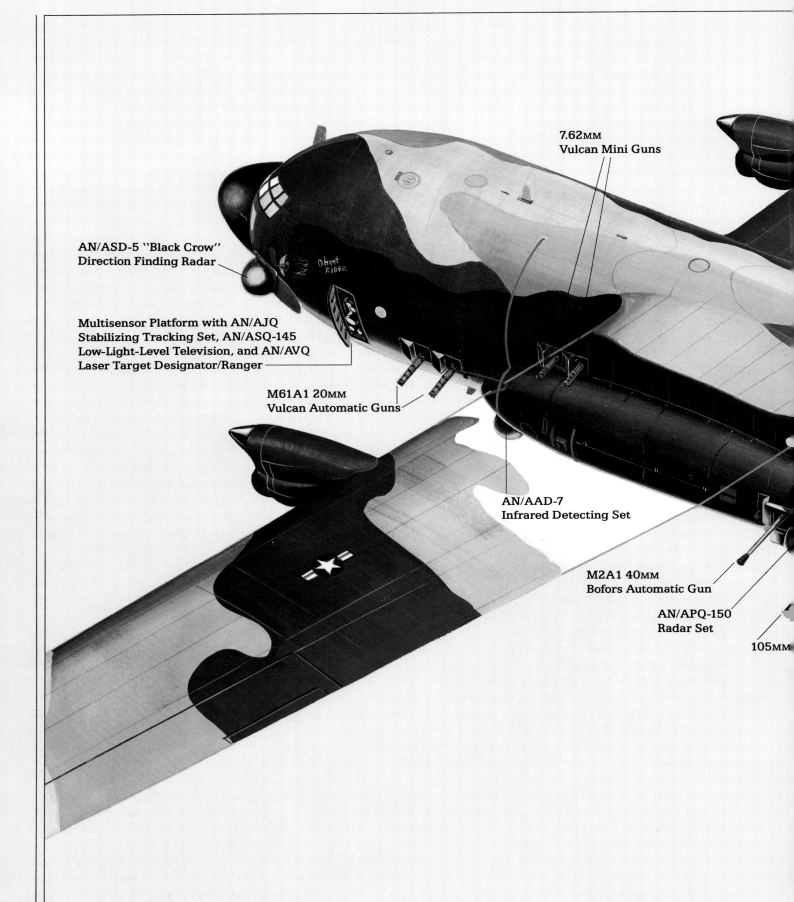

AN/ASD-5 "Black Crow"
Direction Finding Radar

Multisensor Platform with AN/AJQ
Stabilizing Tracking Set, AN/ASQ-145
Low-Light-Level Television, and AN/AVQ
Laser Target Designator/Ranger

M61A1 20MM
Vulcan Automatic Guns

7.62MM
Vulcan Mini Guns

AN/AAD-7
Infrared Detecting Set

M2A1 40MM
Bofors Automatic Gun

AN/APQ-150
Radar Set

105MM

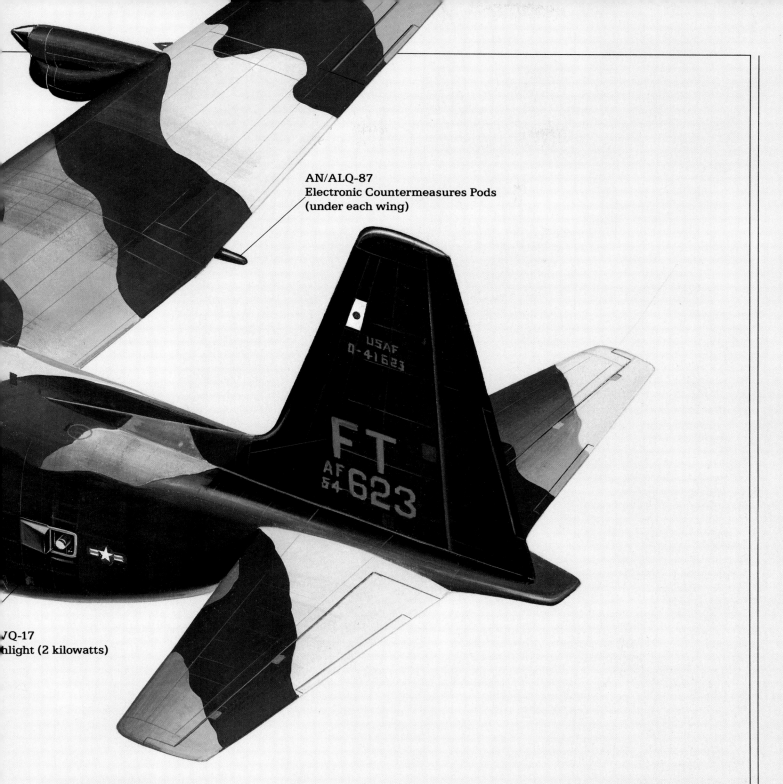

AN/ALQ-87
Electronic Countermeasures Pods
(under each wing)

USAF
0-41623

FT
AF
54 623

VQ-17
hlight (2 kilowatts)

AC-130H Spectre II

Of all the U.S. aircraft flying "interdiction" missions against Communist men and materiel moving down the Ho Chi Minh Trail, none was more successful than the AC–130 Spectre gunship. North Vietnamese truck drivers feared it more than any other plane. As one driver said, "The AC–130 rarely misses its target . . . [and] it needs neither flares nor guidance by recon plane. Moreover, it sticks to us like a leech." What made the AC–130 so difficult to elude was its specialized surveillance equipment, which worked in concert with its powerful guns.

The most advanced of the gunships, the AC–130H Pave Spectre II (or Pave Aegis), is shown here with its left wing partially cut away. Loaded onto its left side is a variety of tracking equipment, including Black Crow radar used to pick up trucks' ignitions, a low–light–level television camera, an infrared detector, ground target radar, and a strong searchlight. The gunship also carried a laser designator to mark targets for laser–guided bombs dropped by other aircraft. Barely visible under the right wing is an ECM pod used to jam enemy radar.

contained an alloy called Mish metal and was found to kindle four to five times as many secondary fires as standard rounds. The ultimate gunship, the AC–130H "Pave Aegis," fielded just before the end of the war with more firepower and from greater distances, replaced one of its 40MM guns with a 105MM army howitzer. Aegis later saw action during the American invasion of Grenada.

The AC–130 owed its tremendous destructive capacity to a combination of its bulk and its elaborate detection and targeting apparatus. The results were impressive: In the first six months of 1969, the first year they were used over the Ho Chi Minh Trail, AC–130s directed by "Moonbeam," the airborne control center flying over southern Laos, destroyed or damaged 54 percent of the enemy trucks they attacked; by March 1971 they were hitting 89 percent of their targets. In all of 1971, AC–130s claimed a total of 6,000 truck "kills." When compared with other attack planes the AC–130 was even more impressive: In 1970 the average for all attack craft was one vehicle hit for every 1.6 sorties; for the AC–130 the average was 7.34 hits per sortie. It may have looked flabby, but Spectre was the most ferocious "truck killer" in Vietnam. The report of North Vietnamese Colonel Le Xi years after the war ended confirmed the effectiveness of the AC–130. The colonel, sent to Transport Station 32 along the trail southeast of Tchepone to investigate U.S. anti-infiltration measures in 1971, had asked truck drivers to describe the gunship's strength. One said, "At times I thought it could hear the noise of our engines. When we stayed quiet it merely circled overhead. But as soon as we started the engine it began firing. If we turned off the engine it would fire a few more rounds, then leave. But if we restarted the motor, it would come back at once." So deadly was Spectre that even the most experienced North Vietnamese drivers feared it, calling it the "Thug."

Given that any commander covets the ability to attack the enemy without risking the lives of his men, Igloo White seemed to represent a technical fulfillment of a military dream. But for all the appeal of its automation, the operation ultimately contributed to an irony that seemed to govern most advanced U.S. equipment in Vietnam: Technologically, Igloo White worked well, proving at least as effective at slowing infiltration as had the Rolling Thunder campaign. But strategically, its accomplishments were limited. Although the absence of the truck-killing aircraft over Laos would have made the battle in the South more difficult for U.S./GVN forces, Igloo White could not have been expected to stop infiltration entirely.

The military itself acknowledged the operation's inherent limitations. The commander in chief of U.S. forces in the Pacific (CINCPAC), Admiral Ulysses S. Grant Sharp, held a conference on infiltration and interdiction in Honolulu in July 1967. The participants, who included General Westmoreland, concluded that unless the North Vietnamese themselves decided to halt infiltration, a marked reduction in the southward flow of supplies "would probably require an unobtainable 99% efficiency on the part of all counter-infiltration programs." A major hurdle to reaching high efficiency was the weather. Even if it worked perfectly the rest of the time, Igloo White could do little during the rainy season, when trucks could slog unmolested down the muddy roads.

In the end, the military itself had difficulty assessing the contribution of the sensor system. The same conflicting analyses that seemed to dog the entire war effort tarnished Igloo White's ultimate performance. Though the DCPG and USAF initially claimed the operation killed 12,000 trucks in both 1970 and 1971 and the same total for the previous two years combined, the USAF estimated that as much as 80 percent of the trucks spotted on the Ho Chi Minh Trail made it through the sensor network. Glowing official reports were not taken seriously by government officials, who discounted the numbers for Laos by 30 percent, according to a report by a Senate Foreign Relations subcommittee. Perhaps most telling of all, in the face of Igloo White's 20,000 sensors, the North Vietnamese managed to move dozens of artillery pieces and tanks and thousands of men down the trail for its attacks on South Vietnam in spring 1972.

Igloo White's failure to stop infiltration can hardly be attributed to the equipment involved, which performed at least as well as hoped. Former DCPG members maintain that the equipment failed only when it was used incorrectly, for example if a sensor were positioned improperly. The operation's main problem was that too much was expected of it. Most top-level U.S. commanders compared the Communist supply system to a funnel with its small end at the docks and shipping yards in Haiphong and Hanoi radiating out to the Ho Chi Minh Trail. They argued that bombing the trail was simply attacking the wrong end of the funnel. Not until mid-1972, with the mining of Haiphong Harbor and the fierce bombing of the North under Operation Linebacker, did the U.S. stop up the funnel's tip, but by then President Nixon was committed to withdrawing the last American forces and leaving South Vietnam to its own ends. Before that, U.S. pilots and the Igloo White sensors were forced to search out or listen for thousands of trucks on the intricate twists and turns of the Ho Chi Minh Trail's 16,000 kilometers of roads. The task became even more difficult after the North Vietnamese caught onto the American technology.

According to NVA Colonel Le Xi's after-the-fact report, by 1969 the Communists had begun to rethink their practice of moving on the trail only after dark, which they had adopted soon after American bombers began appearing over Laos in 1965. In southern Laos where it was used most heavily, the AC–130 seemed to have taken the night back from the North Vietnamese, so Communist trucks reverted to traveling by day along camouflaged roads newly built for the purpose. The new roads apparently not seeded by U.S. sensors also eluded other Igloo White aircraft. By the end of the war, camouflage covered some 3,000 kilometers of the trail, according to the North Vietnamese, who also claim that the tanks used during the Easter offensive of 1972 traveled South under complete secrecy via the hidden routes. When complete, the covered roads carried convoys of as many as 500 trucks in broad daylight. Traveling by day had a further benefit: The truck drivers could keep normal hours, thereby increasing their productivity.

The new camouflaged roads emphasized the herculean nature of Igloo White's charge to track thousands of kilometers of trails in the Laotian jungle. They also proved yet again a truth of warfare accepted by most commanders: that no matter how clever a stratagem is, the enemy can in time devise a way around it.

Despite its estimated annual price tag of $1 billion and its technical achievements, Igloo White increased the cost of the Communists' infiltration effort but could not stop it. One of the original contributors to the sensor system concept, David R. Israel, the former deputy director of DCPG, admitted after the war that Igloo White was terminated in late 1972 in part because too many trucks still made it down the trail. "Technically the sensors worked well. . . . We had no trouble finding targets with our sensors," Israel said. "But destroying them from the air was another [story]. A lot got through."

The Defense Department, however, was undaunted by Igloo White's mixed performance. Some within the military had criticized the idea of an automated, electronic battlefield from the start. General John D. Ryan, air force chief of staff from 1969 to 1973, questioned the system's ability to stop infiltration, later admitting he had "never" favored the system. Civilians in the Pentagon, though, found the idea itself a remarkable tactical advance, claiming it had ushered in a new era of warfare. *Air Force* magazine, for example, called it "a long stride forward in our search for a more effective deterrent to conventional war." Those to whom Igloo White and the concept of automated warfare were appealing took further encouragement from developments in South Vietnam, where electronic equipment also seemed to be broadening the horizon for low-risk ways of fighting the enemy.

The DMZ Barrier

Adjunct to Igloo White was an idea that ultimately fizzled: the physical anti-infiltration barrier across the demilitarized zone (see sidebar, page 152). Because word of "McNamara's Line" reached the American press in 1967, while Igloo White remained secret for another four years, the DMZ barrier's development appeared preeminent at the time. But members of the Jason group and DCPG considered the fence at the Seventeenth Parallel to be secondary to the sensor network of Laos. The barrier itself was

the center of heated debate between the military and the Defense Department. Admiral U. S. Grant Sharp opposed the idea from the start. He doubted that the barrier would be as effective as the Jason planners predicted and felt that the group had underestimated the Communists' capacity to develop methods of countering the defensive line. More emphatically, he believed that the barrier yielded the initiative to the enemy while diverting resources away from the major American efforts, the ground war in the South and the air war in the North.

In spite of Sharp's opposition and the lukewarm acquiescence of the Joint Chiefs of Staff, the barrier was approved, and construction was ordered to begin in 1967. By late 1967 a few sections of the barrier had been completed, primarily to test it, but the expense in dollars, manpower, and equipment was so great that the prospects for additional construction looked bleak. At this juncture an enemy build-up in the northern provinces of South Vietnam forced the American command to funnel more troops into that area, which interfered with work on the barrier. With the onset of the Tet offensive and the siege of Khe Sanh in 1968 the barrier was abandoned, as it turned out, permanently.

To some military commanders in Vietnam the barrier, although itself a failure, bristled with possibilities. Army, marine, and air force commanders all saw uses for its electronic support technology, which would eventually coalesce as the automated battlefield. Ground troops could be deployed more economically and with less risk. The air force could improve its ability to interdict the enemy from above. The commanders' hopes all hinged on the DCPG's work on ground sensors, or UGS—for "unattended ground sensors."

The sensor devices developed for use in Vietnam were probably the most important innovation in detection since radar and sonar. Sensors were the guts of the automated battlefield. The key to their emergence in Vietnam was the development of the tiny but rugged components that made them work. A dazzling variety of sensors was eventually introduced. They operated on several different principles. Seismic detectors, one of the most reliable types, could pick up the vibration of the ground from a footfall or a moving wheel. Some were dropped from the air like the Air Delivered Seismic Intrusion Detector (ADSID), while others had to be positioned by hand, such as the Patrol Seismic Intrusion Detector (PSID). Balanced-pressure sensors released nearly invisible wires that recorded the pressure of anything that passed over them. Magnetic detectors (MAGID) were activated by metal in their immediate vicinity; electromagnetic sensors (EMID) similarly reacted to disturbances in the nearby radio field. Some sensors combined two detection features: One called Acousid, for acoustic seismic intrusion detector, contained both a microphone like an Acoubuoy and a seismic mechanism. And of course some were less faithful than others.

McNamara's Line

The "iron-curtain counterinfiltration barrier" proposed to run across northern South Vietnam and Laos involved enormous technological and logistical challenges. While much of the material originally envisioned—sandbags, barbed wire, guard towers, and searchlights—was relatively elementary, the scale of the project was staggering. In addition, some of the elements, such as electronic sensors and a proposed "small nuclear reactor" to provide power, would have been complicated enough even outside a war zone.

"McNamara's Line" went through several stages on paper before construction began. An early proponent of the idea, Professor Roger Fisher of the Harvard Law School, suggested in early 1966 a land barrier as a counterinfiltration alternative to the costly "Rolling Thunder" bombing program the United States was conducting against North Vietnam. Fisher's suggestion was then submitted to the Defense Department for initial study. Its findings, declassified during General William Westmoreland's suit against "CBS Reports" in 1984, envisioned a static defensive line. As described in a memorandum to Joint Chiefs of Staff Chairman Earle Wheeler from General Harold K. Johnson of the army, dated March 22, 1966, the barrier was to stretch from the South China Sea to the banks of the Mekong River on the Thailand/Laos border, a distance of 360 kilometers—roughly the distance from New York City to Boston, Massachusetts. At first, the technology was kept simple; emphasis was placed on creating a gauntlet of mines, fences, and cleared territory through which it was hoped infiltration from the North would prove difficult, if not impossible.

The plan called first for offensive operations along the east-west axis of Route 9 in South Vietnam, near the Demilitarized Zone, to clear the area of opposition. After allied troops secured the region, construction was to start with clearing a 500-meter-wide strip of jungle from the Vietnamese shore near Dong Ha to Savannakhet in Laos. Troops would then construct twenty-one-foot guard towers at 400-meter intervals along the strip and equip them with sandbags, machine guns, and searchlights. The barrier area would be kept open with defoliants sprayed by aircraft. The strip of cleared territory between towers was designed to include several types of mechanical impediments, such as concertina wire, antipersonnel and antitank mines, and an eight-foot chain-link fence, topped with eighteen inches of barbed wire.

The March 22 memo listed the supplies needed for this relatively simple but rather large barrier. The total material cost was put at $105 million for the barrier, plus $11 million for a service road. Included in these figures were costs for such items as 10,868 antipersonnel mines of all types (claymore, fuse, trip wire), and 412,000 antitank mines, enough mines to seed the District of Columbia with one mine for every sixteen square meters. The total length of chain-link fence required was estimated at 720,000 meters—the distance from Boston to Washington, D.C. Other items included 72,000 floodlights, one for every five meters of territory.

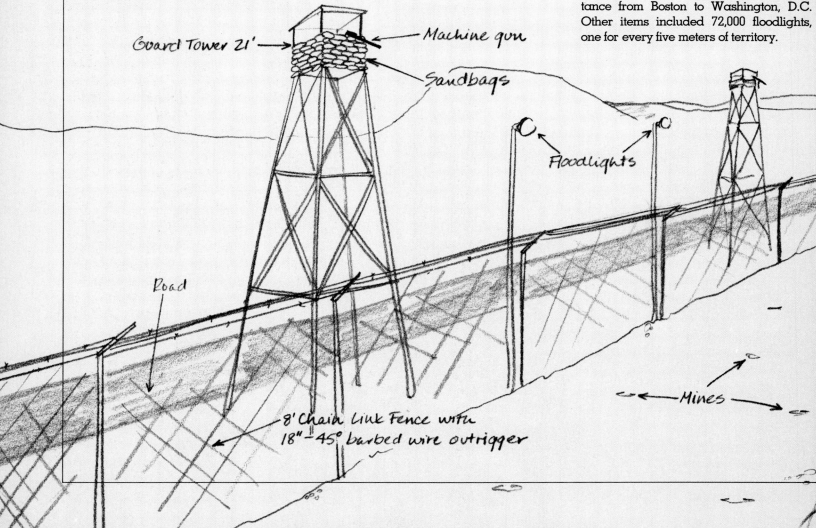

Despite the technological simplicity of this proposal, certain esoteric alternatives were mentioned in the Pentagon study, which noted that its writers had been asked to "disregard political restrictions." One alternative was to seed the defoliated strip with "atomic dust." The memo called this method impractical, since enough radioactive isotopes to saturate the strip would not have been available until 1980. Another option raised was to saturate the area with chemical agents; the memo called for mustard gas. The study described this method as "feasible."

The memorandum also estimated the manpower needs to construct and maintain the fence, and these, too, were large. Initially, the report stated, five divisions would be necessary to secure the barrier area in six months. Two hundred twenty-four "battalion months" would then be spent over one year to engineer and construct the barrier and roads. To maintain and patrol the constructed barrier, the designers estimated a force of five brigades—about 15,000 men—with one division of reserves stationed in the central Laotian panhandle as back-up, and "other forces," unspecified, in reserve from South Vietnam and Thailand.

The March 22 memorandum consti-

tuted the first calculated estimate of the size and scope of a counterinfiltration barrier. Encouraged by the study, McNamara on April 16 commissioned further work on the idea. For the task he brought in the Jason Study Group. The Jason report, delivered to McNamara on August 30, envisioned a shorter, though much beefed-up fence. The new antipersonnel barrier was widened to about 20 kilometers, with an antivehicle barrier twice as wide, and was shortened to run only 100 kilometers along the DMZ and into Laos. The Jason report also added to the fence concept a new element: electronic detection devices.

The primary electronic detection device in the revised fence was to be the air-dropped Acoubuoy, which would pick up sounds made by passing troops or vehicles. Aspirin-sized "button bomblets," too small to cause injury, would also be sown in the area of the sensors; these caused a small "pop" when stepped on, alerting the sensors to infiltration. The barrier zone would also be seeded and reseeded with antipersonnel gravel mines, each approximately the size of a teabag; these had enough punch to mangle a foot. To complete the fence, re-

connaissance planes would patrol the system with radar and infrared night-imaging equipment.

Despite the feeling that added electronic technology would make the barrier more reliable, the amount of weaponry and electronic gear was staggering: each year the line would require 19,200 Acoubuoys, 300 million button bomblets, 240 million gravel mines, 120,000 cluster bombs for air strikes, sixty-eight patrol planes for reconnaissance, and a sharply increased intelligence staff.

Although military men opposed the idea, on September 15, 1966, the defense secretary turned the project over to the Defense Communications Planning Group for further development. The reason for McNamara's pursuit of the idea in the face of opposition was suggested by Leonard Sullivan, at the time a Defense Department official in Saigon: "I guess when you get a man like McNamara, who was not terribly modest about his own capabilities, and very frustrated at the way the war was going, and somebody ran to him and said, 'Look, on analytical grounds I can show you how we're going to win the war,' he would go for that."

Given carte blanche and a "due tomorrow" time frame, the DCPG poured huge sums into developing electronic sensors, mines, and other components of the barrier. As soon as U.S. Marine construction battalions began work on the fence, however, they ran into obstacles, not the least of which were artillery harassment from NVA troops in the nearby DMZ and monsoon mud along the coastal plain. On September 17, 1967, McNamara confirmed that his barrier plan had been trimmed to only seventy-five kilometers in length. Three months later the Pentagon announced that part of the barrier was ready, but when, at last, the fence was put into operation three of the first four guard towers were promptly blown up by Communist sappers. By early 1968 the linear barrier concept was all but dead, and in March 1969 the new defense secretary, Melvin Laird, officially announced the project's termination. By then, however, elements from its stock of supplies—especially the sensors—had already been put to use elsewhere, around Khe Sanh during the 1968 siege and in Laos as part of Igloo White.

← Triple Concertina Wire →

Forest Edge →

Two means of delivering sensors. Top. An airman hurls a Spikebuoy seismic sensor from a CH-3E helicopter. Above. An air-delivered seismic intrusion detector is released by a PV-2 Neptune, used to drop sensors because of its accurate navigation system. As AAA defenses along the Ho Chi Minh Trail grew, delivery by F-4 jets became the norm.

An infrared sensor called PIRID, for Passive Infrared Intrusion Detector, could detect minute temperature changes in its range but also attracted insects, which caused it to malfunction.

All sensors worked on batteries and thus were effective for only a limited time. They could not be recovered or recharged. When picked up or handled in any way they were designed to self-destruct, a feature designed to prevent prying enemy soldiers from learning how they worked. Their miniature transmitters went into action either when something activated them or when they were commanded to via radio. The sensors passed on their electronic impulses or the sounds they detected to relay aircraft hovering nearby or directly to intelligence or command centers in the air or on the ground.

Acoustic sensors often transmitted the sounds around them as reliably as a police "bug." On one occasion a burst of excited conversation told the listening technicians that the enemy had discovered an Acoubuoy. The listeners next heard the sounds of the tree in which it hung being chopped down, then the cry of a soldier who had been hit by the falling tree. Another Acoubuoy recorded the shouts and honks of truck drivers impatient to get under way. While the trucks were still moving out, the airplanes called in by ground controllers monitoring the sensors could be heard approaching, then came the sound of bombs exploding.

Most sensors were camouflaged in some way. Acoubuoys and their small parachutes were mottled with jungle colors. Seismic detectors, which looked like fat darts with their ground-piercing nose and tail fins for stability, had an antenna that was supposed to look like a defoliated branch. Some air-dropped sensors were built to resemble debris on the forest floor. One ingenious model looked like dog feces and was thus called "Turdsid." But before it was put into production someone remembered that few dogs, if any, roamed the Southeast Asian jungles. Turdsid was redesigned to look like a piece of wood.

The success of the sensors depended on a precise knowledge of their location, which was plotted on a map or stored in a computer. A mistake of a few hundred yards could be crucial to the effectiveness of an artillery attack or a bombing raid. When American troops at Khe Sanh came under siege in January 1968, thousands of sensors originally intended for the McNamara Line were distributed in such haste around the base that their whereabouts were not always known. Prop-driven navy P-2 Neptune patrol bombers were favored for sensor drops at first because of their excellent navigational gear, but the slow-moving Neptunes proved to be too vulnerable to antiaircraft gunners. After helicopters and several other craft were tried, the job was finally entrusted to the multipurpose F-4 fighter-bombers.

The pattern and density with which sensors were

seeded were also critical. While a signal from a lone detector provided little useful intelligence, a half-mile-long sensor "field" generated data profiling the size, direction, and speed of an enemy party. Even with a field that large a half-mile-long convoy traveling at ten miles an hour would pass beyond the sensor's signals in only ten minutes. A bomber that needed a half-hour to get from base to target would be too late to hit the enemy.

Finally, sensors proved vulnerable to enemy intelligence. They could be easily destroyed if found and they could also be avoided, since the number of sensors required to saturate all possible avenues of enemy movement would have been astronomical. In addition, they transmitted their intelligence by radio, which was subject to jamming or deceptive imitation. Camouflaging them only reduced the likelihood of their being found. Anti-handling devices—the self-destruct mechanism—provided some protection against the enemy learning how the devices worked. But no device is foolproof, and some intact sensors fell into enemy hands. The more the enemy could learn about them, the greater his chances of devising countermeasures. The enemy's most common countermeasures were also the simplest. One was to hide trails; USAF aircraft could not seed with sensors trails they did not know existed. The other was to use decoy infiltration groups—a fairly hazardous job. Groups too small to be worth hitting would travel selected trails digging shelters. When the decoy group used the trail, the shelters would serve as cover against U.S. bombs. Since most area weapons like the CBU relied on saturating the area with thousands of pellets or fragments, simple earth shelters provided perfectly adequate protection. But despite the successful enemy deception ploys, sensors played a vital role in the U.S. intelligence and interdiction effort. They proved themselves at Khe Sanh.

An electronic ambush

Sensors were still a military secret when General Westmoreland decided to reinforce the U.S. garrison at Khe Sanh late in 1967. But the availability of the new detection devices was a major factor in the general's decision to dig in and defend the outpost against the four North Vietnamese divisions—the 307th, 320th, 327th, and 320C—converging on it. Seed planes were urgently called in and thousands of sensors dropped on the area around the base starting on January 20, 1968. Time was too short to train the marines stationed at Khe Sanh to monitor the electronic gadgets, so air force technicians were flown in to do the job. Carrier-based bombers and nearby heavy artillery stood by to respond to troop movements picked up by the sensors.

The sensor field went to work immediately, helping those inside the base know what was going on around them and preparing them for attacks throughout the siege.

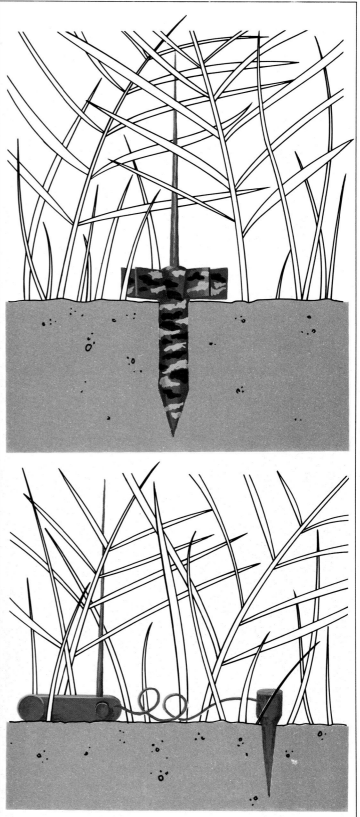

Two sensors used in Southeast Asia were the ADSID (top) and the PSID (above). ADSIDs were part of the Igloo White network, while PSIDs were used by troops to set ambushes. The spikelike object picks up movement and sends signals to the PSID's transmitter (left) which relays the signal to a distant receiver (not shown).

One night in March, sensors near Route 9, the east-west road that was the main approach to Khe Sanh, began to signal that something was afoot. One by one, the sensors came to life. The number of minutes a particular sensor remained activated told the monitors the length of the enemy column: an entire regiment. The sequence in which the sensors clicked on indicated direction: The regiment was headed toward Khe Sanh. The interval between sensor signals showed how fast the troops were moving.

Officers at the Khe Sanh command post added the data from the sensors to information gathered on reconnaissance missions, plotted the enemy's most likely assembly points, and estimated the regiment's probable course for the next few hours. Then they drew a box on their maps around the projected location of the regiment at a specific time several hours hence. The "box" was to be blanketed simultaneously by firepower from aircraft and artillery, each striking a different area within the box.

Six A-6 Intruders on an aircraft carrier at Yankee Station 100 miles out to sea from Da Nang were already on alert and loaded with 15,000 pounds of bombs each. Artillerymen at Camp Carroll, ten miles east of Khe Sanh, stood by their long-range 175MM guns. The marines manning 105MM guns and mortars at Khe Sanh were also counting the minutes. When the predetermined time for the strike arrived, word flashed to the carrier. The Intruders nosed into the sky under radar control. A computer aboard the airborne "sky spot" command center used the target coordinates, desired bomb pattern, and time of impact to calculate the jets' altitude and flight path along with the precise second the bombs were to be released. The computer followed the Intruders' progress by radar. At Camp Carroll, meanwhile, soldiers coordinated artillery shells to arrive at the same moment as the A-6s' bombs on the NVA troops in the computerized box.

The first few companies of the NVA regiment moving along Route 9 were now in the target area. The enemy commanders as yet had no cause for apprehension; all was quiet. Not until the tail end of the regiment entered the box did the first distant whine of a jet engine shatter the stillness. Suddenly 90,000 pounds of explosives rained down on the Communists. The 175s from Camp Carroll hit at almost the same time along with the 105s from Khe Sanh. The "electronic ambush," for that is what it was, set the sky ablaze and turned the gentle green hills of Khe Sanh into an inferno. The heavy guns from Camp Carroll marched their shells in an orderly line along three sides of the deadly box. Marine gunners at Khe Sanh stitched up the fourth side nearest the base.

The NVA regiment, now scattered on either side of the road, disintegrated under the massive firepower. Casualties were so high that only one North Vietnamese company reached the perimeter defenses at the southeast corner of the Khe Sanh base, and it was thrown back by waiting ARVN troops. There were no American casualties.

Firebase Crook

A year and a half later and 650 kilometers south sensors played a large role once again in a similar drama on a smaller and scruffier stage. The scene was a circular scab of bare red earth scraped by American soldiers from the verdant countryside in Tay Ninh Province, a ragged ring of sandbag bunkers and howitzers and poncho tents and lean-tos called Firebase Crook. Barbed wire and claymore mines filled the no-man's land beyond its outer ring. From the air the series of cleared circles around the base gave it the look of a bull's eye.

Earlier firebases had served as everything from artillery emplacements to back-country comfort stations, but Crook, built in spring 1969, and other firebases of its generation existed primarily to lure the enemy into battle. Men on the base were not expected to do the bulk of the fighting; it was surrounded by ground sensors to track the enemy so American firepower from the air and the ground could be unleashed on attacking forces. Patches of cover had been deliberately left around the base to draw Communist patrols. In June 1969, men of the 25th Infantry Division manned Crook with the division's Battery A, 7th Battalion, 11th Artillery, there to operate the base's six 105MM howitzers. The firebase had been quiet all spring, but that was soon to change.

After dark on June 5, seismic detectors beyond the base perimeter picked up signs of movement. Zeroing in on the area in which the sensors were activated, artillery from Crook and other nearby firebases shelled the site. Helicopter gunships and jet aircraft added their muscle to the barrage. The next morning patrols from Crook found seventy-six enemy dead. That night the sensors triggered again. This time ground surveillance radar also detected small bands on the move, corroborating the sensor signals. Again the howitzers and mortars saturated the area. There were signs that the enemy forces were still on the move so Night Hawk helicopter gunships equipped with night-vision devices and rapid-fire miniguns were called in. Crew men on the gunships spotted large concentrations of enemy troops, and more help was summoned from the air force. AC-119 "Shadow" gunships arrived to strafe the ground with their Gatling guns. Enemy soldiers kept advancing, and just before dawn a few reached the outer ring of Firebase Crook where they were quickly repelled. That day, the sun rose over a battleground littered with 323 Communist dead and 10 who were taken prisoner. Only one American had been killed in action and three wounded over the two nights. The sensors had done their job again.

It was primarily the alerts from the sensors and then the firepower that could be called in that enabled lightly manned outposts like Firebase Crook to turn the odds in their own favor. But there were other gadgets not normally found in an infantryman's field pack that proved helpful in gathering intelligence. The ground surveillance radar that was also on duty at Firebase Crook was one such device. The detector known as the "people sniffer" was another.

Ground surveillance radar was used in combat for the first time in Vietnam. Too heavy to accompany troops on patrol, radar rigs were normally assigned to firebases such as Crook. The radar could detect movement as far away as 1,500 meters for the smallest mechanism, 18,000 for the largest. The radar detected moving bodies and transmitted their position to the operator via headphones or on a small screen. Its effectiveness depended heavily on the alertness of an operator detecting the transient indication of movement. Line-of-sight scanners could not penetrate hills or trees or see around corners, but they could pick up moving objects within their relatively narrow range. Ground radar often helped an ambush patrol intercept an enemy detachment. Storms threw them off because the scanners recorded any movement including bushes and branches waving in the wind.

The ground radar was often directly connected to a base's fire direction center, and anything spotted on radar was immediately shelled. This practice harmed civilians venturing out after curfew, as well as nocturnal animals, and it was questionable on military grounds alone. By failing to distinguish between important and unimportant targets, indiscriminate radar-induced shelling of small targets sometimes warned a large, undetected Communist force. It told the enemy which areas to avoid because they were covered by radar.

Late in the war the technology improved; Lincoln Labs at the Massachusetts Institute of Technology developed a radar device that could electronically weed out false signals caused by wind and more accurately detect human movement. The MIT radar also had a 360-degree scanning range, which was especially welcome in a war where trouble could come from any direction.

"People sniffers" attempted to penetrate the jungle canopy with a chemical nose. The most successful people sniffer was mounted on helicopter gunships, but a portable device developed by General Electric Corporation at the army's request included a backpack connected to a hoselike detector. Attached to a rifle, the detector drew in an air sample from the direction the weapon was aimed and sifted it chemically for ammonia, which is present in human sweat and urine; it also searched out engine exhaust fumes. One trouble with the sniffers was that animals emit ammonia too. Explosives leave traces of ammonia as well, so that a shell crater was apt to excite a detector. Ground soldiers thought that their bulk outweighed their usefulness. Many preferred scout dogs, which had more reliable noses and did not weigh down a field pack.

The most intriguing people sniffer was an improbable combination of electronics and insects. Bedbugs become agitated when they detect humans, which they can do from fifty feet away if the humans are upwind of them. The insects were housed in a small box attached to an electronic monitor that recorded the motion of the insects when they detected humans. The monitor then sounded an alarm. This quaint mechanism could be foiled if the wind changed direction or if the bugs died.

Mechanical brains

Sensors and other electronic detectors were "dumb"—they only collected data without processing them or responding to them. The "brains" of the automated warfare were provided by computers, which could rapidly process the reams of information generated by the sensors. The computer revolution that would transform American life in the 1970s and 1980s, however, was still a dim glow on a distant horizon in the early years of the war. One of the first computers ever used to store and analyze military intelligence was the Univac 1005, which the 25th Infantry Division installed at its Cu Chi headquarters in 1966. The men of the 25th fed into the Univac data from intelligence and operation reports broken down by region. The computer stored the information and correlated it on request. The large Univac, which filled a van, had only a few hundred lines of program memory (modern home computers have much more capability). But it proved to be a valuable tool at the time.

One of the 25th's main worries was the location of Vietcong mines. Every time a mine was discovered, data on its type and location were punched into the Univac. When enough information had been accumulated the computer was able to pinpoint the location of undetected mines by correlating data on known sites. Shifts in the enemy's mining pattern could be readily detected. The division's commanders also used the computer to analyze their various tactical options.

The Combined Intelligence Center at U.S. Military Assistance Command in Saigon acquired its first computer soon afterward, the IBM 1400 with a memory of sixteen kilobytes, one-fourth that of the modern Commodore 64 home computer. Others with more power were gradually added, including the IBM 360 and the IBM 1311, which were used primarily for map overprints. The computer accumulated intelligence on the concentrations of enemy troops and printed the information directly on maps that were then distributed to the various commands. The areas where the chance of encountering the enemy was greatest were specially outlined.

Computers also simplified and hastened the painstaking chore of interpreting aerial reconnaissance photos, one of the main sources of intelligence. The AR-85 Viewer-Computer interpreted ground positions, distances, elevations, and other data in aerial photographs. A photo interpreter could set the viewer to roll the film at a specified speed, halt it on command, and magnify any piece of it as much as thirty times without losing resolution. Prints could be made from the film in less than forty seconds. Photo interpreters still needed a great deal of skill, but they could work much more quickly with the AR-85.

Computer-aided photo processes made Vietnam the first war to be illustrated by "pictomaps." Pictomaps were mosaics of aerial photos adjusted to eliminate distortion and overprinted with standard symbols from topographic maps, such as waterways and elevation. In combining the more enduring geographic features of an area with changes in village layouts, trails, and other manmade phenomena, the pictomaps provided accurate and up-to-date pictures of much of Vietnam.

By the time the American command launched Igloo White in 1967, computers had become the centerpiece of the automated battlefield. Igloo White itself became fea-

sible only after sensors were combined with lightweight computers carried on the orbiting relay aircraft and the sophisticated high-speed computers at the command center at Nakhon Phanom, Thailand. The steady refinement and miniaturization of computer technology, especially advances in large-scale integrated circuits, resulted in smaller, lighter, and more reliable machines with memories that expanded geometrically. Between 1962 and 1972, the size of the average airborne computer shrank from two cubic feet to one-tenth of a cubic inch; its power demands declined from 250 watts to 25; its cost dropped from $16,000 to $8,000. Its reliability, meanwhile, increased from 330 hours between breakdowns to 150,000 hours. (Military computers, however, lagged behind the civilian market, which called for more advanced machines.)

It was the development of the microchip that trans-

formed military computers as it revolutionized their counterparts in American offices and homes. Computers were coming into full flower at about the same time that the American commitment in Vietnam was beginning to wind down. By then they were no longer intriguing battlefield accessories but center-stage participants in the most vital decisions. Computers in aircraft gathered and collated intelligence with only minimal human assistance from crew men standing by in case the equipment malfunctioned. They orchestrated the collection of data before an attack and then guided the attack itself, plotting flight paths and bomb release times. And they did it all at maximum speed and with minimum risk to friendly forces.

Vietnam posed unique problems to normal intelligence-gathering techniques. The country itself provided convenient hide-outs for Communist soldiers and made it difficult for reconnaissance patrols to find them without themselves being discovered. It was also nearly impossible to train reliable spies. CIA analyst Sam Adams told a Congressional subcommittee that, at the time of the 1968 Tet offensive, the U.S. had 1 reliable agent in the Vietcong while 30,000 VC spies had penetrated American compounds and the South Vietnamese military and government. As a result, much of the day-to-day business of gathering intelligence was done from the air. The aerial reconnaissance over North and South Vietnam, Laos, and Cambodia was unlike anything practiced in previous wars.

RF-101 Voodoo reconnaissance jets at Tan Son Nhut air base in 1965. One of the near jet's several cameras is exposed. Inset. Air force reconnaissance photo interpreters wear caps and gloves to keep the film spotless.

The techniques for seeing and recording enemy territory, in fact, had evolved beyond the processes identified with the word "photography."

Airborne detection

Images of the foe and his terrain were captured with conventional cameras and television cameras with light intensification devices, with radar and airborne infrared devices, and with the aid of telescopic "target locator" systems and giant "light bombs" that worked like flash bulbs to illuminate the countryside. They were taken from satellites 150 miles up, from SR-71 "Blackbirds" scanning 100,000 square miles an hour as they flew three times the speed of sound at 85,000 feet, from R-F4 Phantom jets, from converted C-47 and C-130 cargo planes, from helicopters, and from prop-driven army OV-1 Mohawks flying as low as 1,500 feet. The images were sometimes snapped by human hands and sometimes registered automatically in pilotless drones and remote-controlled craft, some scarcely larger than model planes. They could be relayed electronically to display screens on the ground while a recon aircraft was still in the air. Or the film bearing the images could be processed back at headquarters, as 3 million feet of it was in Saigon every month at the height of the war.

The expanding technology of aerial image-making made it possible to see virtually anything, from any elevation and in all weather, with remarkable precision. The 150-mile-high spy satellites, taking advantage of the fact that haze and turbulence are less intrusive in high-altitude photography, produced pictures in which individual trucks could be recognized. Photo reconnaissance planes at 15,000 feet could capture a scene in such detail that the fine strands of radio wires were visible. The fireworkslike "light bombs" detonated a few seconds after they were released to turn midnight into noon with a candlepower equivalent to 4,000 sixty-watt light bulbs. The flash lasted just long enough for a photograph to be snapped.

Manned recon planes contained a variety of devices to make visual observation and photography easier. The army's Visual Airborne Target Locator System (VATLS), developed in 1966, was a high-powered telescope mounted on a stabilized inertial platform that automatically recorded its position in relation to its starting point the way a missile or a jet airliner does. When an observer at the scope sighted a potential target, the data on the platform's position together with the angle and direction of the scope combined to pinpoint the site on the ground for artillery or tactical air strikes. VATLS proved far quicker and more accurate than even the best map readers. From 1968 on, air force gunships like the AC-119 and AC-130 were equipped with low-light-level television cameras and screens, which allowed the gunships to track and fire on the enemy at night. Another advanced sensor used in the skies over Vietnam was side-looking radar (SLAR), which used a "synthetic aperture" to form a highly refined radar image of objects on the ground. Some SLAR systems also used moving target indicators to highlight moving objects.

Airborne infrared devices recorded the heat and infrared light emitted by different objects on the ground and converted the radiation to images, either on a photograph or on a screen. In World War II infrared cameras uncovered hidden camps and gun batteries by detecting the difference between freshly cut camouflage and live vegetation. In Vietnam a detailed infrared "picture" of an area was produced with the aid of powerful aerial searchlights covered with filters that permitted only infrared radiation to pass through. While invisible to the unaided eye, a beam from an eighteen-inch searchlight in a helicopter could illuminate an area more than a mile away.

Another infrared detector could identify "hot spots" on the ground, such as engines or campfires, by picking up the heat they emitted, even when they were concealed by the jungle canopy. This form of aerial intelligence-gathering demanded corroboration, however, because a hot spot could just as easily be a fresh shell crater or a herd of water buffalo as a North Vietnamese outpost. As infrared heat sensors gradually became more sophisticated, they provided more elaborate pictures of the area under scrutiny. The use of infrared detection in Vietnam reached its apex with the introduction of "forward looking infrared" sensors mounted on the AC-130 gunships patrolling the Ho Chi Minh Trail.

The film used in air reconnaissance missions was normally processed soon after the plane landed and then sent to photographic interpreters. But in Vietnam even this operation was advanced a notch. Automatic film processors attached to the airborne cameras developed the film on board the aircraft as it was exposed. It was then fed through a scanner that converted the developed film into radio signals that were transmitted to a ground station. There the image was reconstructed from the signals and flashed onto a high-resolution TV screen, and interpreters could get a preliminary look only minutes after the picture was taken.

Most photo reconnaissance planes could fly high enough to stay clear of antiaircraft fire, but planes on visual reconnaissance flights enjoyed no such luxury. The ideal aircraft for low-altitude reconnaissance missions would make no noise whatever, which is why Lockheed produced the almost noiseless YO-3A single-seater in 1970. Powered by a heavily muffled 210-horsepower engine, the propeller-driven plane announced itself to an enemy gunner only when it was too late for him to react. The YO-3A was stocked with various detection devices and for a time was used on night missions. The aircraft proved too specialized for its expense, however, and it quietly faded from use.

Remotely piloted vehicles

The idea of flying a plane by remote control was not new to Vietnam. President John Kennedy's brother Joseph had been killed during an experimental radio-controlled flight in World War II. Kennedy and another crew man were to fly a B-24 loaded with high explosives (making the plane itself a huge bomb) partway to the German missile complex at Peenemünde and then bail out. The B-24 was to be guided to the target by radio from a trailing plane. But Kennedy's bomber blew up before he and the other could escape. The German Luftwaffe experienced moderate success in attacking Allied ships during the invasion of Anzio in February 1943, with guide bombs and missiles controlled via radio by a trailing "mother" aircraft. The radio-controlled bomb was guided to crash into the target ship and explode. It worked if the guiding plane was not shot down and if the pilot in the distant mother ship guessed the correct dive angles and directions. Often he could not and by the time he knew the glider was off target, it was too late to change its course effectively.

The main problem of the radio-controlled plane was that it was piloted from a distant location by a pilot who could not see the target from the plane's perspective. The

Its mission complete, a post–Vietnam Teledyne Ryan RPV reconnaissance model is recovered in midair by a CH-3 helicopter, which will return it to base. The remotely piloted vehicle was launched from a DC-130.

controller in the mother ship also had to keep in view both the target and the remote-controlled plane, making him vulnerable to enemy fire. Americans tried using television to put the controller's eyes back in the cockpit. The first television glide bomb was tested during World War II, but the early, poor-quality television cameras were bulky and proved unreliable in the rough environment of war.

Another kind of pilotless aircraft, the drone, avoids the problems of having to be under the continuous control of a remote operator. They are simple, preprogrammed machines and once launched are beyond control. A drone can take off and fly a programmed route, changing altitude and direction according to a specific schedule, but cannot, for example, see a thunderstorm ahead and "decide" to go around it. The usual drone, serving to conduct aerial photography, flies a routine of oval patterns and returns near the launch point. Some drones, used as practice targets for AA units, can mimic the tactics of an enemy plane but, again, usually in a preplanned pattern.

A sophisticated drone is the cruise missile, actually a

small airplane with a jet engine, warhead, radar, and a computerized TERCOM navigation system. The cruise missile finds its way by scanning the terrain with its radar and comparing it with a preprogrammed route held in its memory. But beyond correcting its course to hold to its programmed route and "recognizing" its destination, a cruise missile cannot change its game plan in midflight. In this sense, even a cruise missile is "dumb."

A major advantage of the drone is that it can be very small. One developed for the marines in Vietnam and used for close support photo reconnaissance missions had a wingspan of only three feet. But once detected by enemy defenses, their predictable paths make them very vulnerable. Their main defense is that their small size makes it very difficult for enemy radar to pick them up.

An RPV combines qualities of a radio-controlled airplane and a drone to avoid the limitations of each. Like a drone it has a "brain"—an onboard microcomputer—that allows it to take preprogrammed actions. Like the radio-controlled plane, it can be "flown" by a remote pilot. Because of the speed and power of small computers, it can be programmed to take contingency actions. For example, if the RPV loses its radio link to the controller the computer can return it to a preplanned flight path or order it to take a series of programmed actions until it regains radio contact. Because the RPV can fly much of the mission on its own, a human controller does not have to be in constant control of it, allowing it to fly long missions that would fatigue a controller or pilot.

Radio-controlled planes always have to be within the controller's sight, otherwise he could not effectively fly the plane. The RPV gets around this by usually including in its sensors a television camera to serve as the distant pilot's eyes. The camera can be swiveled and has a zoom capability. Thus a controller in a remote ground shelter or deep in the belly of a distant mother plane can fly the RPV as if he were in it. He can actively control the RPV, allow it to continue on its programmed course, modify its programmed mission, and search the ground or sky with the RPV's other sensors.

Not having pilots on board, RPVs do not have to carry seats, controls, instruments, life support systems and other paraphernalia to accommodate a flier. This allows the RPV to be much smaller and still have a comparable payload. Additionally, an RPV is not limited to human tolerances in its maneuvering capabilities. For example, in tests over the Pacific in 1974, a Ryan Firebee RPV defeated an F-4 fighter in aerial dogfights. One of its advantages is an ability to execute a high-speed 180-degree turn in just twenty seconds, much faster than any manned high-performance fighter. It is this package of developments, including, in addition to its microcomputers and sensors, a jam-resistant digital radio, that takes the remotely piloted vehicle a quantum jump ahead of radio-controlled airplanes and drones.

RPVs were used in Vietnam starting in 1962. Over 3,000 RPV missions were flown over North Vietnam with a loss rate of only 4 percent with, of course, zero pilot losses. RPVs took 85 percent of the poststrike BDA (bomb damage assessment) photographs in Southeast Asia. High-altitude reconnaissance photography was still best taken with high-performance manned aircraft, such as the RF-4C, which was capable of carrying large, sophisticated camera systems. But successful BDA photography takes place at low altitude immediately after the strike to capture the most detail. For a manned aircraft, such a mission was rather like examining closely a hornet's nest after it had been poked with a stick.

Most air force RPVs were launched from aircraft and recovered by air. Ryan drones and RPVs without takeoff or landing gear were launched from C-130 Hercules mother ships over Laos and Cambodia from 1962 on. The small, black-painted, jet-propelled craft were carried under the mother ship's wings and launched near their mission areas to conduct reconnaissance over infiltration routes. This allowed almost all of the RPV's flying time to be devoted to flying over the target area. When the mission was completed, the RPV flew to a safe recovery area, cut its engine, deployed a parachute, and drifted earthward. Recovery helicopters would then snag the RPV by its parachute lines and haul the machine to base to recover its load of film and prepare it for the next mission. Another common way to launch and recover RPVs was from the ground off of a rail mounted on a truck. The aircraft lands by flying into a net also on board a truck.

Although used mainly for reconnaissance, RPVs in Vietnam were also tested and used in a variety of other roles. They carried chaff or radar-jamming equipment to confuse enemy radar and help manned aircraft get through. They were also tested as bomb and missile carriers and laser target-designators. The effective use of RPVs as weapons platforms or as the control aircraft for guiding "smart" weapons would effectively complete the removal of all humans (except, of course, the enemy) from the battlefield. With that in mind, developments continued on the RPV long after the war with the participation of an increasing number of manufacturers and nations.

Pros, cons, and the future

Modern technology had allowed the U.S. military in Vietnam to cross the threshold of the automated battlefield for the first time. At first appealing primarily to Defense Department civilians, who knew well that political concerns dictated keeping U.S. casualties to a minimum, the technology of remote-controlled warfare worked well enough to convince military commanders of its merits. Especially after American forces began to withdraw in 1969, ground officers began to use sensors to detect the enemy rather than risking their men, and an increasing number of fire

A LANDSAT satellite photo taken from 120 miles above South Vietnam in January 1973 shows the Saigon area with a long plume of smoke marking an oil fire at Bien Hoa.

support bases were ringed with the devices late in the war.

Automated warfare in Vietnam was not without its problems. Many commanders felt that it encouraged U.S. forces to stay on the defensive and react to enemy moves rather than taking the initiative. Also, some critics argue that the use of high-tech weaponry—both unmanned and manned—gave the U.S. military a false sense of superiority and sometimes stood in the way of clear strategic planning. And in the end, the tools of automated warfare brought the U.S. no closer to its goals in Vietnam than any other weapon, simple or sophisticated, could have done.

These drawbacks were not enough to prevent work on the tools of automated warfare from continuing after the war. Before it shut down in June 1972, the last act of the Defense Communications Planning Group was to adapt sensors for use in Europe. Other groups sprang up to carry the technological torch, including the independent Cricket Society, founded in 1974 to further sensor-related technology, and the army's REMBASS, for Remotely Mon-

itored Battlefield Sensor System. These and other groups worked throughout the 1970s on systems designed to take men out of the battlefield and thereby make real a vision of future wars iterated in October 1969 by General William Westmoreland, then the army chief of staff, to the Association of the U.S. Army: "On the battlefield of the future, enemy forces will be located, tracked, and targeted through the use of data links, computer-assisted intelligence evaluation, and automated fire control. Firepower can be concentrated without massing a large number of troops. It can rain destruction anywhere on the battlefield within minutes, whether friendly troops are present or not." In Vietnam, the U.S. had come close at times to fulfilling the general's prediction, but only time will tell whether the tools of automated warfare will continue to be used.

Epilogue: The Legacy of Technology

On June 7, 1965, commanding General William Westmoreland wrote a stark and pessimistic cable to his immediate superior in Honolulu, Admiral Ulysses S. Grant Sharp, a cable that was destined to reach the highest levels of the Pentagon and the Oval Office of the White House itself. In his cable Westmoreland described the devastating effects of the enemy's spring offensive and concluded that South Vietnam "cannot stand up successfully to this kind of pressure."

The result of Westmoreland's cable and a visit to Vietnam by Secretary of Defense Robert McNamara was the decision by President Lyndon Johnson to authorize the deployment of 200,000 combat troops to Vietnam. The first full army division to be sent was the newly organized 1st Cavalry Division (Airmobile). The choice of the 1st Cav was not coincidental, for at the time its troops made up America's, and probably the world's, most technologically advanced maneuver division. When the division landed in South Vietnam it brought with it more than 400 helicopters, more aircraft than all the South Vietnamese armed forces possessed at the time and more helicopters than the entire ARVN would have until 1971.

Westmoreland believed that the deployment of American troops could redress two crucial problems that he had identified. First, American troops would add sheer numbers to the South Vietnamese cause. Second, he believed that U.S. troops could "successfully take the fight to the VC" and "give us a substantial and hardhitting offensive capability on the ground to convince the VC that they cannot win." The 1st Cav's first major encounter with the NVA in the Ia Drang Valley, and many other battles in which U.S. forces emerged victorious, proved the general correct.

The technological superiority enjoyed by American troops as they arrived in 1965 and 1966 was limited when compared to technological advances that would come later but at the time contributed major innovations in the tactics of warfare. Americans could count on the exclusive use of the skies over South Vietnam, a vastly superior, almost unlimited supply of firepower, and a mobility unknown in previous warfare. Before American combat troops arrived, the weapons used in Vietnam were not markedly different from the weapons that the French

and Vietminh had used in the Indochina war of the early 1950s. The Vietcong in many cases were employing the same worn-out weapons inherited from an earlier generation of revolutionary guerrilla fighters, and the ARVN were often equipped with old American equipment turned over to them by the French forces. But the entry of the United States into the conflict, with the commitment of American troops, changed the texture of the war.

The "force multiplier"

The U.S. armed forces have in the past regarded sophisticated weaponry as a "force multiplier." Substantially outnumbered by the Soviet army in Europe in conventional forces, the U.S. military had become convinced that a smaller but better-equipped and better-trained force could handle a larger force equipped with less-sophisticated equipment and manned by less-adequately trained soldiers. This deeply ingrained attitude remained unchallenged in the Vietnam War, and the U.S. armed forces tended to seek deliverance from tactical problems in new or more military hardware.

Even though military, political, geographic, and climatic conditions in Vietnam were substantially different from those confronting U.S. forces in Europe, the force multiplier notion still exerted its soothing hold on American military thinking. The Vietcong and NVA regulars did not have any substantial numerical advantage over the U.S. and its allies, but in view of the experiences of many armies in combating guerrillas, it was felt that an advantage of 10-to-1 in favor of the defender was required. It was politically unthinkable that the U.S. Army in Vietnam would have this quantity of manpower available in view of the war's controversy. U.S. military leaders hoped that the technological edge enjoyed by U.S. forces would act as a force multiplier and diminish the requirement for troops that they knew they could never obtain. Pentagon analysts, in fact, calculated that the advantages of technology could allow the defending force to lower safely its numbers by more than half, to a 3.5-1 defender to guerrilla ratio.

The problem was that the general purpose weaponry and equipment available to the U.S. armed forces in the first years of the war had been developed primarily with a conventional war in Europe in mind. The army lacked tropical weather uniforms. Its soldiers still carried the eleven-and-a-half-pound M14 rifle, a weapon very suitable in Europe but less so in the tropics. Units were outfitted with a great deal of heavy equipment, which made no difference in Europe where trucks could carry it virtually anywhere along roads. Few roads traversed the jungles of Vietnam, and soldiers had to walk through the jungle, so specialized lightweight equipment was sorely needed. It took time, but eventually it came. Ripstock jungle fatigues, Alice packs, lightweight radios, and the eight-pound M16 were developed and fielded to meet the peculiar needs of the war. These new weapons and equipment were not without their problems. GIs found the ripstock fatigues more comfortable in tropical humidity than their cotton predecessors, even though initially they did not wear as well. The adoption of the M16 with its light ammunition made a great deal of sense, even though its new propellant gave it a tendency to jam.

Much of the equipment developed for troops in Vietnam was not very "high tech." Beehive artillery rounds were just a new twist on the centuries-old artillery round known as a "canister" that had been used by the U.S. Army since the revolutionary war. Cluster bombs had been used since the Spanish Civil War of the late 1930s. But advances in ordnance technology made these new variations far more lethal than their progenitors.

The jet fighter, the helicopter, the M113 armored personnel carrier, and artillery all helped establish the texture of the war. Except for the helicopter, these weapons had been developed for fighting against a mechanized Soviet army on the temperate plains of Europe. In many cases, the equipment or the tactics developed for these weapons was inappropriate for Vietnam. The task of adapting these weapons to the new circumstances fell to the soldiers and commanders in Vietnam.

When the M113 armored personnel carrier was first introduced into ARVN service, American advisers taught their Vietnamese students the tactics they had conceived for European plains warfare. In theory, the M113 was to serve as a "battlefield taxi." Its light armor was sufficient to protect its squad only from small-arms fire and artillery airbursts on the approach to the battle line. But when the enemy's force was finally met, the infantry squad disembarked and carried out the infantry attack on foot. Vietnam made a shambles of these tactics. ARVN infantry would pour out into a rice field or into elephant grass, lose all mobility, and be chopped to pieces, as they were at the battle of Ap Bac in 1963. The ARVN's American advisers helped change these tactics, teaching ARVN soldiers to fight from the M113 and use its mobility to overcome terrain difficulties. While APCs in Europe could expect to encounter enemy tanks, early in the Vietnam War the enemy had no armored vehicles, so these offensive cavalry tactics proved very suitable. The M113 was adapted to this new role by the addition of gun shields on the hull roof to protect its troops, who now rode on top of the vehicle. The new vehicle, which was also more heavily armed, became known as the ACAV, for armored cavalry.

Ultimate high-tech weapons like the high-performance jet aircraft were also adapted for new uses in Vietnam. The B-52, developed to wage nuclear war against Soviet industrial targets, was modified to carry tons of simple conventional bombs for tactical purposes in South Vietnam. The F-105 tactical nuclear strike aircraft had its sleek lines interrupted by the protrusion of conventional bomb pylons, ECM gear, and Southeast Asia olive drab and brown camouflage paint.

The helicopter made what many consider the most successful adaptation to Vietnam. The U.S. Army had for some time shown interest in air mobility for its troops but had been unable to battle test thoroughly the new tactic. Vietnam demonstrated that the helicopter was much more than the convenient utility aircraft it had been handy for bringing forward supplies or transporting commanders. The helicopter had become a vital offensive weapon essential in waging a war without conventional battle lines.

Technology became the handmaiden of U.S. strategy in Vietnam. U.S. forces were not permitted to invade North Vietnam to attack the NVA at its roots. Nor were the political leaders of the U.S. enthusiastic about drafting sufficient manpower to permit an invasion and occupation of the Ho Chi Minh Trail in Laos and Cambodia. The use of sophisticated and costly new weapons was politically and diplomatically more acceptable than the more traditional strategic alternative of increased manpower. As a result, in Vietnam high-technology weapons and equipment became more than just force multipliers, they became force substitutes. Jet aircraft bombed military targets in Laos and Cambodia because a conventional invasion was out of the question. Igloo White sensors vigilantly scouted the wilds of the Ho Chi Minh Trail in lieu of human patrols. And AC-130 Spectres and jet fighter-bombers raided the trail's supply lines in the place of a more traditional strangulation of enemy logistics by ground units. In some cases the expectations placed on these technical means were too great. Was it realistic to expect that automated methods could prevent so much equipment and so many men from being sent south on the trail that support for NVA forces in the South would dry up? Was it realistic to expect that *limited* air strikes against military and industrial targets in North Vietnam would cripple their war effort when it had been evident over Germany in World War II that a determined enemy could withstand years of merciless *unrestricted* aerial bombings? The exaggerated expectations placed on these weapons and their crews were often based on the ill-conceived hopes of military and political leaders, lacking any realistic basis in the technical and tactical capabilities of the weapons.

Beyond Vietnam

Inappropriate though some of the new weaponry proved for fulfilling the high hopes of American commanders for success in Vietnam, the technological aspects of the war have had far-reaching effects on the U.S. armed forces. Vietnam subtly changed the nature of modern conventional warfare in ways that were only beginning to be felt a decade after the war. In years to come, it is likely that many a military historian will look back to Vietnam to find the roots of a contemporary tool of war.

Vietnam greatly accelerated the development of military electro-optical systems like the laser and night vision devices. Early laser devices had fairly low-energy outputs, and so their peculiar optical qualities were exploited to develop bomb and missile guidance systems. Laser-guided bombs have become commonplace since Vietnam and soon will be obsolete, partly because laser beams can be deflected or diffused in poor weather conditions or in the smoke and haze of the battlefield. Newer precision guidance systems, on the drawing boards right now, will rely on imaging infrared seekers mated with microcomputers that are able to distinguish targets on the battlefield even on a cloudy, moonless night, all without the aid of a human hand or brain in the guidance circuit.

But there is little prospect that lasers themselves will soon depart the battlefield. One of the least known, but potentially most revolutionary, military uses of the laser received its first test in the U.S. during the later years of the Vietnam War. U.S. bombers over North Vietnam had elaborate means to jam the radar guidance systems of enemy-guided missiles and antiaircraft guns. But the antiaircraft guns could still prove hazardous when aimed by their human crew. No obvious electronic countermeasure existed to deal with a human gunner, or so it seemed until the late 1960s when some unrecognized engineer realized that the beam from a low- or medium-powered laser could temporarily or permanently blind the human eye if properly aimed.

This led to a little-known program (called OWL-D) aimed at developing an aircraft pod with a sensor to detect the flash of antiaircraft fire and a guidance system to aim a medium-powered laser at the gun. A short burst of intense laser light would be fired at the gun, blinding any hapless member of the crew aiming his weapon at the aircraft overhead. Since the late 1960s, work on lasers has continued in the U.S. and the U.S.S.R. in order to field a variety of medium-energy laser weapons capable of destroying optical sensors like tank gun sites and that most vulnerable optical sensor of all, the human eye. Although such weapons may one day change the nature of conventional war, all parties involved in their development are extremely reluctant to discuss this frightening weaponry, knowing that public knowledge of it would result in considerable uneasiness.

Military technology developed as a result of the Vietnam War has affected other, low-tech areas as well. The grim world of ordnance development has also witnessed its own unrecognized revolution. Although sleek fighter planes, imposing battle tanks, and behemoth warships may attract most public attention in war, it is the mundane and simple artillery piece that does most of the killing. On the eastern front in World War II, Soviet artillery accounted for over 80 percent of German casualties. Vietnam saw the first use of a new generation of cluster munitions. These differed from earlier and cruder cluster munitions in the sophistication of their fusing and detonating systems. A bomb could dispense dozens of tiny little mines or bomblets that could explode on impact or land and await the footstep of an ill-fated soldier or civilian before detonating. Until Vietnam, CBUs were designed to be dropped from aircraft, but after the war, a similar kind of projectile was designed for use by ground artillery. Unlike a conventional artillery projectile filled with high explosives, an improved conventional munition, or ICM, contains dozens of self-detonating small grenades, each lethal for several dozen yards. With its newfound ability to use cluster munitions, artillery has become far more deadly than ever before. Indeed, the development of these and other new types of ordnance with increased destructive capability has led some military analysts, including military historian John Keegan, to suggest that a conventional war could cause the deaths of as many people as a war waged with tactical nuclear weapons.

Besides impact-detonating grenades, new scatterable mines have been developed for firing from artillery. Mine warfare had always been a tedious affair of planting mines like so many lethal tulip bulbs. But with an artillery scattering system, a minefield of small but extremely deadly mines can be sprayed rapidly over a wide area. The microelectronics in these mines makes it possible to render them inactive after a set amount of time, making it possible for an army later to transit an area previously made unsafe to an enemy force. The tank's Achilles' heel remains its tracks, which can be blown off by a relatively small explosive charge. These new artillery-scattered mines are cheap and can be deployed in the midst of an attacking tank force, either disabling many of the tanks or forcing them to stop and begin the laborious process of clearing the mines.

Helicopters have also gone through a remarkable transformation since Vietnam. Recent helicopter designs have stressed the incorporation of armor and rugged composite materials into the aircraft's skin to resist the impact of small-arms fire, the main enemy of helicopters in Vietnam. A single rifle bullet in the wrong spot of a Vietnam-era chopper could bring it down. This lesson has been heeded by the developers of newer helicopters, like the heavily armored AH-64 Apache attack helicopter and the UH-60 Blackhawk troop helicopter, the successor to the UH-1 Huey. The UH-60 proved its soundness during the American invasion of Grenada in 1983. During the short attack one UH-60 was struck over twenty times by heavy machine-gun fire. This would have been more than sufficient to destroy a Huey, but the UH-60 successfully completed its mission.

Electronic warfare

After Vietnam, the most dramatic growth in U.S. military technology occurred in electronic warfare and electronic countermeasures, popularly called by the services EW and ECM. ECM gear aims at defeating an opponent's electronic devices, particularly his radars and radio communications. This can be done actively though the use of chaff or jamming or passively in the form of "stealth" aircraft design, as employed by the Vietnam-era SR-71, which makes radar identification of an object more difficult. The U.S. Air Force and Navy were badly stung by North Vietnamese surface-to-air missiles and radar-directed antiaircraft guns during the initial phases of the air war over the North. This bitter lesson led to the acceleration of studies of ECM equipment, to the point where, by 1980, the U.S. led the world in this type of technology. Its battlefield implications were no more evident than during the air war over Lebanon in 1982 when the Israelis, using U.S.-supplied ECM equipment (and considerable tactical skill), shot down more than eighty Syrian aircraft while losing only a single aircraft. EW and ECM gear rendered Syria's air defense missiles nearly useless, and the coordination of its fighters was made impossible by ECM techniques that had been pioneered by U.S. fliers over Vietnam.

While the Vietnam War served as a catalyst to accelerate the development of some new military technologies, it also to a degree distorted the shape of American defense research and equipment procurement. In the 1960s, the army was in the midst of a major modernization program aimed at providing the U.S. forces in Europe with a qualitative edge to compensate for the Soviet army's substantial quantitative advantages. A whole interrelated family of new weapons was in development to accomplish this goal. This included a new tank, the MBT70; a new infantry combat vehicle, the mechanized infantry combat vehicle (MICV); new air defense missile and gun systems, the Mauler and Vigilante; and a new attack helicopter, the AH-56 Cheyenne. These programs and others had to be dropped or postponed in part because of the drain of financial resources into Vietnam. Vietnam did not slow down research and development throughout the military, however, and a host of new weapons was developed during the Vietnam era for use in future air wars. These included the air force F-15 air combat multipurpose fighter, E-3A airborne warning and control system (AWACS), and A-10 close air support aircraft; the navy F-14 long-range interceptor; and a host of long-range cruise missiles. By the 1980s, however, the military had started to make up for any slowdown. Under President Ronald Reagan, the U.S. began spending heavily to modernize its military, stirring no small amount of controversy.

Fundamental questions

While the military remains committed to applying principles of high technology to modern weaponry, the discussion of how well that technology has been used in the past and how it can best be applied in the future is far from over. In the 1970s, the emphasis of American strategic planning swung back to conventional war in Europe and weapons development followed suit, even though many military leaders think limited war somewhere else on the globe far more likely.

In Vietnam, the U.S. committed itself and its technology to just such a limited war, yet faced an enemy that had made a total commitment to victory. Therein lies the major paradox of the war: In spite of the fact that the incredible U.S. arsenal permitted U.S. forces to cause enormous destruction and defeat the Communists in virtually every battle of the war, these victories did not bring the U.S. the outcome it sought. General William Westmoreland maintains that "without the exploitation of technology we would not have been able to accomplish what we did. If we had not used our firepower, I would estimate that we would have taken at least twice as many casualties as we did." America's might had turned the tide when it arrived, and as long as it was used it prevented Communist victory. The technology, however, could bring the U.S. no closer to its goal of an independent South Vietnam.

Part of the problem lay in what some have identified as an American "technological imperative," a philosophy defined by Adam Yarmolinsky, a former assistant to Defense Secretary Robert McNamara, as "If you can do it, do it." A variety of observers have argued that the U.S. succumbed to that approach in Vietnam. British military correspondent W. F. K. Thompson, for example, ascribed the tendency to America's role as "the leading technological country" whose "natural reaction to any problem is to look for a technological answer." Robert Komer, designer of the CORDS program of pacification in Vietnam, also noticed the technological imperative at work. He wrote after the war that commanders were "playing out our military repertoire—doing what we were most capable and experienced at doing." He cited as one example sixty-two amphibious operations mounted in Vietnam between 1965 and 1969 that snared few enemy troops. The marines did it because they wanted practice. The landings, according to a Marine Corps historian, "not only kept the amphibious art alive . . . but advanced it by providing testing and training in a combat environment." Adam Yarmolinsky concluded, "I think that obsession with technology tended to make people overlook more fundamental questions."

The "fundamental questions" were those of strategy, and the country's leaders themselves realized, at least until 1969 when the U.S. began to withdraw, that they had not sufficiently answered those questions. A conference of top-level civilian and military policymakers in Honolulu in the summer of 1967, addressing the problem of infiltration and interdiction, agreed that an overall U.S. strategy in Vietnam was sorely lacking. Its final report stated, "A clear concise statement of U.S. strategy in Vietnam could not be established. . . . A war of attrition provides neither economy of force nor any foreseeable end to the war. . . . The existence of long-range planning for the war was not revealed." The policymakers said: "A statement of overall U.S. strategy is vital if the most effective employment of the full range of U.S. resources is to be realized in attaining U.S. objectives in Vietnam." In the absence of that strategy, it became difficult for troops and their commanders to decide how and when to use their high-tech arsenal most effectively.

Even without leading the U.S. toward its goals in Vietnam, the advanced weapons employed there suggested possible advantages of technology in a limited, counterinsurgency war. It can serve as a great equalizer, neutralizing the insurgents' greatest advantage of surprise, of being able to attack at times and places of their choosing. It successfully multiplied U.S. forces, permitting a half-million American troops to do the work that would have required a much larger force in the absence of technology. At times, especially in Laos, technology served in place of ground troops as a replacement for force, a new aspect of warfare. But technology in the Vietnam War, as in others, was not a panacea and it certainly was not a replacement for a sound, coherent strategy and the will to pursue it.

The enduring validity of this ancient truism of the science of warfare was brought home poignantly to Colonel Harry G. Summers, Jr., a U.S. delegate to the Joint Military Team, established by the peace terms of 1973. Summers was in Hanoi in April 1975, carrying out his official duties while North Vietnamese tanks and troops encircled Saigon. As the conclusion of the long Vietnam War became inevitable, Colonel Summers turned to his North Vietnamese counterpart, Colonel Tu, and with only slight exaggeration reminded him, "You know, you never defeated us on the battlefield." Colonel Tu thought for a moment and replied, "That may be so, but it is also irrelevant."

American firepower in Vietnam. Eleventh Armored Cavalry troops fire machine guns from their M113 ACAVs and M48 tanks during a "mad minute" in the Iron Triangle, War Zone C, northwest of Saigon.

Bibliography

I. Books and Articles

Abt, Col. Alan B. "Battlefield Computers." *Army* (April 1973).
"AC-130 Gunships Destroy Trucks and Cargo." *Air Force* (September 1971).
"A Formidable Antiaircraft Defense." *Army* (December 1980).
"A Guide to Army Equipment." *Army* (November 1968).
"Air Cushion Vehicles." *Army* (October 1966).
Amlie, Thomas F. "Radar, Shield or Target?" *IEEE Spectrum* (April 1982).
"AN-PPS-5 in Vietnam." *Army* (March 1968).
"Antiaircraft Artillery Vs. The Fighter Bomber." *Army* (December 1973).
Arbogast, Capt. Gordon W. "Radio Communications in Vietnam." *Signal* (April 1967).
"Army Missiles: A New Generation." *Army* (June 1973).
"Army Reveals Details on Night Vision Devices." *Aero Technology*, June 3, 1968.
"Army Seeks to Improve Ground Positioning." *Technology Week*, October 17, 1966.
"Army Weapons, Equipment Looking for a Breakthrough." *Army* (October 1971).
Asprey, Robert B. *War in the Shadows*, Vol. 2. Doubleday, 1975.
Atkeson, Brig. Gen. Edward B., "PGM, Implications for Detente." *Parameters: Journal of the Army War College* (February 1976).
Avco Corporation: The First Fifty Years. Avco Corp., 1979.
Baines, T. E. "Transportable Computers Improve Combat Support." *Signal* (July 1969).
Baldwin, Hanson W. *Strategy for Tomorrow*. Harper & Row, 1970.
Bamford, James. *The Puzzle Palace*. Houghton Mifflin, 1982.
Baxter, James Phinney, 3d. *Scientists Against Time*. Little, Brown, 1947.
Baxter, Lt. Col. William P. "Soviet Communications: Bare Bones But Secure." *Army* (August 1982).
"Benning Tests Armed Helicopters." *Army* (December 1957).
Bentley, Helen Delich. "The U.S.-Built Ports of South Vietnam." *Navy* (May 1967).
Berkman, Capt. David S. "Disc Harrow for Land Clearing." *The Military Engineer* (September-October 1969).
Besson, Gen. Frank S., Jr. "AMC's Support of Our Troops in Vietnam." *Army* (October 1967).
Bidwell, Shelford. *Modern Warfare: A Strategy of Men, Weapons and Theories*. Allen Lane, 1973.
Bielinski, Maj. Henry E. "The F-4E—A Pilot's View." *Air Force* (November 1972).
Bonds, Ray, ed. *The US War Machine*. Crown, 1978.
———. ed. *The Vietnam War*. Crown, 1979.
Bradley, M-Sgt. Ernest C. "Bridging by Helicopter." *The Military Engineer* (July-August 1967).
Brindley, John F. "Air Cargo—The Sleeping Giant." *Interavia* (January 1971).
Britt, Lt. Col. Robert W. "Mighty Mouse." *Ordnance* (March-April 1972).
Brodie, Bernard. *Decisive Battles of the Twentieth Century: The Tet Offensive*. Sedgewick & Jackson, 1976.
Broughton, Col. Jack (Ret.) *Thud Ridge*. J. B. Lippincott, 1969.
Brown, Anthony Cave. *Bodyguard of Lies*. Harper & Row, 1975.
Brown, Gen. George S. "Technology: The Mold for Future Strategy." *Strategic Review* (Spring 1973).
Brown, H. E. "Integrated Weapons Concept." *Ordnance* (September-October 1973).
"Bugs of War: Fire From Friendly Sources." *The Nation*, July 8, 1968.
Burke, John T. " 'Smart' Weapons." *Army* (February 1973).
Burke, Kelly H. "Electronic Combat: Warfare of the Future." *Armed Forces Journal* (December 1982).
Canan, James W. *The Superwarriors: The Fantastic World of Pentagon Superweapons*. Weybright & Talley, 1975.
"Cantonement Construction, Vietnam." *The Military Engineer* (May-June 1967).
"Caring for the Wounded: GAO Survey on Treatment of Civilians." *New Republic*, June 8, 1968.
Chapelle, G. L. "Water War in Vietnam." *National Geographic* (February 1966).
Chomsky, Noam, and Howard Zinn, eds. *The Pentagon Papers*. Senator Gravel Edition, Vols. 1-4. Beacon Press, 1972.
Cogol, Capt. Robert M. "Passive Defenses for Air Bases. *The Military Engineer* (November-December 1969).
Collins, Gerald W. "Conex: Logistic Wonder-Worker in Vietnam." *National Defense Transportation Journal* (May 1966).
Collins, Lt. Gen. Arthur S., Jr., "The Best—and Most For the Army's Dollar." *Army* (November 1968).
"Communications Can Corrupt Commanders." *Army* (May 1970).
Cook, Davidson E. "Massive Sealift to Southeast Asia." *National Defense Transportation Journal* (July-August 1966).
Cooke, J. J. "A New Generation of Field Artillery Computer Systems." *International Defense Review* (May 1978).
Coughlin, W. J. "Technological War." *Technology Week*, November 14, 1966.
———. "On the Use of Gas." *Missiles and Rockets*, April 19, 1965.
"C3I" (series of articles on C3I). *Army*, March 1979.
Daley, Maj. Jerome R. "The AH-1G Vs. Enemy Tanks in An Loc." *Armor* (July-August 1972).
Davis, R.M. "Helicopter Mine Sweeping Operations." *International Defense Review* (May 1978).
Deitchman, Seymour J. *New Technology and Military Power: General Purpose Military Forces For the 1980s and Beyond*. Westview Press, 1979.
Dickson, Paul. *The Electronic Battlefield*. Indiana Univ. Press, 1976.
" 'Different' War—Same Old Ingenuity." *Army* (September 1968).
"Dredging in Vietnam." *The Military Engineer* (November-December 1969).

Drendel, Lou. *C-130 Hercules in Action*. Squadron/Signal Publications, Inc., 1981.
Dunstan, Simon. *Vietnam Tracks: Armor in Battle 1945-75*. Presidio Press, 1982.
"Efficiency is the Key to U.S. Logistical Support in Vietnam." *Army* (September 1970).
"Electronic Reconnaissance in Vietnam." *International Defense Review* (August 1972).
Eliot, Maj. Gen. Fielding. "Construction in Vietnam." *Ordnance* (September-October 1966).
"Enemy Napalm in Vietnam." *Army* (August 1968).
"Equipment Review." *International Defense Review* (February 1972).
"Event Log." *Sea Power* (May 1972).
"Extraction Without a Landing Zone." *Army Aviation Digest* (April 1972).
Fallows, James. *National Defense*. Random House, 1981.
"Floating Assault Force." *Army* (February 1968).
"Fort Benning Tests Armed Helicopters." *Army* (December, 1957).
Freedman, David H. "Mini-Drones Spy Behind Enemy Lines." *High Technology* (August 1983).
Frisbee, John L. "Electronic Warfare." *Air Force* (July 1972).
———. "The Air War in Vietnam." *Air Force* (September 1972).
The Military Laser and Night Vision Market. Frost & Sullivan, 1974.
Geddas, J. Philip. "A-10—USAF Choice in the Close Air Support Role." *International Defense Review* (February 1973).
"General Abrams Listens to a Different Drum." *New York Times Magazine*, May 5, 1968.
"General Westmoreland Reports on the Vietnam Military Situation." *Department of State Bulletin*, June 17, 1968.
Gervasi, Tom. *Arsenal of Democracy II*. Grove Press, 1981.
Giap, Gen. Vo Nguyen. *How We Won the War*. Recon Publications, 1976.
Glover, Walter P. "Air Armament." *Ordnance* (May-June 1972).
Gordon, Col. Don E. *Electronic Warfare: Element of Strategy and Multiplier of Combat Power*. Pergamon Pr., 1981.
Goure, Daniel, and Gordon McCormick. "PGM: No Panacea." *Survival* (January-February 1980).
Grant, Z. "Vietnam By Computer." *New Republic*, June 15, 1968.
Green, William, and Gerald Pollinger. *The World's Fighting Planes*. Hanover House, 1959.
Griffiths, Maurice. *The Hidden Menace*. Conay Maritime Press, 1981.
Gunston, Bill. *Rockets & Missiles*. Crescent Books, 1979.
Hackworth, Col. David. "Our Great Vietnam Goof!" *Popular Mechanics* (June 1972).
Hallion, Richard P., and the editors of Time-Life Books. *Designers and Test Pilots*. Time-Life Books, 1983.
Haldeman, Steve. "Jungle Medevac." *Army Digest* (August 1969).
Halloran, Bernard F. "Soviet Armor Comes to Vietnam." *Army* (August 1972).
Hanna, Lt. Col. Robert K. "A Flyer's View on Fighter Design." *Air Force* (August 1972).
Harris, Richard, and William Ward. "A Different Kind of Courage." *Army Digest* (May 1971).
Haseltine, William. "Automated Air War." *New Republic*, October 16, 1971.
Hartmann, Gregory K. *Weapons That Wait: Mine Warfare in the U.S. Navy*. Naval Inst. Press, 1979.
Hawkins, Gains B. "Vietnam Anguish: Being Ordered to Lie." *Washington Post*, November 14, 1982.
Hayes, Maj. Gen. T.J. III. "Army Engineers in Vietnam." *The Military Engineer* (January-February 1966).
———. "A New Map for Vietnam; The Pictomap." *The Military Engineer* (1966).
Hazen, Capt. Donald E. "Pipe, Sand & Hustle." *The Military Engineer* (March-April 1969).
Heaton, Lt. Gen. Leonard D. "Medical Support in Vietnam." *Army* (October 1966).
"Helicopter Radar System." *Army* (November 1966).
Henton, Leonard. "Medical Support in Vietnam." *Army* (October 1966).
———. "Medical Support of the Soldier." *Army* (October 1969).
Hillsman, Maj. Gen. William J. "C3I Communications Vital in Integration of Force-Multipliers." *Army* (March 1979).
Hottenroth, Col. J. H. "Army Troop Construction." *The Military Engineer* (September-October 1966).
Hubbell, J. G. "Brave Men in Frail Planes: Forward Air Controller." *Reader's Digest* (April 1966).
"Huey Cobra Armed With the Tow." *Army* (December 1970).
Hunt, Richard A., and Richard H. Schultz, eds. *Lessons From An Unconventional War. Assessing U.S. Strategies*. Pergamon Pr., 1982.
Howard, Maj. John D. "An Loc: Study of U.S. Power." *Army* (September 1975).
Howze, Gen. Hamilton H. "Vietnam: An Epilogue." *Army* (July 1975).
Hymoff, Edward. "Technology Vs. Guerrillas." *Atomic Science* (November 1971).
Isby, David. *Weapons and Tactics of the Soviet Army*. Jane's Publishing Company Limited, 1981.
Joiner, Susan, and John Batchelor. *Fighting Aircraft Of World Wars One and Two*. Phoebus Publishing Co., 1976.
Kaldor, Mary, and Asbjorn Eide, eds. *The World Military Order*. Praeger.
Keegan, John. *World Armies*. Facts on File, 1979.
Kellerstrass, Lt. Col. E. J. "Drones, RPVs and Aerospace Power." *Air University Review* (September-October 1973).
Kinnard, Douglas. *The War Managers*. University Press, 1977.
Kissinger, Henry. *White House Years*. Little, Brown, 1979.
Langord, A. C., ed. *Low Light Level Imaging Systems*. Society of Photographic Scientists and Engineers, 1970.
"Laser Guided Missile Tests." *Army* (February 1972).
"Laser Printer." *Army* (December 1972).
Leslie, E. "Starlight Scope Sees in the Dark." *Radio-Electronics*, August 7, 1968.
Levy, Milton L. "Naval Air Reservists Aid Vietnam Effort." *Navy* (June 1967).

Lewy, Guenter. *America in Vietnam*. Oxford Univ. Press, 1978.

"Lifting the Fog of War (AN/TSQ-73 Missile Minder)." *Army* (July 1972).

Lippincott, Maj. W. Reeves, Jr. "RPV: Tomorrow's 'Armchair' Giant Killer." *Army* (May 1976).

Littauer, Raphael, and Norman Uphoff, eds. *The Air War in Indochina. Report of the Air War Study Group, Cornell University*. Beacon, 1972.

"Logistics for Vietnam." *Navy* (February 1966).

"Looking For a Breakthrough." *Army* (October 1971).

Loory, Stuart H. *Defeated: Inside America's Military Machine*. Random House, 1973.

Ludvigsen, Eric C. "Army Missiles: A New Generation." *Army* (June 1973).

Lussier, Maj. C. C., Jr. "The Portable Foxhole." *The Military Engineer* (July–August 1969).

Macbain, Merle. "Mines: The Forgotten Weapon." *Sea Power* (May 1980).

"Mac: Command With Airlift For Its Middle Name." *National Defense Transportation Journal* (May–June 1966).

Maclear, Michael. *The Ten Thousand Day War*. Avon Books, 1981.

Macmillan, Lt. Col. David C. "Technology: The Catalyst For Doctrinal Change." *Air University Review* (December 1977).

"McNamara's Fence." *Army* (August 1968).

Mahaffey, Maj. Gen. Fred K. "C3I for Automated Control of Tomorrow's Battlefield." *Army* (March 1979).

Manaker, 2d Lt. A. M. "Engineering Developments in Artillery Technology." *Field Artillery Journal* (January–February 1975).

Manning, Robert, and Michael Janeway, eds. *Who We Are. An Atlantic Chronicle of the United States and Vietnam*. Little, Brown, 1969.

"Manpack Personnel Detector." *Army* (November 1966).

Marshall, Brig. Gen. S. L. A. *Bird: The Christmastide Battle*. Cowles, Inc., 1968.

Mason, J. F. "Great Wall of Vietnam." *Science Digest* (April 1968).

McKinney, Col. John A. "Hai Van Pass." *Army* (June 1969).

McNeill, William H. *The Pursuit of Power*. Univ. Chicago Pr., 1982.

"Meal, Combat, Individual." *Army* (April 1971).

Menzel, Capt. Sewall H. "Automatic Ambush." *Armor* (September–October 1972).

Meselson, Matthew S. "AAAs Report on Military Use of Defoliants in Vietnam." *Scientific American* (February 1971).

Mesko, Jim. *Armor in Vietnam*. Squadron/Signal Publications, Inc., 1982.

Messey, Maj. Curtis L. "Night on the Trail." *Air Force* (January 1972).

Middleton, Cdr. W. D. "Seabees in Vietnam." *Proceedings of the Naval Institute* (August 1967).

"Military Airlift in Southeast Asia." *Air Force* (October 1972).

Millis, Walter. *American Military Thought*. Bobbs-Merrill, 1966.

Momyer, Gen. William W. *Airpower in Three Wars*. GPO, 1978.

"Monsters That Float On Air." *Army* (June 1968).

Nalty, Bernard C., George M. Watson, and Jacob Neufeld. *The Air War Over Vietnam; An Illustrated Guide*. Arco Publishers, 1981.

Narmic. *The Components and Manufacturers of the Electronic Battlefield*. American Friends Service Committee, August 1, 1971.

Nelson, B. "M.I.T.'s March 4; Scientists Discuss Removing Military Research." *Science*, March 14, 1968.

Newport, Capt. Henry S. "Inventory Controls in a Combat Zone." *Army* (August 1967).

"New Weaponry, Two Fronts." *Commonweal*, March 1, 1968.

"Night Fire Control System For the Cobra." *Army* (December 1970).

Norman, Lloyd. "Debating the Future of 'Flying Tanks.' " *Army* (February 1972).

Oberdorfer, Don. *Tet!* Doubleday, 1971.

Oliver, Capt. Edward F. "A Chain of Ships." *Proceedings of the U.S. Naval Institute* (November 1969).

Ordway, Frederick I., III, and Ronald C. Wakford. *International Missile and Spacecraft Guide*. McGraw-Hill, 1960.

O'Rourke, Lt. Cdr. B. F. "The LST in Vietnam." *Proceedings of the U.S. Naval Institute* (October 1966).

"Oval Wheels, Trucks That Walk and Tanks That Move By Touch." *Army* (June 1968).

Padfield, Peter. *Guns At Sea*. Hugh Evelyn, Ltd., 1973.

Palmer, Dave Richard. *Summons of the Trumpet*. Presidio Pr., 1978.

Pawle, Gerald. *Secret Weapons of World War II*. Ballantine Books, 1967.

Picou, Lt. Col. Lloyd J. "Call 'Falcon' For Prompt Aerial Fire Support." *Army* (June 1967).

Pisor, Robert. *The End of the Line: The Siege of Khe Sanh*. Norton, 1982.

Pitman, Dale E. "This LSD Is No Dream For Marines." *Navy* (February 1967).

"Port Bottleneck in Vietnam is Broken." *The Military Engineer* (May–June 1966).

"Precision Weaponry: The Changing Nature of Modern War." *Army* (March 1974). 17, 1965.

Prisma, L. Edgar. "Smart Bombs and Menacing Mines." *Sea Power* (June 1972).

"R&D In An Uncertain World." *Army* (September 1969).

Rasor, Dina, ed. *More Bucks Less Bang: How the Pentagon Buys Ineffective Weapons*. Fund for Constitutional Government, 1983.

Rather, C. J. "Geneva in Eclipse: Medicine as a Weapon." *The Nation*, September 9, 1968.

Robinson, Anthony, Anthony Preston, and Ian V. Hogg. *Weapons of the Vietnam War*. Bison Bks., 1983.

Ropp, Theodore. *War in the Modern World*. Duke Univ. Press, 1959.

"Safer in Vietnam." *Science Digest* (May 1968).

Sallagar, Frederick M. *Lessons From An Aerial Mining Campaign*. Rand Corp., 1974.

Schevitz, Jeffrey M. *The Weaponsmakers. Personal and Professional Crises During the Vietnam War*. Schenkman Publishing Co., 1979.

Schmid, Capt. Karl F. "Improvisations at Special Forces Medical Facility, Vietnam." *The Military Engineer* (1966).

Schultz, Mort. "A Fast Fleet That Rides on Air." *Popular Mechanics* (February 1972).

Schultz, M. "They Hunt For Floating Death; VC's Exploding Mines." *Popular Mechanics* (April 1968).

Shapley, Deborah. "The Army's New Fighting Doctrine." *New York Times Magazine*, November 28, 1982.

Sharp, Adm. U. S. Grant. *Strategy For Defeat: Vietnam in Retrospect*. Presidio Press, 1978.

"Shore Bombardment Target Location Still Plagues Navy." *Missiles & Rockets*, March 28, 1966.

Simmons, Brig. Gen. Edward H. "Marine Corps Operations in Vietnam 1969–1972." *Proceedings of the U.S. Naval Institute* (May 1973).

Smith, D. A. "Educated Missiles." *Ordnance* (1972).

Sommerberg, G. J. *Radar and Electronic Navigations*. Newnes-Butterworth, 1970.

South Carolina VFW News (November–December 1982).

"Soviet Missile Doctrine Response to Anti-tank Missile Threat." *Army* (August 1980).

Spore, John B. "Floating Assault Force: Scourge of the Mekong Delta." *Army* (February 1968).

Stallman, Lt. Cdr. T. J. "Pre-Engineered Structures." *The Military Engineer* (September–October 1967).

Stambler, Irwin. "The Changing Status of Remotely Piloted Vehicles in the U.S." *International Defense Review* (April 1974).

Stanton, Shelby N. *Vietnam Order of Battle*. U.S. News Books, 1981.

Starnes, Col. W. L. "Cam Ranh Army Airfield." *The Military Engineer* (September–October 1967).

"Steel Walls in Vietnam." *The Military Engineer* (1966).

"Stick Launching Pad." *Army* (June 1968).

"Stratcom is Worldwide." *Army* (October 1966).

Stubblebine, Brig. Gen. Albert N., III. "C3I For Automated Focus On Intelligence Picture." *Army* (March 1979).

Sturm, Ted R. "They Call It Lataf." *The Airman* (April 1966).

Summers, Harry G., Jr. *On Strategy: The Vietnam War in Context*. Army War College, 1981.

Sundarm, G. S. "Anti-jam Communications: The Spread Spectrum Solution." *International Defense Review* (May 1978).

Taylor, John W., ed. *Jane's Pocket Book of Major Combat Aircraft*. Collier Books, 1974.

Taylor, Michael J. H., and John W. R. Taylor. *Missiles of the World*. Ian Allan Press, 1972.

"The Battle For Surveillance." *Army* (November 1967).

"The Navy's Matchless Seabees at 25." *Navy* (March 1967).

"The See Capability." *Army* (May 1966).

"The Technology Explosion and The Coming Generation of Weapons and Equipment." *Army* (October 1969).

Thompson, Capt. Paul Y. "Aircraft Shelters in Vietnam." *The Military Engineer* (July–August 1969).

Thompson, Sir Robert. "Military Victory: Political Defeat." *International Defense Review* (1975).

———. "Revolutionary War in Southeast Asia." *Orbis* (Fall 1975).

Thompson, W. Scott, and Donaldson D. Frizzell, eds. *The Lessons of Vietnam*. Crane, Russak & Co., 1977.

"Tomorrow's Gunships." *Army* (March 1972).

"Tow in Vietnam." *Army Aviation Digest* (October 1972).

"Tow Missiles in Vietnam." *Ordnance* (September–October 1973).

Traffalis, J. J., and J. J. Hromadik. "Freeway to the Beach." *The Military Engineer* (January–February 1966).

"Turbine Engine Supply Management." *Army Aviation Digest* (April 1972).

Ulsamer, Edgar. "How Computers Will Fly Tomorrow's Airplanes." *Air Force* (July 1972).

———. "The 'Flyable' Smart Bomb: Adding Another Dimension to Airpower." *Air Force* (August 1972).

Verble, Keith E. "Precision Laser Target Designator: A Breakthrough." *International Defense Review* (April 1974).

"Vietnam and the Scientist; Appeal From the Left Bank." *Science*, March 1, 1968.

"Vietnam Has Lessons For Today's Army." *Army* (November 1968).

Vietnam. The History and the Tactics. Crescent Books, 1982.

Wagner, William. "Lightning Bugs and Other Reconnaissance Drones." *Armed Forces Journal International* (1982).

Wakebridge, Charles. "Electrons Over Suez." *Ordnance* (March–April 1972).

Walker, Paul F. "Precision-Guided Weapons." *Scientific American* (August 1981).

———. "Smart Weapons in Naval Warfare." *Scientific American* (May 1983).

Wallick, Paul. "Today's Arsenals." *IEEE Spectrum* (October 1982).

Walt, Gen. Lewis W. *Strange War, Strange Strategy*. Funk & Wagnalls, 1970.

"War Balloons." *Army* (April 1964).

"Weapons and Equipment: Outlook For the 1970s." *Army* (October 1970).

"Weapons Directory." *Army* (October 1966).

Weller, Jac. "Arms for Guerrilla War." *Ordnance* (November–December 1972).

Welsh, Douglas. *The History of the Vietnam War*. Galahad Books, 1981.

Westmoreland, Gen. William W. *A Soldier Reports*. Doubleday, 1976.

WGBH-TV. "America Takes Charge," Episode 5, *Vietnam, a Television History*, 1983.

Whitside, Thomas. *The Withering Rain: America's Herbicidal Folly*. E.P. Dutton, 1971.

Winchester, J. H. "Our Fabulous Choppers." *Popular Science* (February 1966).

Wolf, Charles, Jr., *The Logic of Failure*. Rand Corp., October, 1971.

Yens, 1st Lt. David P., and Capt. John P. Clement, III. "Port Construction in Vietnam." *The Military Engineer* (January–February 1967).

Zaloga, Steven J. *Modern Soviet Combat Tanks*. Osprey Publishing Ltd., 1984.

———. *Soviet Tanks Today*. Arms & Armour Press, 1983.

Zimmerman, R. "From a Dead Stop to 40 Knots in 75 Seconds: Patrol Gunboats." *Popular Mechanics* (September 1968).

II. Government and Government-Sponsored Reports

Albright, John, John Cash, and Allan W. Sandstrum. *Seven Firefights in Vietnam.* OCMH, 1970.

Ballard, Jack S. *Development and Employment of Fixed-Wing Gunships 1962-1972. United States Air Force in Southeast Asia.* Office of Air Force History, 1982.

BDM Corporation. *A Study of Strategic Lessons Learned in Vietnam.* National Technical Information Service, 1980.

Buckingham, William A., Jr. *Operation Ranch Hand: The Air Force and Herbicides in Southeast Asia 1961-1971.* Office of Air Force History, 1982.

CINCPAC. *Report of CINCPAC.* Infiltration/Interdiction Conference, July 24-26, 1967.

Dorland, Peter, and James Nanney. *Dust Off: Army Aeromedical Evacuation in Vietnam.* Vietnam Studies, Department of the Army, 1982.

Eastman, J. N., Walter Hanak, and L. J. Paszek, Eds. *Aces and Aerial Victories. The United States Air Force in Southeast Asia 1965-1973.* Office of Air Force History, 1976.

Eckhardt, Maj. Gen. George S. *Command and Control 1950-1969.* Vietnam Studies, Department of the Army, 1974.

Hay, Lt. Gen. John H., Jr. *Tactical and Material Innovations.* Vietnam Studies, Department of the Army, 1974.

Heiser, Lt. Gen. Joseph M., Jr. *Logistical Support.* Vietnam Studies, Department of the Army, 1974.

Internal Medicine in Vietnam. Vol. II of *General Medicine and Infectious Diseases.* Offices of the Surgeon General and OCMH, 1982.

Kelly, Francis John. *U.S. Army Special Forces 1960-1971.* Vietnam Studies, Department of the Army, 1973.

Komer, Robert W. *Bureaucracy Does Its Thing: Institutional Constraints on US-GVN Performance in Vietnam.* Rand Corporation 9-967-ARPA, 1972.

McChristian, Lt. Gen. Joseph A. *The Role of Military Intelligence 1965-1967.* Vietnam Studies, Department of the Army, 1974.

Momyer, Gen. William W., USAF (RET). *Air Power in Three Wars (WWII, Korea, Vietnam).* GPO, 1978.

Myer, Lt. Gen. Charles L. *Division-Level Communications 1962-1973.* Vietnam Studies, Department of the Army, 1982.

Neel, Maj. Gen. Spurgeon. *Medical Support 1965-1970.* Vietnam Studies, Department of the Army, 1974.

Ott, Maj. Gen. David Ewing. *Field Artillery 1954-1973.* Vietnam Studies, Department of the Army, 1975.

PACOM Report on the War in Vietnam as of 30 June 1969. Department of Defense, HQ, Pacific Command, 1969.

Pearson, Lt. Gen. Willard. *War in the Northern Provinces 1966-1968.* Vietnam Studies, Department of the Army, 1975.

Principles of Naval Ordnance and Gunnery. GPO, 1971.

Rienzi, Maj. Gen. Thomas M. *Communications-Electronics 1962-1970.* Vietnam Studies, Department of the Army, 1972.

Sharp, Adm. U.S. Grant, Jr., CINCPAC. *Report on the War in Vietnam 1964-1968.* GPO, 1968.

Shore, Cpt. Moyers E., III. *The Battle of Khe Sanh.* Historical Branch, HQ, USMC, 1969.

Tilford, Carl H. *USAF Search and Rescue in Southeast Asia 1961-1975.* Office of Air Force History, 1980.

Tolson, Lt. Gen. John. *Airmobility 1961-1971.* Vietnam Studies, Department of the Army, 1973.

United States Embassy, Saigon. *The Impact of the Sapper on the Vietnam War. A Background Paper.* U.S. State Department, October, 1969.

U.S. Congress. Hearings of the 95th Congress, 2d Session. *GBU-15 Modular Guided Weapons System.* GPO, 1979.

U.S. Congress. House. Subcommittee on Medical Benefits. *Hearings on Herbicide "Agent Orange."* GPO, 1978.

U.S. Congress. Senate. Committee on Armed Services. *Investigation Into the Electronic Battlefield.* GPO, 1971.

U.S. Naval Aviation 1910-1980. NAVAIR 00-80P-1. GPO, 1981.

III. Unpublished Material

Brooks, J. L. *Experience With the OH-6A in Vietnam.* Internal Report. Hughes Helicopters, Inc. June 1, 1983.

Craddock, William P. Bell Helicopter Textron. Letter. May 23, 1983.

Dendy, John C. Hughes Helicopters, Inc. Letter and Materials. June 1, 1983.

Lyon, Matthew. Breeze Corporation. Letter. May 6, 1983.

Perdue, Richard M. Texas Instruments, Inc. Letters. August 29, 1983.

Savenelli, Louis P. Avco Lycoming Division. Letter and Materials. June 20, 1983.

IV. Newspapers and Periodicals Consulted by the Author

Air Force Times; Aviation Week; Commander's Digest; Newsweek; Time; U.S. News and World Report (1966-1975 inclusive).

V. Interviews

Col. James P. Brown, U.S. Army.

Lt. Gen. Kenneth Cooper, U.S. Army (Ret.), DCPG.

Mavis Dezolovich, Electro-Optics Lab, Fort Belvoir.

Lt. Gen. Edgar C. Doleman, U.S. Army (Ret.), DCINCUSARPAC.

Col. Dale Eppinger, USAF SOS.

Gerald Ewing, former helicopter pilot.

Dr. John Foster, TRW Corporation.

Maj. Avery Jackson, U.S. Army.

Harry Keene, Natick Laboratories, MA.

Col. Leo G. Kohler, U.S. Army.

Robert Komer, former deputy COMUSMACV for CORDS.

Leonard Sullivan, former Defense Department deputy director, Southeast Asia, Office of the Director, Defense Research and Engineering.

Gen. William Westmoreland, U.S. Army (Ret.), former COMUSMACV.

Maj. John D. Wiggins, U.S. Army (Ret.).

Charles Williamson, Natick Laboratories, MA.

Wallace R. Winkler, Retired NSA.

Adam Yarmolinsky, former assistant to Defense Secretary Robert MacNamara.

Credits

All illustrations by John Batchelor unless otherwise indicated.

Cover Photograph: Marc Riboud—Magnum.

Chapter One
p. 7, Co Rentmeester—LIFE Magazine, © 1966, Time Inc. p. 9, Imperial War Museum. p. 10, Bildarchiv Preussischer Kulturbesitz, West Berlin. pp. 12-13, Library of Congress. pp. 14-15, John Loengard—LIFE Magazine, © 1964, Time Inc. pp. 16-17, AP/Wide World.

Technology in the Great War
pp. 18-19, Imperial War Museum, courtesy John Batchelor Collection. p. 20, top, BBC Hulton Picture Library; bottom, Imperial War Museum. p. 21, Imperial War Museum. p. 22, top and bottom, BBC Hulton Picture Library; middle, Imperial War Museum. p. 23, top, Imperial War Museum; bottom, BBC Hulton Picture Library. pp. 24-25, top, U.S. Air Force Museum, Wright-Patterson Air Force Base. p. 24, bottom left, BBC Hulton Picture Library; bottom right, Imperial War Museum. p. 25, Imperial War Museum.

Chapter Two
p. 27, U.S. Air Force. pp. 29-31, U.S. Army. p. 32, Philip Jones Griffiths—Magnum. pp. 34-35, U.S. Army. p. 41, James H. Pickerell—Black Star; inset, Dick Swanson—TIME Magazine. p. 44, left, U.S. Army. pp. 44-45, Don McCullin—Magnum. p. 47, Robert Ellison—Empire News, courtesy Black Star. p. 49, U.S. Army. pp. 51-53, Co Rentmeester—LIFE Magazine, © 1967, Time Inc. pp. 54-55, U.S. Army.

Chapter Three
p. 65, AP/Wide World. p. 66, Walter Reed Army Institute of Research, Washington, D.C. p. 67, James H. Pickerell—Black Star. p. 68, UPI/The Bettmann Archive. p. 69, Walter Reed Army Institute of Research, Washington, D.C. p. 71, top, Robert Ellison—Black Star; bottom, Robert Ellison—Empire News, courtesy Black Star. p. 73, UPI/The Bettmann Archive. pp. 74-75, Library of Congress. p. 76, Philip Jones Griffiths—Magnum. p. 77, Walter Reed Army Institute of Research, Washington, D.C. p. 78, U.S. Army. p. 79, Walter Reed Army Institute of Research, Washington, D.C.

Chapter Four
p. 81, Camera Press Ltd. p. 82, Marc Riboud—Magnum. p. 83, Eastfoto. p. 87, U.S. Army. pp. 88-89, Eastfoto. pp. 90-91, James H. Pickerell—Camera Press Ltd. p. 93, Camera Press Ltd. pp. 96-97, Eastfoto. p. 99, AP/Wide World. p. 103, Marc Riboud—Magnum. pp. 104-5, Sovfoto. pp. 106-7, Roger Pic.

Chapter Five
p. 115, Mark Godfrey—Archive Pictures Inc. p. 117, Bill Ray—LIFE Magazine, © 1965, Time Inc. p. 121, Jay Miller—Aerofax Inc. pp. 124-26, U.S. Air Force. p. 131, U.S. Navy. p. 132, UPI/The Bettmann Archive. p. 134, left, U.S. Air Force. pp. 134-35, © Larry Burrows Collection.

Chapter Six
p. 143, Roger Pic. p. 146, U.S. Air Force. pp. 152-53, illustration by Diane McCaffery. p. 154, U.S. Air Force. p. 155, illustrations by Diane McCaffery. pp. 158-59, U.S. Air Force; inset, © Larry Burrows Collection. p. 161, U.S. Air Force. p. 163, NASA.

Closing Photo: Co Rentmeester—LIFE Magazine, © 1967, Time Inc.

Acknowledgements

Boston Publishing Company would like to acknowledge the kind assistance of the following people: James Canan, *Air Force Magazine,* who read the manuscript, and Dr. Robert J. T. Joy, Uniform Services College of Medicine, Bethesda, Maryland; Maria Vincenza Aloisi and Josephine du Brusle, Time-Life Bureau, Paris; Dorothy Bacon, Time-Life Bureau, London; Carolyn Chubet and Christina Lieberman, Time-Life Bureau, New York; Elisabeth Kraemer-Singh, Time-Life Bureau, Bonn; Dana Bell, National Air and Space Museum; Edward B. Doctoroff, Head, Circulation Division, Widener Library, Harvard University; Charles W. Dunn, professor and chairman, Department of Celtic Languages, Harvard University; Feuerwache, Freie und Hansestadt Hamburg; Chief Warrant 4 Ron Gerner, Historical Department, Grumman Aerospace, Bethpage, Long Island, New York; Harry Klein, Lois Lovisolo, and Fred Puglisi, Historical Department, Grumman Aerospace, Bethpage, Long Island, New York; Heidi Klein, Bildarchiv Preussischer Kulturbesitz, Berlin; J. S. Lucas and M. J. Willis, Imperial War Museum; Meinrad Nilges, Bundesarchiv, Koblenz; Heinz Nowarra, Babenhausen; Ed Marolda, Naval Historical Center; Specialist 4 Ed Ramirez; Dale Weaver, Teledyne-Ryan Aeronautical, San Diego, California; Captain Edward Wilbur.

Index

Weapons and Equipment

Order of Battle

Air Force
390th Tactical Fighter Wing, 134

Army
1st Cavalry Division (Airmobile), *7*, 26, 28, *29*, 31, *32*, 38, 39, 47, 48, 68, 78, 98, 164
8th Cavalry
  1st Battalion, 83
12th Cavalry
  2d Battalion
    Company C, 64, 66
5th Special Forces Group (Airborne), 39, 82
9th Infantry Division, 78
Mobile Riverine Force, 52
11th Armored Cavalry, 27, *168, 169*
  3d Squadron, *52, 53*
25th Infantry Division, 90, 156, 157
  4th Cavalry (Armored)
    3d Squadron, 54
  5th Infantry (Mechanized)
    1st Battalion, 54
  11th Artillery
    7th Battalion
      Battery A
27th Engineer Battalion (Combat), 55
33d Maintenance Squadron, *126*
83d Artillery
  1st Battalion
    Battery B, *49*
101st Airborne Division (Airmobile), *87*
  320th Artillery
    2d Battalion, *30*
    Battery B, 31
173d Airborne Brigade, 43
199th Infantry Brigade (Light)
  12th Infantry
    4th Battalion, 44, 45
Mobile Riverine Force, see 9th Infantry Division

Marines
3d Marine Division
  3d Marines, 92

Navy
Seventh Fleet, 11
Task Force 77, 11

U.S. Army structure (to company level)		
Unit	Size	Commanding officer
Division	12,000–18,000 troops or 3 brigades	Major General
Brigade	3,000 troops or 2-4 battalions	Colonel
Battalion*	600–1,000 troops or 3–5 companies	Lieutenant Colonel
Company	150 troops** or 3-4 platoons	Captain

* Squadron equivalent to battalion.
** Size varies based on type of unit.

Names, Acronyms, Terms

AA—antiaircraft.

AAA—antiaircraft artillery.

ABCCC—airborne battlefield command and control center.

ACTIV—U.S. Army Concept Team in Vietnam. Evaluated problems confronted by army units in the field and devised solutions with the aid of modern technology.

APC—armored personnel carrier.

ARM—antiradiation missile. Designed to destroy enemy radar sites.

ARVN—Army of the Republic of Vietnam (South Vietnam).

AWACS—Airborne Warning and Control System. A surveillance, command, control, and communications system which combines sophisticated radar with advanced data processing and communications relay equipment. It is capable of all-weather, long-range surveillance over all kinds of terrain.

BDA—bomb damage assessment.

beehive—artillery rounds filled with thousands of small metal fléchettes which burst in a 30 degree arc.

bouncing betty—a land mine that springs an explosive 60MM mortar round up to waist level before detonation.

C&C—"Charley-Charley." Slang term for command and control ships, airborne operations centers, usually in helicopters, from which commanders were linked to every element of an invading force and could scan the battlefield below.

CBU—cluster bomb unit.

CIA—Central Intelligence Agency.

CINCPAC—Commander-in-Chief [of U.S. Forces in the] Pacific.

claymore mine—A command-detonated, antipersonnel land mine which explodes in a sixty-degree fan-shaped swath.

CORDS—Civil Operations and Revolutionary (Rural) Development Support. Established under MACV in 1967, CORDS organized U.S. civilian agencies in Vietnam within the military chain of command.

COSVN—Central Office for South Vietnam. Communist military and political headquarters for southern South Vietnam.

CS gas—A riot control agent, or tear gas, used in Vietnam primarily to flush Vietcong agents and civilians out of tunnel complexes.

DCPG—Defense Communications Planning Group. A top-secret, low-profile research group which reported directly to the secretary of defense. In its five-plus years of operation the DCPG sparked an entire generation of new weapons, virtually creating the electronic battlefield.

DMZ—Demilitarized Zone. Established by the 1954 Geneva accords, provisionally dividing North Vietnam from South Vietnam along the seventeenth parallel.

ECM—electronic countermeasures, especially jamming and deception of radar.

FAC—forward air controller. Pilot or observer who directs strike aircraft and artillery.

FDC—fire direction center. Translates a request for fire support into data for ground artillery.

FLIR—forward looking infrared device. Registers minute thermal differences among objects.

GCI—ground control intercept stations.

IIR—imaging infrared sensors. Allows gunships to locate targets at night.

Iron Triangle—An area to the northwest of Saigon that was the scene of heavy fighting between U.S. and Communist forces.

LAW—M72 light antitank weapon. A shoulder-fired 66MM rocket with a one-time, disposable Fiberglas launcher.

LGB—laser-guided bomb. First used in quantity in March 1972 on targets in North Vietnam, the bomb homes in on a target that has been illuminated by a laser beam.

LLLTV—low-light-level television.

MACV—Military Assistance Command, Vietnam. U.S. command for all U.S. military activities in Vietnam.

MEDCAP—Medical Civic Action Program. Established in fall 1965. A program in which units made up of several medical corpsmen escorted by an armed squad extended outpatient care and basic medical services to Vietnamese civilians in the villages.

MICV—mechanized infantry combat vehicle.

MiG—Russian-built fighter aircraft developed by designers Mikoyan and Gurevich.

MILPHAP—Military Provisional Health Assistance Program. A health program for Vietnamese civilians set up by the medical command in Vietnam. Its main purpose was to assist Vietnamese medical staffs and help to improve clinical and surgical services through the introduction of American methods and technology.

MUST—Medical Unit, Self-contained, Transportable. A rubberized, inflatable ward designed to be moved as the scene of battle shifted.

NLF—Communist National Liberation Front in South Vietnam.

NVA—North Vietnamese Army.

ROTC—Reserve Officers Training Corps.

RPG-7—Russian-designed rocket launcher.

RPV—remotely piloted vehicle. Small, unmanned aircraft flown via remote control and/or along a preprogrammed flight path.

SAM—surface-to-air-missile.

sortie—a single aircraft flying a single mission.

TFR—terrain following radar installed on A-6, F-111, and other U.S. aircraft. Maps the ground ahead and detects any obstructions. Should a hazard appear the radar instantly flashes a course correction to the aircraft guidance system. TFR enables planes to operate in any weather.

TOW—tube-launched, optically tracked, wire-guided missile. An American antitank-guided missile.

UGS—unattended ground sensors.

USAF—United States Air Force.

VATLS—The army's Visual Airborne Target Locator System. A high-powered telescope designed to pinpoint ground sites for artillery or tactical air strikes.

Vietcong—Common reference to a member of the NLF; a contraction of Vietnam Cong San (Vietnamese Communist).

WAAPM—wide area antipersonnel munition.